Liberalization and Culture in Contemporary Israel

Liberalization and Culture in Contemporary Israel

Ari Ofengenden

LEXINGTON BOOKS
Lanham • Boulder • New York • London

Published by Lexington Books
An imprint of The Rowman & Littlefield Publishing Group, Inc.
4501 Forbes Boulevard, Suite 200, Lanham, Maryland 20706
www.rowman.com

Unit A, Whitacre Mews, 26-34 Stannary Street, London SE11 4AB

British Library Cataloguing in Publication Information Available

Library of Congress Cataloging-in-Publication Data Available

LCCN 2018945752 | ISBN 9781498570350 (cloth:) |
ISBN 9781498570367 (electronic)

Contents

Acknowledgments

Writing this book from abroad (with frequent visits to Israel) had its advantages, as I could see the way in which Israel has been radically changing in ways that perhaps those living there could not. It also necessitated much help in terms of research. I want to thank my father, Uri On, for referring me to relevant books and films as well as for his knowledgeable comments on the book. Deep gratitude to my mother, Malka On, for her love and support. To Noa Cnaan On for a long running conversation on Israel that has helped clarify many things. Thanks to Lidia Averbukh for her discerning comments on the first chapters. To the love of my life, Tzofit Ofengenden, for everything else.

Introduction

The origins of the 21st century lie in the economic and technological changes brought about in the late 1970s. During the late 1970s leaders around the world made an active decision to undertake a policy of marketization and global integration. Statesmen as different as Ronald Reagan, Margaret Thatcher, Deng Xiaoping, and in Israel Menachem Begin and Shimon Peres have undertaken to allow both global and local markets to have an increasingly dominant role in the control and allocation of both material and cultural resources.[1] The fall of the Berlin Wall in 1989 and the collapse of the Soviet Union were only the most dramatic outward consequences of processes that have started earlier. The late 1970s also signaled the rise of the knowledge economy, based largely on rapid developments in computer technology, the first applicable uses of internet (then called ARPNET) and the first rapid sequencing of DNA.[2] Knowledge economy can be defined as an economy in which value creation, productivity, and economic growth are dependent on knowledge, information, and innovation. The 1970s thus inaugurated a new global post-industrial era in which both a world integrated market and knowledge production stand at the forefront of change.

Corresponding to these economic and technological developments in the 1970s, culture had rearticulated itself as series of "posts" and "neos": Postmodernism, Postnationalism, Neo-nationalism, and most importantly Neoliberalism. This time saw an unprecedented dissemination of commercial culture assertively actualizing itself across the globe. This era has also witnessed an unexpected reemergence of both cultural and political manifestations of religion and Neo-nationalism. Religious ideology to the surprise of social scientist, intellectuals, and political leaders moved to the public sphere and offered new meanings and solutions to conditions generated by the new changes. Neo-nationalism articulated itself against the adverse effects suffered by the working class of outsourcing and immigration, which is the effect of increased global flow of goods and people.

All these changes, diverse and yet paradoxically interconnected, signify the decline and displacement of the enlightenment project itself. This project, embodied in the 20th century by socialism and progressive nationalism, came under sever critique, and was essentially replaced by identity politics of gender and race, and by multiculturalism. Needless to say such global changes expressed themselves very differently in different countries. While the transition to global economy has stood at the base of these changes, the main argument of this book will be that it was precisely cultural interventions that dismantled of progressive nationalism in both its civic and as well as left-wing varieties. Cultural interventions have undone both types of nationalism and have articulated a new kind of cultural hegemony complete with contrasts and antagonisms of its own. This culture compensates for the privations associated with globalization and liberal internationalism by a redrawing of rigid lines between Jewish and non-Jewish people in Israel.

In this book I intend to show that in many ways it is less distorting to view the cultural interventions that took place in Israel as the outcome of a combination of global and local forces than to view these changes as wholly singular to Israel itself as have been the case of many writers who have concentrated on the Holocaust or the Arab-Israeli conflict in order to explain Israel. More perhaps than most countries, Israel is widely recognized as the vanguard of these new economic, technological, and cultural developments. It stands at the forefront of the global changes enumerated above, especially the transition to the global knowledge economy. Branded Start-Up Nation, Israel is at the same time deeply engaged in controversies around nationalism and the resurgence of religion. Drawing much of its military and diplomatic support from the United States, the primary agent of cultural and economic globalization, Israel finds itself as one of the countries most influenced and influencing these global trends. This book specifically looks at the role that mainstream culture has played in these developments and how it came to embody a new ideology, sensibility, and self-understanding.

This book defines mainstream culture as those films, television series, and books that receive most popular and critical attention in Israel and abroad, mainstream culture can further be defined by the relative power of institutions that propagate this culture, it is the culture that is disseminated by the major television channels and newspapers. Mainstream culture can be negatively defined as a culture that does make explicit appeals to a certain subculture in Israel. That is, it does not explicitly appeal to some specific subculture of Israeli society such as Orthodox, Mizrachi, Druze, Russian Immigrants, Palestinians with Israeli citizenship, and so on.

Though there are differences in mainstream culture between popular culture and more highbrow culture, both have contributed to the cultural restructuring that accompanies the transition to globalization and knowledge-based society. The transformations that both have gone through are dramatic and entail changes in both form and their content. Israeli films, for example, have completely overhauled their production values and consequently their look in the early 2000s. Gone are Israeli films that seem unpolished or that suffer from technical problem of lighting, sound, framing, and acting. Israeli films have also changed their content to suit the interests of a more global art house audience. Like the most successful Israeli novels they often mediate the particularities of Israeli existence such as the Arab-Israeli conflict or Jewish religious experiences to audiences abroad. Israel's most successful films such as *Waltz with Bashir* (2008), *Lebanon* (2009), *Zero Motivation* (2014), *Gett: The Trial of Viviane Amsalem* (2014), and *Foxtrot* (2017) as well as Israel's most successful novels such as *A Tale of Love and Darkness* (2002) and *To the End of the Land* (2008) narrate for Western audiences what is seen by these audiences as most characteristic of Israeli existence. In a seeming paradox, globalization has made the content of Israeli films and literature less universal and more particular. Israeli television series while geared more toward local audiences have also found their own way of globalizing. Several of Israel's most successful series have been sold and adopted to the United States and elsewhere, becoming global: good examples being *Homeland*, *In Treatment*, *The A Word*, *Greenhouse Academy*, *Dig*, *Hostages*, and *Fuada*. Much of the success of these television shows has to do with the global vision of producers, their relatively modest budgets, and the willingness to take risks and provide character-driven stories.[3]

Covering the culture of a nation-state and the way that global marketization has transformed it is well beyond the scope of one book. Though this book provides examples from various segments of Israeli society it concentrates on mainstream culture in Israel, especially film, television, and literature. Television, film, and to a certain extent also literature are not only the media that have most radically altered their form by increasing dominance of the global market economy, they have been the quickest to represent those changes as they influence Israeli society. This book examines the complex interplay between Israeli culture and the profound transformations that Israel went through as it adopted itself to a global market knowledge economy.

The first chapter of this book delineates the historical background to the process of the marketization of Israeli society and culture from the 1970s until the second decade of the millennium. It articulates the economic and cultural context for this process. The social background is mainly characterized through the control and influence of the state of Israel on Israeli society. Until globalized marketization started roughly in the late 1970s the state of

Israel saw itself as controlling or supporting many realms of citizen's lives including education, defense, economy, and culture. The chapter then sets the immediate cultural context for this book, the forming of a distinctly non-state culture of the 1960s and 1970s. Though economic and societal model was statist, the 1960s and 1970s culture have already reinvented individualism in values and worldview. The core posture and values of this culture was expressed in a playfully defiant individual everydayness. It was a culture that attempted to valorize and celebrate quotidian lives in explicit contrast to grand nationalist narratives of Holocaust, resurrection, and birth of a new Jewish man. Subjectivities were articulated and represented in a way that went against national duty and military sacrifice. In their stead they affirmed and valued simple enjoyments. While the 1970s concentrated on the withdrawal of the individual from national and collective sensibilities and from duties like settlement and army service, by the late 1980s and early 1990s collective national sensibilities came under explicit critique. Historians and intellectuals took on the job of reforming nationalism along the lines of liberalism. This was done either explicitly by introducing new post-Zionist approaches to Israeli history and theory or in more subtle ways by narratives that sought either to parody or to therapeutically treat certain kinds of amplified militarist expressions of Zionism. This book argues that this cultural intervention has had a lasting effect on both Israeli society and culture ever since. The 2000s have inaugurated an unprecedented surge in Israeli commercial television programming. It has also seen the first Israeli television series that were sold for export to the United States and Europe. The film industry that was in decline in the 1980s and 1990s saw a surge of successful films. This chapter thus looks at the way that culture and subjectivity has been at the forefront of marketization, at the decline in political and social participation that has given rise to a more market-oriented individualism informed by commercial culture and the pressure for gainful employment. New kinds of narratives that represent the vicissitudes, joys, and frustrations of work under global market conditions came to the fore. The chapter ends with examining the ways that global integration has created opportunities to which Judaism, Zionism, and Israeli democracy have reasserted themselves in newly complex ways.

The second chapter concentrates on representations and interventions in national identity in the 1990s and early 2000s. I claim that fiction has attempted to transform and reform national identity in two major ways: through therapeutic narrative and through satire. In therapeutic narratives national identity is represented as ultimately rooted in the trauma of the Holocaust that the hero works through. The chapter employs Melanie Klein's object theory in order to interpret Amos Oz's *Tale of Love and Darkness* as a therapeutic intervention that sublates or collapses the dichotomy of Old Jew New Jew. This dichotomy was created as an internalization of and an answer to anti-Semitism. The resultant conception of the New Jew that ultimately found its ideal in the figure of masculine solider is at the same time both a fantasy of the disempowered and has outlived its practical use. Oz calls his readers to see him and themselves as displaced cosmopolitan European Jews. At a time in which soldierly masculinity comes under critique from both feminism and from the decline in the ideals of nationalism, Oz articulates a global diaspora-like identity for both his Israeli and largely European and American-based readership. A second example of a therapeutic intervention comes from the popular film *Walk on Water* that takes an Israeli intelligence agent and pairs him up with a gay grandson of a Nazi war criminal. The meeting facilitates the turning of a violent and heterosexual Mossad agent into a soft maternal figure, a husband and father in a mixed Jewish-German family and working in agriculture in the Kibbutz. The therapeutic meeting with the German "other" is an over determined global occurrence both on the level of the narrative of the film itself and on the level of its production and distribution. The film includes dialogues in Hebrew, German, and English, and was largely produced on German funds and has premiered in Berlin.

To exemplify satiric narratives the chapter uses Yoram Kaniuk's *Nevelot*, a satire about two retired, aging paramilitary Palmach members. The two are marginalized and resentful of contemporary society around them and see today's youths as over-sexualized, selfish, and thoroughly commercialized. The narrative shows the irrelevance of the values informing the Palmach, such as comradery and selfless sacrifice for contemporary Israel. Another satiric narrative of national identity is Orly Castle-Bloom's *Dolly City*. The novel relates a story of an abusive single mother and her relationship with her son. Her abuse is a parody of nationalist socialization, a critique of violent over-controlling mothers. Finally the chapter looks at Sayed Kashua's satiric sitcom *Arab Labor*, the first prime-time Israeli program that depicts the Arab-Israeli minority in Israel. The show pokes fun at its main character—an Israeli Arab who is desperate to mimic and assimilate into mainstream Jewish-Israeli culture. In his successes and failures he implicitly criticizes the forces of inclusive-exclusion that would have him become an Israeli but yet keep him apart from the mainstream.

The third chapter provides a succinct image for the changes Israel went through since the 1970s. In it I argue that Israel has been distancing itself from the European model of the secular social democratic nation-state and its culture of realism and modernism. I conceptualize the changes that Israel went through by depicting the country's development as an active negation of the European model. Instead of imitating the classic European nation-state, Israel began emulating the United States and the countries of the Middle East. Since the 1970s religious nationalism gradually replaced secular nationalism. Global capitalism superseded social democracy. In this chapter I have chosen a popular Israeli song called "It Ain't Europe Here" that exemplifies all of these changes. The chapter argues that at the base of all these transformations stand the marketization of Israeli society and its integration into the global knowledge economy.

The fourth chapter looks specifically at the ways that the Israeli media has stood at the forefront of marketization and the development of the knowledge economy. It starts with the explosive fragmentation and pluralization of newspapers as each newspaper appealed to a special niche. It then shows that while local media that is directed toward domestic audience has experienced a fragmentation, cultural producers of film have transformed from adopting European culture to Israeli audience to that of exporting Israeli realities to a global audience. I argue that this change has paradoxically entailed a highlighting of national themes (Arab-Israeli conflict, orthodoxy, etc.) in Israeli books and films. I elaborate on the decline of both realism, modernism, and ultimately postmodernism as well that were deemed unmarketable. I show the increasing influence of commercial media and provide examples from Israeli reality television and celebrity culture. I closely read the Israeli reality television series *Connected* in which participants, bent on achieving celebrity status, are asked to film themselves, and the series *Very Important Man* that problematizes celebrity lifestyle in an ironic self-reflective way. Then I discuss how marketization and its moral conundrums are rendered in Nir Baram's novel *World Shadow* that explicitly deals with those who stand both at the forefront of global capitalism and those who are wholly marginalized by it and attempt to overthrew it. I also analyze *Google Baby*—a documentary that portrays an Israeli bio-tech start-up company that uses sperm from Israel, egg donors from the United States, and surrogate mothers from India to "produce" babies for childless gay couples and others in Israel.

The fifth chapter examines the cultural reaction to the liberal intervention in the shape of Neo-nationalist discourse. The chapter specifically looks at the fiction and political writings of Gadi Taub, who long before recent Neo-nationalist trends (Trump and Brexit) provided an intellectual framework for Neo-nationalism as a force against privatization, multiculturalism, postmodernity, and liberal post-Zionism. The chapter disentangles these aspects of Taub's critiques. It then examines Taub's political worldview and literary practice. Taub's political worldview is a sophisticated articulation of a new kind of ideology in Israel—National conservatism or neo-nationalism. In terms of literary practice Taub marries this ideology with a reinvigoration of the tradition of literary realism and the role of the politically committed realist writer who exposes the societal ills that come with liberalization and Westernization of society. Taub's attempt to resurrect secular nationalism in a new conservative mold allows us to examine its fate and transformations in a globalized interconnected world.

The sixth chapter argues that another cultural effect of liberalization and globalization is the surge in dystopian imagination in recent Israeli fiction.

The chapter begins with outlining the social, political, and environmental contexts that have contributed to this genre becoming a popular way of narrating reality. Among the most important features of this context are the second intifada and Gaza conflict, the growing cost of living and economic inequality, environmental degradation, religious fundamentalism, and the devaluation of the secular-nationalist worldview. I argue that the dystopian novel gives shape to anxieties and articulates both intellectually and emotionally a present lacking in a clear progressive future horizon. Contemporary novels deal with a diverse set of direct causes for dystopia including natural catastrophes such as earthquakes and rising oceans, wars and religious fundamentalism. In contrast to the classical dystopias of the past that represented the over-rationalization of an administrated, iron-cage society the contemporary dystopian imagination features fragmentation, uneven development, disorientation, and chaos. Ultimately the chapter argues that the dystopian imagination is due to the breakdown in belief in progress and the decline in realism and modernism that was associated with it.

The seventh chapter deals with liberal presentations, made for a global audience, of the Arab-Israel conflict in films and documentaries. The chapter focuses on films that represent the second intifada. The chapter interprets several films that have suicide bombing at their center and examines the interrelationship between ideological and aesthetic choices that are made in the film. The film *The Attack* (2012) represents an example of the complex and very political reception and sharp critique by the Arab world. The film's very political reception also reveals the constraints on those who want to represent the conflict from a European humanist perspective. The constraints of Arab and Israeli filmmakers who live in the West are shown to be the result of globalization of the conflict itself that creates heterogeneous multiplicity that mixes participants and audiences geographically. The chapter moves to examine the classical trope of trauma as a focus of liberal interventions. The film looks at the results of hostilities and the ways in which those who have experienced loss of their child attempt to derive meaning from their loss: that is, the politics and social construction of bereavement. The chapter analyzes three documentaries that feature bereaved Israeli mothers who attempt to meet the other side: *Encounter Point* (2006), *One Day after Peace* (2012), and *To Die in Jerusalem* (2007). The chapter shows the difficulties involved in meeting with the Palestinian "other" but more importantly how global integration has altered the way in which bereavement is construed. Participating in these documentaries serves as supplemental "global" commemoration for these mothers in an age in which the value of specifically national commemoration has declined. The last part of the chapter is devoted to another kind of meeting and relationship with the other, the relationship between a Shin Beth agent and his informant. The chapter looks at two representations of this relationship: one fictional and one real. Both *Bethlehem* (2013) and the *Green Prince* (2014) relate the relationship between a likable Shin Beth agent and his younger informant. These films use the trope of father-son like relationships and the complex emotions that they evoke, in order to give shape to international Western audiences' wish to personalize the Israeli-Palestinian conflict while providing audiences with the drama of an impossible love.

This book ends with a reconceptualization of cultural interventions in Israel in terms of a transition to a globally integrated knowledge economy. This movement entails a radical break with the past on the ideological, economic, and cultural levels. I broadly characterize the new kind of culture as active participant in a kind of dematerialization and deterritorialization within global assemblages of work and cultural production. Work and culture have detached themselves from the land and from material. The Tel-Aviv metropolitan area, the economic engine of the country, produces software, scientific and technological knowledge, entertainment, and services. This represents a dramatic reversal of previous national ideals of working the land and the valorization of material labor. This whole immaterial production in which the differences between culture and economy have been effaced has been integrated into heterogeneous global networks. This transition has been highly volatile and has resulted in a succession of new kinds of cultural articulations, narratives, and subjectivities from late modernist, postmodernist, and finally contemporary global realism. Finally, I look at what the emancipatory possibilities for culture are.

NOTES

1. In her book *Strange Rebels: 1979 and the Birth of the 21st Century*, Christian Caryl posits and identifies the year 1979 as pivotal for all these changes. That year saw the election of Margaret Thatcher and the subsequent unleashing of "Thatcherism" within Britain and beyond, the visit by Pope John Paul II to his homeland in Poland, the beginning of the unraveling of Eastern European communism and the rise to power of Deng Xiaoping and China's opening up. I would add that only two years before saw loss of power of labor in Israel. See Christian Caryl, *Strange Rebels: 1979 and the Birth of the 21st Century*, 1st ed. (New York: Basic Books, 2013).

2. Some of the cultural consequences of the digital revolution are already foretold by Lyotard in his famous 1979 book *The Postmodern Condition*, his first chapter being "Knowledge in Computerized Societies" see Jean-Francois Lyotard and Fredric Jameson, *The Postmodern Condition: A Report on Knowledge*, Translated by Geoff Bennington and Brian Massumi, 1st ed. (Minneapolis: University Of Minnesota Press, 1984), 3–6.

3. "Top 7 Reasons Israeli TV Shows Are Smash Hits Abroad," accessed December 13, 2017, http://www.israel21c.org/top-8-reasons-israeli-tv-shows-are-smash-hits-abroad/.

Chapter 1

Economics and Cultural Globalization in Israel

A Historical Introduction

THE ERA OF BIG STATE

Disagreements on how best to organize the economy have characterized the Zionist movement from its inception into the late 19th century. Like many national movements there has been a lively debate on the role of the state versus the market in the economy as well as over fundamental questions concerning ownership of property and division of labor.[1] Historically there was a broad spectrum of positions regarding these issues ranging from a traditionalist emphasis on family ownership of small business, Herzel's mixed, statist economy, to Ber Borochov Zionist Marxist stress on inverting the class pyramid that is having Jews partake in what Borochov considered productive labor rather than in commerce and professions. However broad the spectrum of opinions was, it is undeniable that in the formative period of the creation of Israel, the state and collective public institutions have exercised formidable control over the economy. Even before statehood, it was political and public, not private, institutions which controlled and mobilized capital coming from the Jewish diaspora that was used for purchasing land and maintaining a policy of Hebrew labor. Both systematic purchasing of land and the maintaining of Hebrew labor were not possible without the centralized political organizations like the Jewish National Fund. Though political control of the economy was especially suited to the specific and relatively unique aspects of land acquisition, some kind of political control of the economy was also the dominant practice during that time in both developing countries and in Europe. The determinative pre-state years that overlapped with the interwar years were marked by a worldwide rejection of liberalism and capitalism and a global affirmation of national, anti-colonial, or socialist collectivism, most often a combination of the three. Political control of the economy and

1

collectivism were perceived as more rational, effective, and just way to develop and make full use of the productive forces of society.[2] Essentially it was seen by many, at the time as the fastest path to modernization and progress even for countries that formed the previous core of laissez-faire liberalism such as England.[3] Central economic planning and collectivism were also understood as crucial for the specific problems that mandatory Palestine and the early years of the state faced. These problems included limited natural resources, lack of sovereignty over land, the initially small population of Jewish settlers and the hostility of the native population to the new endeavor. Central decision-making and planning has relatively effectively dealt with all of these difficulties.[4] During the late 1960s it could look back on its achievements and say that it has efficiently mobilized scarce resources both in Palestine and abroad, has settled a proportionately vast number of immigrants and refugees, has incorporated much of the land of historical Palestine, has effectively dealt with defense, and has provided universal health care and social security as well as almost full employment.[5] That many of these achievements were facilitated from the 1950s onwards by reparations from Germany as well as military and financial support from the United States, both necessarily going through government channels, has also furthered the government's control over the economy. Consequently, from its inception until the 1980s Israel was marked by collective ownership, political control, and central planning of the economy. Political control of the economy was achieved not solely by the state but by powerful labor organizations that worked closely with the state and often had more power than some state institutions and structures. The main labor organization of Israel, the Histadrut, organized 25,000 members in mandatory Palestine, which accounted for 75 percent of the Jewish workforce. In 1983 its members counted 1,600,000 (including dependents), accounting for more than one-third of the total population of Israel and about 85 percent of all wage earners. The Histadrut became one of the most powerful institutions in the state of Israel. Aside from being a trade union, its state-building role made it the owner of key of businesses and factories owning 25 percent of the economy and the largest employer in the country.[6] The 1980s inaugurated dramatic changes in Israeli economy and society on all fronts. These economic changes have impacted the totality of life and culture in Israel. From being predominantly employed by the state, Israelis have turned to being mainly employed by business, often international business, from living in a kind of socialist asceticism to becoming hyper consumerist. Israelis who before the 1980s grew up and were socialized within a secular national culture are now significantly socialized by the mass global entertainment industry and news media on the one hand and by religion on the other, from living a kind of socialist asceticism to becoming hyper consumerist. Many of these changes have their historical origin in what is called the Israel Economic Stabilization Plan.[7] The roots of the plan go back to the oil embargo of the Yom Kippur war of 1973. In reaction to Operation Nickel Grass, a strategic airlift operation conducted by the United States to deliver weapons and supplies to Israel during the Yom Kippur war, members of Organization of the Arab Petroleum Exporting Countries raised the price of oil by 70 percent. In response to the inelastic demand of oil, market prices rose dramatically and the world financial system began a phase of recessions and inflations. In Israel inflation went up from an average of 2.0 percent between 1967 and 1971 to 36.6 percent in the years 1974–1977. In 1984 inflation reached 400 percent. The decade between 1973 and 1985 became known as the "lost decade" for its hyperinflation and large government deficit.[8] The global economic crisis was an unrecognized historical "causality" of the Arab-Israeli conflict. The crisis has resulted in the implementation of a transition toward market economy around the world, including Israel. The economic changes that Israel went through in the 1980s have had far reaching societal and cultural effects on every level. A good way to look into the human significance of these changes is to examine the way that individuals from the Zionist mainstream perceived themselves in relationship with state and society before and after liberalization. Liberalization of the economy has expedited a shift in public discourse from articulating social issues from a collective point of view to a more individualist perspective. Before the process of liberalization began people perceived themselves as a kind of "we," often explicitly articulated as such in their discourse. There was a strong willingness to postpone or repress individual needs for the collective needs of both family and nation. The relationship with the state was intense and articulated itself all through the life span. One was very likely to have worked for the state, to have served in the state army for two to three years, enjoyed universal health care and social security, attended state schools and universities, watched television on the one and only state channel, listened to state radio channels where army bands were popular, and received one's pensions through the state. Precisely because the state has organized so much of life, it has never been perceived as a foreign or somehow threatening force for the majority of the Jewish population.[9] A liberal "night watchmen" state was an alien concept since the state's involvement has been crucial in immigration, healthcare, defense, and employment in the formative years. Many segments of the population such as Mizrachi and various religious groups who perceived themselves as being coerced or threatened by the state usually articulated their grievances as new demands from the state, rather than a demand to diminish the role of the state itself.[10] Citizen's critique of the state was often very intimate; citizens expressed anger at politicians for making mistakes, but held a basic belief that the political system is looking after general well-being. While many of these attitudes still prevail in Israel, this intense relationship with the state has weakened in the last thirty years. Less and less people work for the state or for public institutions, children of those who have been public servants are very likely to work for either multinationals or various service industries catering to these multinationals. These newer generations do not see public service as attractive enough in terms of remuneration, but perhaps more importantly such work does not correspond to internalized images of success and fame produced by the culture industries and the media. Culture that used to be produced through state institutions became largely commercial. Both health and education have been strongly affected by these changes. Those who can afford it turn to private health care; but in any case, all have to deal with the staggering cost of medicine imposed by multinational pharmaceuticals. Private colleges requiring full tuition have sprung up all over Israel. Army service has been rearticulated either as individualist self-realization, an option for a future career, or a burden rather than a contribution to the public good. The perception of the state has also altered; most groups now see the state not as serving the greater public good but as serving sectarian special interests. All of these increasingly create a distance between person and state and draw closer to what is conceived as the alternative to the organizing principle of the state, the market. The individual thus transitions from being in an important and fundamental relationship with the nation-state to being in a fundamental relationship with the job and consumer market. These changes in subjectivity are particularly visible in the realm of narrative, both literature and film, in which biographical lived experience and sensibilities are given a heightened form. This transformation of subjectivities as expressed in narrative can be divided into successive generations that form ideal types.[11] The first generation of Hebrew writers in Israel are often called the statehood generation. They were born in Israel in the 1910s and 1920s and began their literary career in the 1940s. Most of these writers were actual party members of Mapam, a Marxist-Zionist party. This pro-Soviet party was ideologically aligned on all issues with the Soviet Union except on the issue of Zionism itself where soviet anti-Zionist policy was considered a mistake that will eventually be recognized.[12] This very leftist statehood generation was a leading force in Israel. Its life-changing event has been the participation in the war of 1948 that was perceived as a war for survival. The war that had an extremely high casualty rate relative to the population was perceived as an unavoidable sacrifice in creating the state.[13] This is the generation of the "founding fathers" of Israel and its "greatest generation" combined. Having witnessed the Holocaust, they were the most committed to state building and defense. The narratives of their literature followed their central experiences of growing up in collective groups in Kibbutzim and Moshavim and active of traumatic combat in the war of 1948.[14] The style of their literature has been very much been informed by social realism, the dominant style of most socialist states. Israeli social realism often figured idealistic Kibbutzniks and soldiers torn between their dedication to society and their romantic longings.[15]

THE IMMEDIATE BACKGROUND: INDIVIDUAL SENSITIVITY IN THE 1960s AND 1970s

The cultural generation following were born around the time that the state was created and came into their own in the late 1960s and early 1970s. They have not experienced the birth of the state as adults nor have they participated in the war for independence. From a contemporary point of view their generation forms a transition between two life-world systems: the national one and the global-capitalist one.[16] In terms of their economic situation the middle class usually worked in government jobs, while the lower class ran small very local businesses. However, their culture has already transitioned away from state. Though this generation looks transitional in many ways it has been the most persuasive in articulating what we have come to think of as the quintessence of Israeliness. We can shorthand this generation by a long list of writers, film makers, artists, and musicians whose work became both popular and the canonical core of Israeli culture. In fact their work has been deemed representative of Israeli culture well into the early 1980s: In film the New Sensibility of Uri Zohar, David Perlov, Avraham Heffner; in music the soft rock of Erik Einstein, Shalom Chanoch, Matti Caspi, Shlomo Grunich, Ariel Zilber; in literature and poetry the works of Yaakov Shabtai, Yona Wallach, Yehuda Amichi, Natan Zach, and Amos Oz. What characterizes their work is a withdrawal from the big themes of national redemption and a focus on private everydayness, an everydayness that was in fact enabled by a strong interventionist welfare state and was shielded from strong market forces. The typical heroes of this kind of culture were marginal figures, who do not participate in state building or culture.[17] Uri Zohar's heroes are hedonistic beach bums, sexually frustrated reserve soldiers, sports coaches, and others who fail to represent the ideals of society.[18] Amos Oz portrays latter day Chekhovian provincial figures whose economic situation in life is modest but stable, which enables his characters to concentrate on repressed libidinal longing or expressed romance and sexuality.[19] Amichi's poetry explicitly deals with the rejection of being subjugated to the history of the nation and its attendant violence and to clear a space for the individual and his or her everyday life experience. His poems express a wish to die on his bed ("I want to die in bed") instead of in a heroic battle, not to be politically right but to flourish and live everyday life ("The Place Where We are Right").[20] Israeli rock and pop of that generation is also filled with celebrating small everydayness. Erik Einstein is perhaps Israel's most canonized male singer, who sings songs dedicated to driving slowly or his fondness for sleeping. In his song "Get Out of It," explicitly he sings:

> Perhaps you should stop fighting with the world then you would feel much more stable.[21]

Shalom Chanoch, Israel's quintessential rock musician, famously sings:

> What do you do when you wake up in the morning? The same things but slowly.[22]

Later in a more introspective mood Shalom Chanoch sings:

> A man lives inside himself, inside himself. Sometimes he is sad or bitter, sometimes he sings, sometimes he opens a door to receive someone he knows, but for most of the time man shuts himself inside himself.[23]

While such a song that Chanoch himself has written was most obviously related to a poetic rendition of personal loss (a divorce that he went through), still such lines were unimaginable just twenty years before. Their expression would have been considered too individualist, too disengaged from the collective efforts, almost reactionary. Arial Zilber is another seminal figure of Israeli rock who from the beginning articulated a kind of zany Israeli vitality quips:

> I used to have principles, I have sold them all. A great deal for me and good for them. Now that there is nothing to believe in I sink often in hallucinations on sex.[24]

It is as if this generation was insisting on everydayness and normalcy in defiance of the "melodramatic" narratives of the Holocaust, Arab-Israeli wars, and state building. In their cultural making they were in a sense saying "let us be, leave us alone with your demands for sacrifice, we want to experience ourselves, our everyday life, our individuality." This explosion of creativity, this innovative exploration of subjectivity and authenticity was enabled by a juxtaposition of several related conditions both national and global. On the global international level the late 1960s and early 1970s have seen an explosion of creativity in film, literature, and music. Rock has gained universal appeal through the likes of the Beatles. French new wave and art film has also burst unto the world stage. These creative impulses are then creatively mediated, adopted, glocalized, and "made native" for an Israeli audience.[25]

They express both a distinct Israeli style and articulate distinct Israeli specific meanings. While the cultural explosion of the late 1960s and early 1970s had a clear political meaning of rejecting the values and practices of existing society, such as in the United States, Germany, and France; in Israel the culture of the 1970s did not engage in culture in the name of rebellion but as we saw before sought a kind of individual disengagement from the demands of the state. Artists were mostly nonpolitical and sought to appease their audience. They have not taken a stand on contested political issues. It is for this reason that most culture of the late 1960s and 1970s was not rebellious but conciliatory.[26] Not political, not "enlisted" to the state, artists work and sensibilities were nevertheless enabled by the very support that the state provided in employment, health, and education. It is in this context that artists could explore subjectivity and everydayness relatively free from market pressures. Their works seems free from the struggle to secure employment or the need to generate wealth. The structure of feelings that permeate their work is not affected by ideals and aspirations of consumerist culture. For example, their characters and their persona never present themselves as aspiring for aura and status accrued by Western rock stars, celebrities, famous actors, or sport stars. In their art, they take pains to represent themselves and their main characters as everyday people, similar and not above their audience. The audience itself had no desire to be famous and thus there was no need to provide it with the mediated experience of being famous. In a society in which wants are relatively modest and many of the basic needs are supplied by the state, and where one was surrounded and recognized by relatively tight knit group of peers, being famous did not have the many added incentives material and symbolic that characterize contemporary Israel. Materially, since the 1990s, being famous has come to mean escaping economic uncertainty, the ability to afford housing, health, education, and travel as well as upper end consumer goods. In the symbolic realm being famous provides recognition and affirmation of self-worth at a time when recognition by one's peers has declined. However, in the 1970s the artist and performer presented a kind of joyous and self-contented everyman. In many ways the artist celebrated both self and locality, an artistic pleasurable rendering of normal provinciality. Though their styles have often been imported and adopted (rock, new wave) the content, the human experience rendered was very local and not global, meetings with various Others in their art are relatively rare, and their work does not represent significant experiences abroad. Their very local horizons are perhaps best symbolized by their linguistic competencies. This generation is perhaps the most monolingual generation in Israel. Previous generations were likely to be immigrants who know several languages (Yiddish, Arabic, Polish, Russian, English, etc.). While subsequent generations have had to master at least English and often learn another language for economic reasons (e.g., German, Chinese, Japanese) and Arabic for military service. Indeed, this linguistic and cultural simplicity and lack of cultural and material resources was celebrated in a variety of mediums. Two good examples are Uri Zohar's films and Israeli art movement "Want of Matter." Uri Zohar's best films feature very local "barren" settings like the beach in *Peeping Toms,* dilapidated apartment buildings in *Big Eyes* and *Three Days and a Child.*[27] Perhaps the most fitting description of this cultural trend has been the concept "Want of Matter," a term coined by curator Sara Breitberg-Semel, who has identified this art as using local low-cost materials such as plywood, cardboards, industrial paints, writing, and scribbling. In her influential essay Breitberg-Semel compares painter Raffi Lavie's works to the pop art of Robert Rauschenberg:

> Rauschenberg put into his works ridicules objects and photographs, while the background for his work are the towers of glass and steel of the biggest and most alienated city in the world. In social terms one can see this as a declaration of rebellion and a statement of other values. In Lavie's works in contrast, there is no discrepancy between the world in the picture and the world outside of it—small intimate city at the rim of the Mediterranean Sea. The great Zionist experience, full of pathos, value laden, shrinks, that is to a physical falling in love with the city. To the child of Tel-Aviv there is no religion, no people, no country, there is a city. No ideology, just vitality. Beyond all of these, beyond the scribbling and the want of matter, the works present the figure of the dispossessed Sabra: the one who placed Judaism under malignant Diaspora; shook off the Zionist myth with it pathos, like any other myth, symbol or phrase; is full of contempt for European bourgeois decadence with all its worldly possessions, and clings to the behavior of torn patches, tattered rages as authentic expression.[28] (My translation)

Part of this localism this "no religion, no people no country" is also the lack of contact with others. For mainstream artists and writers of that generation there was little contact with those outside of their social milieu, which was Ashkenazi, secular, and middle class. This provincialism was sometimes celebrated as a kind of patriotic, narcissistic self-sufficiency, a hedonistic localism as we saw in the quotes from popular music above, at other times it was viewed more critically as a constraining provincialism in Chanoch Levin's or Amos Oz's novels. In any case Israel is distant from the rest of the world. To relate both distances Oz translates the provincial sensibilities of Anton Chekov and Sherwood Anderson into an Israeli idiom.[29] Levin uses theater of the absurd as his stylistic model and relates the same sense of provincialism in a much more explicit manner.[30] The existence that they relate is always one of distance, distance not only from other places but distance from other kinds of people. If there is a meeting with someone from abroad, it is not a normal everyday affair but an amplified occasion. The meeting is essentially an occasion for persuasion, where the Israeli partner takes pains to explain and justify himself. The foreigner (most usually an American or a European) is implicitly being persuaded to support the Zionist endeavor. A good example of this is Uri Zohar's film *Every Bastard a King* (1968), which follows an ultra-masculine Hemmingway-like writer called Roy Hemmings who comes to report on the war of 1967. Roy is chaperoned all across Israel by the Yoram (Yehoram Gaon) who takes him to bohemian parties but also gets him to meet the idealistic and charming Raphi Cohen (played by Oded Kotler), a peace activist who flew without authorization to Egypt in an attempt to meet Gamal Abdel Nasser and prevent what was to be the six-day war.[31] However ideologically committed films like *Every Bastard a King* were quite rare in the late 1960s. Zohar's own opus is as we have seen not overtly ideological. Meetings with global others are rare and only serve to provide perspective on the Zionist project itself. There is never a serious consideration of the life of the other in and of itself, and culture remains very local.

To recapitulate, the background for the changes that this book deals with can be characterized as a combination of a very strong state with strong political control over the economy, schooling, and culture while at the same time a new culture is formed that tries to articulate a movement away from grand narratives toward the sensitive individual in his or her everydayness. This is the immediate cultural background against which the rapid changes starting in the 1980s take place.

LIBERALIZING ISRAELI SOCIETY IN THE 1990s: A BRIDGE TO THE PRESENT

The individualism of the 1970s was a cultural project seemingly lacking in political significance, a celebration of the everyday and the individual without clear political repercussions. Though the injunction was for everyday enjoyment, it was presented as a kind of temporary reprieve from the demands of nation building. By the early 1990s this essentially cultural project has turned into a full-fledged project of liberalization of state, society, and culture on all fronts. A good example of this is the actions of the Supreme Court in the 1990s. The Supreme Court started its work on a future constitution through basic laws that were to articulate basic human rights. In 1992 two basic laws were articulated: freedom and dignity of persons and freedom of occupation. In the early 1990s the Supreme Court ruled in several instances against military censorship and use of excessive violence, and promoted equality between different sectors in Israeli society. For example, the year 1994 saw a ruling that states that employees cannot discriminate between heterosexual and homosexual couples in their provision of benefits. This year saw another ruling that stated that the Israeli Defence Forces (IDF) couldn't discriminate based on gender in terms of acceptance to elite units.[32] The year 1993 saw the signing of the Oslo accords on the White House lawn that was supposed to put an end to Israeli rule over the territories and thus make almost all of those who live under Israeli rule full citizens of the state. Revisionist histories were written on the policy of the state regarding Holocaust survivors, Palestinians, and Mizrahim, and a wide-ranging discussion in the newspapers and in academia took place regarding the tensions between Jewish and democratic articulations of the state. In film, television and literature, and the media, as we shall see later, an active reform of nationalist identity was taking place. Postmodern writers like Etgar Keret, Orly Castle-Bloom writing in colloquial Hebrew attempted to reform national identity through satire. Palestinians with Israeli citizenships like Sayed Kashua and Anton Shamas attempted a critique of the contradictory forces of inclusion and exclusion of mainstream national culture. Even an older generation of writers like Amos Oz and Yoram Kaniuk attempted to "treat" the excess causes of national violence and attempted a liberal reform often drawing from Jewish traditions of the diaspora. Television shows like the *Chamber Quintet* (Hahamishia Hakamerit) satirized sacred cows or controversial or extremely touchy issues of Israeli culture including the IDF and its rituals, instrumental use of the Holocaust, the settlement movement, public diplomacy also known as Hasbara, and the murder of Yitzhak Rabin. The early 1990s saw an active process of liberalization on many fronts, a political peace process, a legal articulation of inalienable human rights, culture, and research that reveals various problems with nationalism and aims at reforming them. This book argues that this intervention and its repercussions and reversals has been the most important event in Israel in the last forty years. It is at the core of the antagonism that Israel has been experiencing ever since between international liberalism and neo-nationalism. In contrast to theorists in the 1990s who thought of a smooth transition to liberal internationalism (e.g., End of History) and recent theories of populism and neo-nationalism, the book makes an argument to the irreversibility and disruption of the cultural changes brought about in the 1990s. It claims that contrary to the intentions of those who undertook these cultural interventions, they in fact inaugurated an irrevocable transition away from civic nationalism and its culture. The second intifada has acerbated this trend. By the early 2000s the Supreme Court lost influence, the peace process ground to a halt, critique of illiberal aspects of nationalism and militarism has been repressed. However, in contrast to the cessation of cultural and political aspects of liberalization, the 2000s saw economic liberalization and ensuing marketization continue unabated. From the 2000s life narratives in Israel are strongly coupled with both the opportunities and pressures of marketization, globalization, and commercialization. Israeli culture is no longer about personal expression and subjectivity as it was in the 1970s nor is it transformative politically, but mainly reflects pressures of the local or global market and of the precarious subject. The horizon of expectations informing much of the work being produced, as well as the global conditions of production itself, exert economic pressures that preclude the kind of "indulgent" psychological realism and romantic individualism of the culture of the 1970s, or even the stress on liberalization, critique, and satire of the 1990s. Though Israeli culture has transitioned from collective identity to the individualism of the everyday and then to economic individualism, it is faced with severe problems that pertain to the public good. The nation-state and its demands and difficulties do not disappear; Israel's place in the world and in the Middle East is not "naturalized" and is not seen as legitimate by many across the world, least of all by Palestinians. Israel also faces challenges in terms of immigration, environment, education, health, and economic inequality. Many sectors of Israeli society especially the Orthodox Hardi and the Arab population are underdeveloped. However, at the same time public mindedness, and new articulations of the common good are not a predominant aspiration, and are not portrayed as such. There are several underlining causes for the decline in ideals of citizenship and civic virtues. One main cause is that economic and technological development that used to take place under various public and political bodies, such as the state, worker unions, Kibbutzim, cooperatives is undertaken largely by corporations and private enterprise. As a consequence, innovation, what was conceived in the past as progress, is wholly independent from citizenship. Innovation, development, and progress express themselves in the world market, outside of the framework of the nation-state. They contribute simultaneously to worldwide technological capabilities and to the economic well-being of a relatively small sector of technology professionals. Innovations impact on Israel is relatively small as it does not transform or develop the nation-state as a whole. This stands in contrast to the past in which technological developments in agriculture, textile, and other light industries had developmental effects on almost the whole nation-state. Military service is another major aspect with which civic virtues and public mindedness were expressed in Israel. Up to and through the war of 1973 military service was perceived as essential to the collective survival of the state. From the state's creation until that time it was one of the most venerated institutions in Israel. However, since that time it has undergone significant changes in some of its most salient tasks, and therefore in the way that it is perceived. These changes occurred as a result of broad global transformations such as the decline of ideologies and growth of individualism coupled with very specific national reasons. The Lebanon War of 1983, that was costly in lives, was seen by many as a superfluous war, a war of choice as the expression went. The protests in Tel-Aviv over the IDF indirect involvement in the massacre in

Sabra and Shatila were the largest Israel had seen until this time. While the territories acquired in the war of 1967 have not presented themselves as a particular problem to most Israelis, by the first intifada (1987–1993) and the second intifada (2000–2005) it was clear that a major task of the IDF is to control and police the population in the territories. Decline in the importance of ideology and individualism and the changing role of the military have eroded its allure among mainstream population, and have created a new attitude toward military service. These implicit changes were finally made public and explicit in the elections of 2013. When the issue of lack of recruitment of Haredim and Arabs exploded into the public sphere and was a significant issue in the election itself,[33] it is quite telling and significant that the term that everyone used in the media was "equality in the burden" (שוויון בנטל). Thus, everyone who participated in this discourse saw military service through the conceptual framework of the term "burden." This is very instructive since Israeli culture offers other terms. The term "service" (שירות), for instance that is already used in such combinations such as "national service" (שירות לאומי). One could also have used the word "enlistment" (גיוס). One could easily imagine that the contested rallying cry would be "equality in service" or even "equality in enlistment," both are imbued with feelings and conceptions of republican citizenship, which the word "burden" explicitly lacks. Thus, it seems that citizenship often articulated in Israel as the heroic and existentially essential military service is not something which is conceived as an inspiring ideal but on the contrary, it is articulated as a burden. In contrast to the "sensitive" generation of the 1970s, the ambivalence regarding the burden and sacrifice is not articulated in the name of self-expression and individuality, but mainly because it detracts from economic survival or success. In a sense, the very antinomy between commitment to the nation and self-expression of individuality has been superseded by the tension between serving the state and success or failure in the market. Since the market from the very beginning valorizes the individual, individuality is not an aspiration like in the 1970s, but a hard economic and social fact of positive self-reliance or its obverse economic insecurity. This individuality however is not an internal "sensitive," "lyric," "romantic" individuality nor is it hedonistic and marginal appealing to the simple (though thoroughly chauvinistic) pleasures of woman, friends and nature that were articulated in the film and music of the 1970s. It is a precarious individuality heavily influenced by commercial culture, by the job market, and by desires for fame and fortune. The individual both directly feels their insecure position in the market but also has been socialized to be attuned to the market itself.

In the contemporary socialization process in Israel that culminates in adulthood, three very persistent socializing forces exercise their decisive long-term pressures of parents and teachers and an all-pervasive popular and consumer culture. Parents and teachers try to have children acquire marketable skills as well as a viable Jewish identity. In terms of marketable skills, parents and teachers stress math, technology, and increasingly biology. In this way, parents, teachers and increasingly the children themselves have internalized the job market perspective, more precisely the perspective of a future employer. Parents especially are aware of the need to provide comparative advantage for their children in relation to peers in a future competitive job market. Jewish identity on the other hand can be conceived as a kind of fixed asset. Though it is almost always conceived as biologically given, it is in actuality reproduced through practices that enhance Jewish identity such as holidays, remembrance ceremonies, Bible class, and trips to Poland or Jerusalem. Parents and teachers attempt to reproduce their own kind of Jewish identity. Secular parents and teachers, for example, are usually weary of significant extension or elaboration of Jewish identity (becoming "Born Again") or what is conceived of as the diluting or diminishing of Jewish identity by intermarriage. This desire for cultural reproduction may succeed or may fail in various ways that are related to the broader changes taking place in Israel. The natural expectation that their "brand" of Jewish identity will be reproduced has been problematized by what sociologists Urlich Beck, Anthony Giddens, and Scott Lash call reflexive modernization of identity.[34] Under reflexive modernity, individuals feel entitled and empowered to critically reflect, adopt, or reject tradition and ways of life that were reproduced automatically so to speak before. In Israel, this includes marrying and having a family, circumcision, the extent of study of Judaism and Bible, and most importantly the choice of staying or leaving Israel. All of these choices have been affected by globalization and liberalization. Secular Israelis might choose to elaborate on their Jewish identity in ways that their parents did not, for example by studying post-biblical texts. On the other hand, circumcision has become a subject of discussion in Israel, it is no longer the automatic thing to do. Globalization coupled with reflective modernity has made staying in or leaving Israel a conscious choice. Staying in one's country which has been seen as natural is becoming a conscious choice. This choice often needs a discourse of justification attached to it. Staying or leaving Israel of course has important ramifications for Jewish as well as Israeli identity. Jewish identity in the diaspora is significantly different than its counterpart in Israel. In Israel, a secularized Jewish identity is dispersed in all spheres of life; media, culture, education, army service, and use of Hebrew. Jewish identity in the diaspora focuses mainly on the synagogue and Jewish day school. Leaving Israel thus has important consequences for Jewish identity. The liberal intervention of the 1990s has not only made all of these individual reflective choices in need of explicit justification, it has also devalued those who culturally or socially reproduce "unthinkingly."

The other socializing force that saw its impetus in the 1990s is an all-pervasive consumer culture.

Since the 1990s this takes the form of an increasingly invasive media that articulates pleasure, enjoyment as well as worldview. Though parents and teachers may signal that commercial entertainment is not to be taken seriously and may even be critical of it for a variety of different reasons (religious, humanistic, etc.), nevertheless commercial media has both obviously direct and indirect effects on the way that children are socialized in Israel. Many sophisticated accounts from Frankfurt school to cultural studies have been captivated by analyzing content, message, and ideology of popular culture and often miss a more fundamental influence: the way in which popular culture enthralls and squeezes out other forms of socialization, rendering other forms of education and even other forms of entertainment, a kind of drudgery that is less "fun" and less "cool." In this way it precludes access to history, culture, and politics, and to the wider world outside of popular American culture. In addition to squeezing out other kinds of media and content, popular culture compensates, forms an ersatz for contemporary life. Sitcoms and talk shows compensate for lack of friendships. Identification with the hero in action films compensates for lack of agency in lives and work, popular music either placates (e.g., ambient, coffee house, or elevator music) or gives vent to frustrations (e.g., rock, metal, and hip-hop).[35] Commercial culture however not only squeezes out other interests or engages in compensation, it also elicits desires and dreams; it forms the model of what one finds valuable and who we aspire to be like. Children growing up in a market economy live under two conflicting injunctions. One from their "realist" parents and teachers who are trying to instill skills needed in the future job market, and the other originating in glamorous role models of famous actors, athletes, celebrities, musicians; in short, those that rosrising above the anonymity of contemporary life. Commercial culture in Israel as elsewhere generates enjoyment, compensates, and presents a normative model. While much of the effects of popular culture are global, their context of implementation is always particular. As presented above, aside from market culture that is either mediated through socializing agents or through popular culture, Israeli children imbue some combination of old and new forms of national and religious culture. National and religious culture and socialization are for most people in contemporary Israel both complimentary and antagonistic to this basic capitalist culture. Many political theorists have commented that liberal capitalism is unable to provide key emotional and social needs. According to Jürgen Habermas liberal capitalism "offers no support, in the face of the basic risks of existence (guilt, sickness, death) or interpretations that overcome contingency; in the face of individual needs for wholeness [Heilsbedürfnisse], they are disconsolate . . . [it] permits no intuitive access to relations of solidarity within groups or between individuals, allows no real political ethic in any case in political and social life."[36] Habermas is explicating the social and emotional deficits in liberal capitalism. Liberal capitalism does not offer support in case of many kinds of loss. For example, in case one experiences death or sickness of loved ones there are no communal or supportive elements, which inhere in liberal capitalism. A religious worldview overcomes negative feelings associated with contingency; "why was I born in this time and place, to these parents, in this station?" A religious worldview also provides a godly plan or direction that overcomes negative aspects of contingency and a sense of wholeness with the world. Since liberal capitalism is essentially an ideology that protects the individual, his privacy, property, and other rights, it finds it hard to articulate a collective mobilizing political ethos. It also finds it hard to connect individuals with each other and with something greater than themselves. It is these lacks that national or religious worldviews come to complement. One can add that socialization under capitalism compounds isolation and competition in the job market with the hedonism of consumerist market.[37] Religious and national communities, discourses, and rituals offer real or imagined connection and solidarity with others while at the same time generating pride at the postponement of pleasures.[38] However for exactly some of the same reasons, national and religious culture and practices stand in an antagonistic relationship with capitalism. While in some influential accounts, capitalism itself originates from religious innovation (Weber's Protestant ethic) and in other no less famous accounts religion is the soothing ideology that keeps capitalism from being overthrown (Marx's opium), it seems today that capitalism is increasingly more independent from religion, and that it wears away at the fundamental attributes underlining religious practice. Capitalism is inseparable from key attributes of modernity that have been radically transformative since the Renaissance including individualism, entrepreneurship, rationality, and experimentation. Many of these basic value orientations stand in friction with traditional religion. Individualism for instance leads people to prefer their own short-term good over a willingness to make sacrifices for groups such family and religious community. A highly dynamic global job market that encourages flexibility and gender equality necessarily leads to a significant reduction in people who opt to create and stay in families and religious communities. When considering a host of issues, individuals are likely to look at their own benefit quite narrowly conceived and to take up opportunities like immigration or intermarriage that threaten or disrupt the continuity of religious, ethnic, and national community. Experimentation and rationality are alternative sources of authority and praxis than religious tradition. When experimental rationality takes over as a major source of authority, most dramatically in society's account and manipulation of the natural world, in its economic and legal behavior and in technology, religious tradition often withdraws and concentrates on "core" competences of relations with the divine, religious ritual, and community building. However even this "core" is threatened by an onslaught of synergies of global entertainment, the internet and hyper commercialism. Global entertainment and consumerism create a totally ubiquitous and compelling world of enjoyment that forcibly "pushes" out other content. In many ways, the liberal intervention of the early 1990s and its corresponding culture have pushed religious as well as national culture aside. National culture in the form of folk songs, folk dances has been wholly jettisoned by commercial entertainment.

It is perhaps because of this withdrawal that both religion and nationalism in Israel have sought to reassert themselves in new modes, such as Chabad's ultramodern ways of outreach and religious Zionism's intensive and increasing participation in key institutions of the state especially the army and the education system. In terms of socialization both institutions have a captive audience; that is, they can exercise control of education outside the market forces. While both strategies have been partially successful in drawing people into the religious and national sphere of influence, these same populations whether as consumers or as workers are increasingly subject to global economic imperatives that undermine them. Both religious and civic republican virtues become largely irrelevant or even weigh down with their commitments on those who actively participate in wider global economic production networks. These networks produce and consume for populations vastly more numerous than the small domestic Israeli market or of most other nation-states. Increasingly people in Israeli society are very active participants in a global network of economy, knowledge production, technological development, and consumption on one level while taking part in a distinctly national or religious community whether in the army, school, or synagogue as a kind of "extra" outside of the global economic rationality governing life. In thought and discourse as well, a split exists between a kind of general, global calculated, "cool" and functional economic and liberal "common sense" articulated toward the world in general and a much "hotter" discourse that pertains to nation and religion that has been compartmentalized. Globalized Israelis function with this functional "cool" set of facilities in their global work only to sometimes transition into a more specific "hot" and relatively emotional set of discourses, mental schemes and affects when dealing with "their" nation in particular. This set of discourses is "hot" in that it is imbued with emotions that stem from its partially imagined nature. Imagined not in the sense in which Benedict Anderson used the term, a community imagined through the print capitalism, but an imagined community in the sense that the nation-state no longer constitutes an effective social and political unit and that therefore one's attachments and hopes regarding this unit, one's belief in the sovereignty of the people and their common fate are partially based on illusion. As the nation-state becomes less and less autonomous in culture and economy, as it is more and more integrated globally the very ideals of the nation-state and what it can achieve become vague and unclear. It is worthwhile to try to formulate the normative ideals of the state of Israel and see how they fair under globalization. Israel has often been normatively characterized as a Jewish democracy. Indeed, the Jewish state has provided citizenship rights, and the protection afforded by those rights, to European Jews who were either without citizenship (east Europe) or those whose formal citizenship failed to offer protection when anti-Semitism became a powerful force in Western Europe.[39] Israel has also provided full citizenship to those Jewish Middle Eastern Jews who enjoyed no such rights as well as to Palestinians inside the green line. Israel however has not extended those rights to Palestinians living in the territories conquered in the 1967 war. Regardless of its mixed track record on individual citizenship rights, it is important to stress that the Zionist project was and is geared toward Jewish collective national rights. Israel is the state of the Jewish people. In its declaration of independence we read:

> This recognition by the United Nations of the right of the Jewish people to establish their State is irrevocable. This right is the natural right of the Jewish people to be masters of their own fate, like all other nations, in their own sovereign State.

In attempting to legitimize sovereignty the declaration harks back to the pioneers who have come to settle the land especially the second and third Alyia:

> Pioneers, ma'pilim [(Hebrew)—immigrants coming to Eretz-Israel in defiance of restrictive legislation] and defenders, they made deserts bloom, revived the Hebrew language, built villages and towns, and created a thriving community controlling its own economy and culture.

These are the ideals with which the Jewish state has been normatively conceived, as a thriving and democratic autonomous community. However, both democracy and Jewish sovereignty, fair badly under marketization and globalization. As we have seen various kinds of having sovereignty, of being "masters of their own fate" and "controlling economy and culture," have diminished by marketization and globalization. In the last four decades the Israeli state has rearticulated and reduced its mission to that of state security, and guaranteeing property rights. Rather than being a relatively autonomous unit with its own purpose it has increasingly become an important arena for furthering of global agendas. One such agenda can be called global liberal culture. This agenda, shared by liberal elites worldwide, furthers a normative horizon of non-coercion and racial and gender equality.

The leading global economies including the United States and Europe are committed to basic human rights and equality before the law and sometimes even aspire to have equality of opportunity. Local Israeli representatives of such trends include human rights organizations, Israeli feminism, LGBT movements, Mizrachi organizations, the liberal left and liberal Arab political parties, Jewish reform movements, and so on. One can see all of these movements as sharing a common agenda of basic legal rights and freedom accorded by liberal doctrine. These trends contain a democratizing trend in Israeli society. Not democratizing in the sense of the greater sovereignty and agency of the people but in the sense of greater freedoms for individuals and groups from coercion and discrimination. The introduction of liberal values coupled with market economy in the early 1990s by Israel's elite and its repercussions to this day are at the center of this book. While globalization and marketization further the democratic principal of equal rights, they undermine other forms of equality. Marketization causes a growing gap in incomes but more crucially a growing inequality between the concentrated wealth generated from owning capital, to the income generated by work itself. Both the concentration of wealth and the lack of proper compensation for work undermine democracy in various ways. The erosion in salaries has translated into a cost of living crisis. Outside those who own capital and those who are well positioned in very specific industries (hi-tech, banking, entertainment, energy), most are struggling with a growing discrepancy between relatively modest incomes to very high cost of living. Large concentrations of wealth have started to distort political process in general and representation of reality in the media in particular. It has skewed the way that the media represents reality from the interest of the many toward the interest of a few very wealthy families.[40] A good example is the way that Israel's perhaps most influential documentary of all time *The Shakshuka System*, a 2008 documentary created by investigative journalist Mickey Rosenthal, was almost not screened or aired in Israel under pressure of the Ofer family. The film reveals the relationship between the political leadership of Israel and the Ofer family, one of the wealthiest in Israel. It shows how government officials who carried privatizations on behalf of the state became senior employees of the Ofer group after retiring from the public sector. Among others the films interviews Ram Caspi, a lawyer who represented the Ofer group in negotiations on the acquisition of the state owned Zim, the biggest cargo shipping company in Israel and the 10th largest in the world. The Ofer group was the only company to participate in the auction over Zim's shares. Some have estimated that Zim was sold to the Ofers at a price of about one-fourth of its actual value. The Ofer family has tried at first successfully to suppress the production and later the showing of the film. It has filed a lawsuit against Rosenthal and his wife (who has not been involved in the film). Wide public support for Rosenthal was expressed by more than a thousand people in the internet who committed to paying one thousandth of the sum which Rosenthal would be asked to pay if the Ofer family would win the claim. Rosenthal has also received death threats. The media conglomerate *Yes* which initially helped finance the film withdrew its backing and cancelled its broadcast. Due to a conference and organization of filmmakers on the theme of censorship under the pressure of wealthy industrialists, the Tel-Aviv Cinematheque agreed to show the film even though it received letters from the lawyers of the Ofer family, later on the film was also screened in the Jerusalem Cinematheque. Only then did Channel 10 and Channel 1 (the state channel) express interest, however they too received letters from Ofer family lawyers and decided not to screen it. The association of citizen's rights then appealed to the Israel's Broadcasting Authority with the claim that the intense pressure of preventing the screening are creating a precedent and have become a decisive issue for freedom of speech and democracy in Israel. Channel 1 ultimately decided that the film will be screened with a response film by the Ofer family. Ofer's film had a large budget and cost half a million dollars. Both were screened in a special broadcast on July 28, 2009. The production and reception of the film itself were indicative of the way that cultural production in Israel stands in power field in which private interests threaten not only material public goods such as Zim itself but also immaterial public goods such as free speech. The difficulties that this film has met reveal how difficult it has become to go against strong private interests in Israel. Though the film was ultimately successful it hints at the countless of other cases in which self-censorship sets the tone. The fact that the national public channel was hesitant about showing a film that clearly dealt with a key public concern has revealed the weakness of a public institution that Israelis have relied on to represent the public interest. In fact the story highlights the radical transformation of the mediascape in the last thirty years. Though the state has energetically privatized public enterprises like Zim and natural commons (e.g., the Dead Sea) giving over its shared natural resources for commercial use (e.g., gas) no industry has been so quickly and thoroughly marketized and privatized as the media in Israel.

CULTURE AND MARKETIZATION OF MEDIA

This book argues that cultural and technological elites in the early 1990s have introduced both liberalism as a cultural ideology and global market knowledge economy to Israel. I argue that this introduction has inaugurated a dynamic that has transformed culture in Israel. It has resulted in new freedoms as well as new hardships for individuals as well as in a neo-nationalist backlash. In the realm of cultural production, it has resulted in the internationalization of film, the commercialization of television, and the fragmentation of culture according to ethnicity, language, and religion. It is to these structural effects of the marketization of the media that this chapter is devoted.

The marketization of Israeli media can be discussed on two levels. One level is the general bird's eye view of the way in which capitalism effects the production, mediation, and consumption of media production in Israel. Such a view seeks to answer questions such as what are the effects of the implementation of a market economy on Israeli cultural production? How has it affected the production of culture in terms of quantity and diversity? How have commercial technological innovations impacted culture in Israel? The other level deals with the way that the "content" of cultural products themselves has been shaped by the market economy. How do narratives present lives that have been strongly influenced by market economy? What points of view and what interests are represented in different media? Answering the first set of questions on the first level is a complex task since the effects on culture of marketization and globalization have been complex and diverse. Still one can attempt to give a general picture that can be completed by further research.

PRODUCTION, DISTRIBUTION, AND CONSUMPTION OF CULTURE: GENERAL PARAMETERS

The introduction of a market economy and attendant values of individual choice, diversity, and multiculturalism in the 1990s has had an explosive effect in terms of quantity and diversity of cultural production in Israel. Market strategies have sought to fit cultural products to existing audience niches. Culture now seeks to reaffirm audience expectations rather than form an agenda for the formation or transformation of new subjectivities. Privatization has often created, a media devoid of substantial long-term agenda, while market strategies have reaffirmed a cultural niche. Thus, the centripetal cultural forces of the first fifty years of the state have been replaced by strong centrifugal forces. Culture thus divides the political body. This plurality is celebrated as a new freedom, freedom from the coercive regime of the culture of the secular Ashkenazi labor-Zionist elite, while at the same time this same cultural freedom entails a depolitization of the figure of the people.[41] Multicultural discourse in the 1990s has celebrated cultural freedom without acknowledging that this same cultural freedom accorded to different groups in Israel has had a detrimental effect on the ability to create what Michael Hardt and Antonio Negri describe as the Common.[42] Culture thus presents itself as the locus of freedom, however this freedom is articulated as negative liberty, the liberty not to be coerced to do things you don't want to.[43]

The fragmentation of the media allows one not to be obligated to participate or even consume hegemonic secular, Ashkenazi culture. However at the same time control of production is not really in local hands but has been privatized. A process of privatization of identity and political worldview has taken place throughout the 1980s and 1990s. This process has had complex effects on cultural production. It is undeniable that cultural production like every other kind of production has grown in scale and complexity. However, at the same time in that period it has stopped articulating a republican common good and has established direct relationships between communities in Israel and similar communities abroad.[44] In the period between the 1970s and the 1990s Israel has changed from a society whose connection to the world is largely mediated by various elites to a society where almost the whole population is intensely connected to the world. A useful way to show this transition is the different way in which culture has been typically disseminated before and how it's disseminated today. In the past, what can be called cultural mediators either came from the centers of European capitals or they went on extensive physical "pilgrimage" to the cultural center (usually in Paris and Berlin but sometimes in New York) there they learnt of the recent cultural movements and only then came to Israel.[45] In Israel they undertook the complex difficult task of creating a persuasive local variant of the most recent international artistic trend. Between the 1920s and 1980s life trajectories and biographies all looked quite similar. In literature Abraham Shlonsky, Natan Alterman, Yosef Shemuel Agnon, Yoram Kaniuk all spent a significant amount of time in one of Europe's capitals learning of contemporary trends and then quite creatively adopted them to Hebrew letters. This could mean adopting symbolist poetry into Hebrew and Israeli experience like Natan Alterman, or Chanoch Levin's adaptation of Antonin Artaud theater of cruelty to Israeli historical experience. Israel's pioneering and most influential film maker, for example, Helmar Lerski was born Israel Schmuklerski in Strasbourg in France, moved to Zürich in his youth to study, immigrated in 1893 to the United States as an actor in a German speaking theater in Chicago. In 1915, he immigrated to Berlin and worked in the most important German studio, UFA, on films such as *Opium* (1918) and *Meteropolis* (1926). In the 1930s and 1940s, he directed some of the most celebrated films in Israel including *Work* (1935), *Children of the Sun* (1939), and *Earth* (1947) all of who creatively adopted European styles to local setting and audience. Such adaptations are highly original and complex and indeed such non-European expressions of modernism are gaining prestige, recognition, and canonization around the world.[46] Popular culture was highly mediated and went through a process of complex adaptation to an even greater degree. Popular folk songs in Israel were a kind of adaptation of Russian and East European folk song.[47] This pattern of cultural adaptation has changed significantly. The general effect is less mediation between global currents and local adaptation and a greater awareness of global currents themselves as they exist side by side with local hybrid adaptation. Mediation and the process of what can be anachronistically called glocal adaptation used to be a slow, synchronic, labor-intensive process. A highly skilled elite adopted and localized global forms in music, painting, and theater and made them into an Israeli art form. The relationship with sources of inspiration sometimes remained obscure often intentionally. A good example is folk singing in Israel, that was creatively adopted from Russian folk songs but due to nationalistic reasons this very adaptation has been obscured. A more transparent model was that of pictorial art that was directly and clearly traced to European artistic movements.[48] However even in the case where influence was not denied, both access to precursors and to further developments in Europe has been very limited and the work of mediation has been very labor intensive and largely in the hands of the elite of culture producers. The distance of European models and the work involved in adaptation and bridging this distance meant that developments in Israel lagged behind those of Europe.

Often this lag in time meant that Hebrew artists and poets borrowed European forms while these forms have been challenged and replaced by other forms. Practically this has meant that modernist poets in Israel have borrowed freely from several styles. Thus, for instance modernists such as Alexander Penn, Abraham Shlonsky, Uri Zvi Greenberg, David Fogel, Yokheved Bat Miryam, Esther Raab and Rachel have borrowed freely from groups as stylistically antagonistic as symbolists, expressionists, futurists, creating a unique combination that reflects their experience and their audience.

From the 1990s onward this slow and labor-intensive mediation has largely been superseded. It is no longer the job of cultural producers in Israel to bring and adopt the West to the East. Even when it might look like an artist is bringing an international style to Israel it is no longer really the case. Israeli hip-hop, for example, is a response to a demand of enjoying a specifically local version of a global style. Those who make Israeli hip-hop are not bringing American music to Israel, American hip-hop is highly accessible and widespread in Israel. They are in fact producing a creative local version of the original with different political meaning, originating from a different social position. The majority of Israeli hip-hop artists do not originate from the working class but from upper-middle class that is perhaps most attuned to global trends. Their social position in Israel is not like those of African Americans in the United States nor of Mizrahim in Israel itself. This social position of enunciation strongly affects the overall meaning of the genre in Israel, and makes it very different than its counterparts in the United States. However more different than the classical role of bringing European and American trends to Israel in order to build a new Hebrew culture is the new role of the Israeli artist. This role is not to bring the West to the East but to bring the East to the West. Increasingly the role of representational arts in Israeli, especially film and literature, is to bring Israeli experience to a global audience. For example, many writers and filmmakers are responding to the opportunities of transporting the experience of the Arab-Israeli conflict to European and American audiences. In the 2000s Israel's main writers and filmmakers did just that. David Grossman, A. B. Yahushua, and Amos Oz wrote books on potentially bereaved mother, on the second intifada and on the war of 1948 respectably and there was a spat of films effectively dealing with the Arab-Israeli conflict that garnered both critical acclaim and popularity including: *Waltz with Bashir, Bethlehem, Five Broken Cameras, The Gatekeepers, The Green Prince* as well as many others. Instead of mediating innovative Western styles to Israel, these artists are mediating the drama of Israeli-Palestinian conflict in a relatively popular style to the West. Thus, the globalization of cultural production has created an exoticization of Israeli culture aimed for export. Internally it has seen the implosion of progressive civic nationalist cultural practices. In their place a logic of exporting the exotic for elite global audience and an internal multiculturalism has taken hold. International liberalization that saw its impetus in the early 1990s oversaw the implosion of two of the most important genres of high culture in Israel: modernism and realism. It is to the decline of these two cultural practices that we need to turn to now.

THE CULTURAL CAUSALITIES OF MARKET CAPITALISM: THE DECLINE IN MODERNISM AND REALISM

Market pressures and opportunities have significantly affected the role of the writers and filmmakers, the style and content of the works themselves. Though the market diversified culture it has diversified it toward the popular and the easily digestible as well as toward export. These two trends have seen the decline of two major genres that have been pillars of Israeli culture: classical realism and modernism. Both are deemed "difficult" for contemporary readers and viewers. This "difficulty" is a direct result of the regime of subjectivities under liberalization. Realism is often "difficult" emotionally, in content. Its plots often revolve around identification with the hardships suffered by individuals and families, due to universal human travails such as sickness, poverty, and death but also more specific causes like Holocaust, immigration, unemployment, Arab-Israeli conflict, and racial discrimination. Often it holds a critical mirror in the face of society demanding its transformation. The decline of realism is part and parcel of what Baudrillard called the death of the real. That is the general effacement of connection with social reality in (post-)capitalist consumer culture.[49] However, in contrast to the United States where consumerism and pop culture have developed at least since the end of World War II, such that suburban life and culture in the 1950s seemed unreal or artificial to many, in Israel the death or implosion of the real was inaugurated in the early 1990s with the birth of multichannel popular television. The decline of realism essentially meant the decline in sustained, careful attention and consideration of the life of ordinary people. A regime of narrative attention to the poor, to agricultural or urban workers, that has started in Europe right after the failed revolution in 1848 with bourgeoisie realism and spanned more than a hundred years up until social and socialist realism, has come to an abrupt end. Under this narrative regime ordinary people were seen as having something to teach us, perception of social reality is cultivated as a practice and a virtue, and subjectivities are constructed that aspire for broad societal change. In contrast when subjectivities are constructed in a way that aspires to becoming famous and wealthy (that is an essential wish to leave rather than to change mainstream society), there is little to be gained from depiction of regular people. Given values of commercial culture such depiction becomes unbearable. Its call for empathy and sustained engagement with and attention to everyday life of working-class people becomes intolerable for those who are precisely seeking to leave working-class life, not as a collective but as "special" and "gifted" individuals. In the attentional regime of today's fiction realism becomes confining, producing what is essentially an unendurable boredom. Realism is thus experienced as an emotional difficulty with difficult content. The liberal intervention of the 1990s has unwittingly ushered in a new age and a new taste in Israel.

Modernism and its offshoots are difficult in form. The audience needs to be sophisticated and playful but also has to be willing to face difficulty: that is, to invest the mental energy and openness in order to come up with possible meanings for modernism's puzzles. Audiences must also be willing to frequently contain modernism's negativity as well as its lack of accessibility. Such preconditions are often difficult to meet for a variety of audiences and for various reasons. Modernism, like realism, entails audiences whose motivations and expectations transcend the simple effects of suspense or comic relief. They must develop expectations that go beyond comic relief and excitement. Modernism from Expressionism to Dada to the Theater of Cruelty has stressed intense kinds of experimentation with form, while at the same time often depicting abstract and philosophical ideas on the human condition or the limits of art. Both realism and modernism challenge audiences: they must take culture seriously and go beyond the emotional staple of romantic comedies and action heroes. Audiences that take culture seriously and are willing to forgo simple identifications and affects were difficult to come by in the past as well. However, while artists suffered lack of understanding and lack of popularity in the past, many modernist writers and filmmakers had the confidence that their work is part of the inevitable progress of culture itself. The audience may not understand and appreciate them today but will in the future. The narrative and aesthetic ideologies of their different groups (symbolism, expressionism, futurism, abstract art) very persuasively argued why a certain literary form is better than the one before it. Modernist aesthetic ideologies as they might be called were also couched in Israel as elsewhere in broader visions for a just and progressive society and writers and filmmakers saw themselves as leading the culture forward. This ideology enabled them to resist popular pressure and persevere in creating both thematically and stylistically difficult works. Once this certainty was undermined and the style of modernism itself waned, culture increasingly articulated itself in a direct relationship with the market of cultural consumers and of opportunities for funding. The ideological supportive back-drop of modernism, socialism and even of progressive kinds of nationalism has been undermined, and writers, filmmakers, and artists have found themselves "naked" and often alone: that is, without artistic movements to support them, in a direct contact with economic pressures and opportunities of local and global markets and funding agencies.

COMMERCIAL CULTURE AND ITS DETRACTORS

Global marketization has created a whole new context and environment for Israeli culture with distinct ways of producing and consuming culture, and with unique problems and opportunities. The pressures, prospects, and effects of the market have been felt at every level of Israeli culture. However, despite the loss of artistic movements, marketization has created various positive outcomes as well. When viewing the effects of the market and capitalism on culture in general it is important not to succumb to totalizing negative vision and to cultural pessimism. Cowen Tyler has typified commercial culture positively thus:

> Profit and fame incentives, decentralized financial support, the possibility of financial independence for some artists, the entrepreneurial discovery of new artistic technologies and media, and the ability to profit by preserving the cultural creations of the past.[50]

Tyler and others have offered to examine the effects of the market on culture by bracketing prevailing cultural pessimism of the conservative right and of the anti-commercial left. Both would like their own culture to be hegemonic, both are likely to miss the fact that although their cultures are indeed visibly marginal in fact they are being produced and consumed on a scale that was never known before. While Tyler makes a strong argument regarding the increased cultural production of all kinds of culture, what he misses and what the right and the left both perceive correctly is the increasing domination and hegemony of commercial culture itself. Commercial culture monopolizes attention, conquers both the internet and public space while other types of culture are relegated to "ghettos" of special institutions and media. These include schools and universities; religious institutions such as synagogues, churches, and mosques; the army; libraries; and special internet sites. All of these are becoming less visible and less present than films, computer games and television series, social media, and so on. However, it is important to stress that the combined socialization power of these institutions is still very influential. In Israel both the liberal left and the religious right have made effective use of institutions in order to pursue their agenda. Universities in Israel have become a stronghold of liberal ideals. The demand for full equality for Arabs, women, LGBT, and other Others in Israel and historical, sociological, and internal critiques of dominant culture have all originated there. While religious nationalists have made effective inroads both in think tanks, schools and in the army in pursuit of their agenda of reviving Zionism and strengthening Judaism in Israel, the institutions stated above are not at the forefront of what could be called invasive or ubiquitous socialization. Technological developments are currently making commercial media omnipresent and ever more emotionally persuasive. Many technological platforms are increasingly engaging, they are both highly interactive and highly individualized. Social media create a culture that is on the one hand empowering for participants, since it is they who create content, but are often based on self-promotion, lack depth and complexity and are socially isolating. In fact one can say that though one belongs to groups in social media, the medium itself is highly individualistic. Many more recent developments increasingly approximate helpful entertaining friend themselves. This connection does not exist in the background of a real social world and social institutions and values, but essentially in a neutral field of cyber space. Other media like the spectacle of blockbuster films, interactive computer games, or reality television mobilize the strong effects of identification, curiosity, suspense, and surprise to such a successful degree that it is hard for classical mass institutions like schools and universities to compete for attention against these types of media. In fact, if we look historically both at the short history of Israel and at long trends around the world it is clear that commercial media is becoming more and more pervasive at the expense of more traditional institutions that mediate culture. Cowen Tyler's counterargument for commercial culture rests on plausible premises of the absolute quantity of cultural production. Indeed, in absolute terms cultural production has risen, as culture itself became one of the most important economic sectors and an important contribution to other sectors as well.[51]

However change in subjectivity is often not reflected in absolute terms. When we look at subjectivity in Israel in the last forty years we can see a shift take place between subjectivities that are constituted by socially aware realist culture and ones that are constituted by commercial culture. This is a pervasive change from a culture of social republicanism to a culture of global commercialism. It is to the different stages of this process that we should turn to next.

INDIVIDUALIZATION, LIBERALIZATION, AND GLOBAL MARKETIZATION IN ISRAELI CULTURE

One can divide this process into three distinct stages. The 1970s and early 1980s mark the first stage of what can be called individualization. Writers and filmmakers explicitly articulated the preoccupations and interests of the individual and everyday experiences against the concern of the collective. Film makers like Uri Zohar dealt with sexuality and male desire, poets like Yehuda Amichi and Amos Oz with frustrations and joys of everyday life, while even highly political writers like Hanoch Levin often stressed the concerns of the individual in the face of death. These writers and filmmakers adopted European intellectual trends of existentialism and psychoanalysis and have examined subjectivity through the lens of everyday life, sex, and death. This type of ideological individualism could only be articulated with a background of collectivism that was provided by the state and other collective institutions. It was the stability of being employed by the state that has moved a significant percent of Israelis to the middle class, whose concerns are more individualist. Strong articulations of individualism were also seen as a bulwark against the implicit threat of communist totalitarianism. The end of the cold war in the 1980s and the collapse of the Soviet Union finally dispelled many fears regarding collectivization. The 1990s inaugurated a period of a kind of triumphalist liberalization. Liberalizing projects expressed themselves as call for the impartiality of the state in relations to its Jewish and Arab citizens, the Oslo accords, a feminist and LGBT agenda, articulations of multiculturalism, and critiques of militarism. It also saw the differentiation and an explosion of consumer choice both domestic and international in television and the media, and the start of mass use of the internet. The early 2000s saw a surge in the global integration of Israeli culture. Israeli film, and television were often coproduced and competed for prizes and recognition with works from around the world. Often, they were explicitly made with an international audience in mind. At the same time Israel adopted and localized global forms of mass entertainment like reality television. Israelis could watch in real time not only sport events and political debates but witnessed the debut of television series and films that premiered around the world and in the United States at the same time. This has not created an erasure of "difference" as religion and nationalism have also been evolving and adopting, both going along with global marketization and providing compensation for it. The 2000s saw reactions to agendas of liberalization. Individuals and institutions with a strong program of liberalization in universities, media, and high culture came under pressure both from other institutions as well as from government.[52] While the project of liberalization has seen successes and setbacks in the last thirty years, the marketization of the media has continued unabated. This global marketization of the media has had dramatic effects not only in terms of diversity of medium but importantly on the content and form of films, novels, and television shows. It is to these effects that I turn to in the next chapter.

NOTES

1. Baruch Kimmerling, *Zionism and Economy* (Cambridge, MA: Schenkman Pub. Co., 1983); Yair Aharoni, *The Israeli Economy (Routledge Revivals): Dreams and Realities* (Routledge, 2014); Yakir Plessner, *Political Economy of Israel, The: From Ideology to Stagnation* (SUNY Press, 2012).

2. For some historians the prevalent and popular combination of nationalism and socialism/communism stem from their mutual source in the French Revolution, see J. L. Talmon, *The Origins of Totalitarian Democracy*, Books That Matter (New York: Praeger, 1960); J. L. Talmon, *The Myth of the Nation and the Vision of Revolution: The Origins of Ideological Polarisation in the Twentieth Century* (London: Berkeley: Secker & Warburg; University of California Press, 1981).

3. Francis Spufford, *Red Plenty* (Minneapolis, MN: Graywolf Press, 2012).

4. Anita Shapira, *Israel: A History*, The Schusterman Series in Israel Studies (Waltham, MA: Brandeis University Press, 2012).

5. Regardless of which political perspective is taken, expansion of control of land and military success have marked Israel's history from the beginning until at least 1973.

6. Lev Luis Grinberg, *Ha-Histadrut Me-'al Ha-Kol* (Yerushalayim: Nevo, 1993).

7. Stanley Fischer, "The Israeli Stabilization Program, 1985–86," *American Economic Review* 77 (1987), 275.

8. "Melnick Mealem.Pdf," accessed October 12, 2016, http://www.jewishvirtuallibrary.org/jsource/isdf/text/Melnick%20Mealem.pdf.

9. This of course discounts two major segments of the population that have seen the state as a threatening force, the Palestinians and the orthodox Jews. Since they are mostly traditional societies both have not had a classically liberal agenda. The orthodox defending against secularization shy away from full participation in what they perceive as a mainly secular state, while most Palestinians adhere to some combination of nationalism, Islam, or Marxism. Both orthodox Jewish and Palestinians have not held a classically liberal agenda.

10. Aside from the relative minority of Anti-Zionist orthodox, communists, and some binationals, most Jews in Israel after 1948 have come to think of their very physical survival in the Middle East that is hostile to the Zionist project as dependent on the state and the army. Such perception reinforces the prevalent statist perspective.

11. I am using Max Weber's account of "Idealtypus," Max Weber, *Methodology of Social Sciences* (New Brunswick, NJ: Transaction Publishers, 2011), 90.

12. Mapam party was a significant force in Israeli politics and society. It received 19 MPs out of 120 in the first Knesset and was second only to Mapai (labor party).

13. Israel has lost 6,373 people in the war of 1948, about 1 percent of its population most from exactly the milieu of the statehood generation. See Benny Morris, *1948: A History of the First Arab-Israeli War* (New Haven, CT: Yale University Press, 2008), 224.

14. Most famously in S. Yizhar (Yizhar Smilansky) masterpiece of that era "Days of Ziklag."

15. A classic example of this genre is Moshe Shamir's novel, Moshe Shamir, *He Walked through the Fields* (Jerusalem: World Zionist Organization, Dept. for Education and Culture in the Diaspora, 1959).

16. I am using Jürgen Habermas's concept of life-world (Lebenswelt) that he appropriated from Edmond Husserl's phenomenology. For Habermas the life-world is more or less the "background" environment of competences, practices, and attitudes; it is the lived realm of informal, culturally grounded understandings and mutual accommodations, see Jürgen Habermas, *Theorie Des Kommunikativen Handelns* (Frankfurt am Main: Suhrkamp, 1981); Pierre Bourdieu and Jean Claude Passeron, *La Reproduction; Éléments Pour Une Théorie Du Système d'enseignement*, Collection Le Sens Commun (Paris: Éditions de Minuit, 1970).

17. A good characterization of this marginality was provided by Reviel Netz. נ״ץ, מקום הטעם.

18. Hedonistic beach bums are featured in Uri Zohar *Metzitzim*, see Uri Zohar, *Peeping Toms*, Comedy, 1973; for marginalized reserve soldiers see Uri Zohar, *Boys Will Never Believe It*, N/A, 1973; in his most autobiographical film *Big Eyes* he plays a sports coach, Uri Zohar, *Einayim G'dolot*, Comedy, Drama, 2009; even in his first film *Hole in the Moon* (1964) Zohar parodied pioneering Zionism and represented his characters as opening kiosks in the desert, a small business attitude that was frowned upon as petty-bourgeoisie Uri Zohar, see *Hole in the Moon*, Comedy, N/A; for on new sensibility Judd Ne'eman, "The Death Mask of the Moderns: A Genealogy of New Sensibility Cinema in Israel," *Israel Studies* 4, no. 1 (November 1, 1999), 112.

19. Amos Oz has quite explicitly articulated this as his poetics in *A Tale of Love and Darkness* where he claims "I understood where I had come from: from a dreary tangle of sadness and pretense, of longing, absurdity, inferiority and provincial pomposity, sentimental education and anachronistic ideals, repressed traumas, resignation, and helplessness." Oz understood that this experience can be turned into literature only after he has read Sherwood Anderson's *Winesburg Ohio*. It is this collection of provincial stories that released him from the need to present sophisticated urban characters. "*Winesburg, Ohio* taught me what the world according to Chekov was like even before I encountered Chekov himself: no longer the world of Dostoevsky, Kafka, or Knut Hamsun, of that of Hemingway or Yigal Mossensohn. No more

mysterious woman on bridges or men with their collars turned up in smoky bars." Amos Oz, *A Tale of Love and Darkness*, 1st U.S. ed. (Orlando: Harcourt, 2004), 493.

20. For this typical kind of reception of his poetry see Jonathan Wilson "The God of Small Things," accessed October 12, 2016, http://www.nytimes.com/books/00/12/10/reviews/001210.10wilsont.html.

21. Erik Einstein Sa le'at.

22. Erik Einstein and Shaolm Hanoch *Shablul.*

23. Shalom Hanoch *Adam betoch Atzmo.*

24. Ariel Zilber, *Ariel Zilber.*

25. On this process in Music see "The invention of Israeli Rock" in Motti Regev and Edwin Seroussi, *Popular Music and National Culture in Israel* (Berkeley, CA: University of California Press, 2004), 137–60.

26. Ibid.

27. Zohar, *Peeping Toms*; Zohar, *Einayim G'dolot*; Uri Zohar, *Shlosha Yamim Veyeled*, Drama, 1969.

28. "דלות החומר כאיכות באמנות הישראלית"

29. Oz, *A Tale of Love and Darkness.*

30. Almost all of Levin's comedies represent provincial life and a yearning to be elsewhere. The protagonists often dream of living a more erotically and financially fulfilling life in what they perceive as the more glamorous life in Europe or in the United States.

31. The character and the flight is based on real life peace activist Abie Nathan, see Mordechai Bar-On, *In Pursuit of Peace: A History of the Israeli Peace Movement* (Washington, DC: United States Institute of Peace Press, 1996), 202–3.

32. Assaf Meydani, *The Israeli Supreme Court and the Human Rights Revolution: Courts as Agenda Setters* (Cambridge; New York: Cambridge University Press, 2011).

33. The issue of army service for the orthodox has been on and off the Israeli agenda for many years. It is only on July 2, 2012, that the then prime minister Benjamin Netanyahu dissolved the Plesner parliamentary committee also known as the commission for equality in the burden. The committee originally recommended having 80 percent of Haredim at the age of eighteen serving for a significant amount of time in the army or civil service. For equality in the burden in the election see, Azulai and Freedman "Weaving a Coalition: Everybody Is Talking about Equality in the Burden."

34. Ulrich Beck, Anthony Giddens, and Scott Lash, *Reflexive Modernization, Reflexive Modernization: Politics, Tradition and Aesthetics in the Modern Social Order*, 1st ed. (Stanford, CA: Stanford University Press, 1994).

35. The most powerful analysis of popular culture as compensation was provided by Freud in his "Der Dichter und das Phantasieren" (often inaccurately translated as "Creative Writers and Day-Dreaming") in which he traces the motivations for writing and reading what was known in the late 19th century as Schundliteratur (trash or popular literature). With its serialized format and its themes of heroism, Schundliteratur was the late 19th century equivalent of today's television series and serial blockbuster

films. Freud analyzes exactly this kind of literature (and not high art) and shows the way in which it compensates for various lacks.

36. Jürgen Habermas, *Legitimation Crisis* (Boston: Beacon Press, 1975), 78; Benedict Anderson makes a similar argument in *Imagined Communities*: "The extraordinary survival over thousands of years of Buddhism, Christianity or Islam in dozens of different social formations attests to their imaginative response to the over-whelming burden of human suffering—disease, mutilation, grief, age, and death. Why was I born blind? Why is my best friend paralysed? Why is my daughter retarded? The religions attempt to explain. The great weakness of all evolutionary/progressive styles of thought, not excluding Marxism, is that such questions are answered with impatient silence." He then goes on to base the success of nationalism with fulfilling exactly the same functions of religion in a secular time. Benedict R. O., G Anderson, *Imagined Communities: Reflections on the Origin and Spread of Nationalism*, Rev. ed. (London; New York: Verso, 2006), 10.

37. Slavoj Žižek has analyzed today's society as standing under a new oppressive regime structured around a new superego injunction to enjoy that bombards the contemporary subject creating new kinds of suffering. Slavoj Žižek, *For They Know Not What They Do: Enjoyment as a Political Factor*, Phronesis (London; New York: Verso, 1991).

38   In his analysis of Judaism, Freud sees triebverzicht (drive renunciation) around images and sensual pleasure as an especially prominent source of pride. See Sigmund Freud, *Der Mann Moses Und Die Monotheistische Religion. Drei Abhandlungen* (Amsterdam: A. de Lange, 1939).

39. The failure of France the land that was most committed to implementing universal rights regardless of race or creed, to protect its citizens of Jewish origin in World War II is particularly a painful failure of European liberalism.

40. For a short commentary, see Daniel Doron, "Crony Capitalism in Israel," *Wall Street Journal*, October 9, 2010, sec. Opinion, http://www.wsj.com/articles/SB10001 4240527487046573045755402218884462554.

41. The cycle of protest of 2011 has tried to recapture and resuscitate the political figure of the people under the banner "the people demand social justice" a counterpart to the American "we are the 99%."

42. Michael Hardt and Antonio Negri, *Commonwealth*, Unknown edition (Cambridge, MA; London: Belknap Press, 2011).

43. For negative liberty see Isaiah Berlin, *Four Essays on Liberty* (London; New York: Oxford University Press, 1990).

44. For the Zionist ethos the very word "community" Kehila is diasporic in the negative sense and was thus avoided. People preferred to use the term "group" Kvutza or the Kibbutz or use a general "we" that designates the secular Jewish, citizens of the state, but very rarely in terms of community.

45. For the global trend of see Pascale Casanova, *Le Republique Mondiale Des Lettres* (Paris: Editions du Seuil, 1999).

46. For a recent example see Mark A. Wollaeger and Matt Eatough, *The Oxford Handbook of Global Modernisms* (New York: Oxford University Press, 2012).

47. For this process see "Shirei Eretz Yisrael" ("Songs of the Land of Israel") in Regev and Seroussi, *Popular Music and National Culture in Israel*, 49–71.

48. Sometimes major participants in European currents simply moved to Palestine and continued their work. Dadist Marcel Janko is a good example.

49. Jean Baudrillard, *Simulacra and Simulation* (Ann Arbor: University of Michigan Press, 1994); Jean Baudrillard and Jean-Louis Violeau, *The Ecstasy of Communication*, Translated by Bernard Schütze and Caroline Schütze (Los Angeles: Semiotext, 2012).

50. Tyler Cowen, *In Praise of Commercial Culture* (Cambridge, MA: Harvard University Press, 1998).

51. Though there aren't figures for Israel creative industries have been playing an increasing role in the economy worldwide, see Richard L. Florida, *The Rise of the Creative Class: And How It's Transforming Work, Leisure, Community and Everyday Life* (New York: Basic Books, 2004); "Hollywood, Creative Industries Add $504 Billion to U.S. GDP | Hollywood Reporter," accessed December 23, 2017, https://www.hollywoodreporter.com/news/hollywood-creative-industries-add-504-662691.

52. A good example is the extra-parliamentary group called "If you will it" (Im Tirzu), that has battled what it sees as post-Zionist bias in academia and was seen by many Israeli academics as a kind of latter day McCarthyism. In 2011 it came out with the "Nakba Nonsense" Campaign that blames Arabs for their expulsion. See "Im Tirtzu," *Wikipedia*, October 9, 2016, https://en.wikipedia.org/w/index.php?title=Im_Tirtzu&oldid=743327619.

Chapter 2

Marketization in Israeli Television, Film, and Literature

ISRAELI REALITY TELEVISION AND CELEBRITY CULTURE

Marketization of culture makes itself felt not only at the level of medium such as the proliferation of television channels, but strongly effects the message or content that these types of mediums disseminate. Marketization is reflected and inflicted in the content of most of what the media has on offer. A good example of the direct and massive influence of commercial culture in Israel is that of reality television. Reality television has been for the last decade the most popular cultural event in Israel. It has consistently garnered the highest ratings in the last decade and is de facto the cultural event that most Israelis have in common on a weekly basis.[1] Some have viewed reality television as a kind of valorization of ordinary people. A democratization of culture that is now not in the hands of professional actors and screenwriters but in the hands of everyday people who entertain other regular people. While there is some truth to this claim, reality television's message is best revealed by contrasting it with the kind of realism that was the dominant format in television until the 1990's. This kind of realism expressed itself first and foremost in the dominance of the news but has also expressed itself in television shows for adults and children. Both characters in reality television and those of previous realism are supposed to be "just like you and me," however in this their similarity ends. Israeli realism redeemed the life that it portrayed. As we saw before in film, poetry, and lyrics culture in the 1960s and 1970s affirmed simplicity and everydayness. A typical example for television is the series *Children of Chaim Neighborhood* (שכונת חיים). Its opening song included the lines "it's not a fancy neighborhood and not a poor one, and it has children just like you and me. Let's tell how children live in Chaim Neighborhood." Or "Here everyone knows the neighbor and says good morning at morning. Women ask each other how do they feel, and how is the laundry and how is the baby. There are no fashion houses here or fancy stores, and people go to work every morning and don't buy things that are expensive."[2] The show that was aired in 1978 in black and white was already unimaginable fifteen years later. Rather than valorizing everyday public life in the neighborhood, on the beach or in the army, reality television invokes ordinary life as something that should be left behind. In talent shows like the *Israeli Voice, A Star Is Born, Dancing with the Stars, X-Factor*, we get the social background of the contestants only for this background to be actively negated and left behind for the glory of competition in front of a national audience. Often the show revels in the contestants' lowly social status, films them filling gas or waitressing, or providing security at an old age home. In a show like *X-Factor* this background is left quickly as we see participants move from their ordinary life to a realm that can be called "off stage." This is the place of the in-between, a "corridor," the introduction to the "holy of holies" of the stage. There they are with family and friends or with a beautiful hostess Bar Refaeli (a symbolic prize for male contestants). Then participants truly move to the main stage which doubles as a stage for the audience in the auditorium and the audience at home. The stage at talent shows is profitably viewed as a kind of social scared space. A contemporary embodiment of Durkheim's "collective effervescence," the stage embodies a kind of social "electricity," an energy which leads to a high degree of emotional excitement. This excitement transports individuals and makes them feel as though they are part of something that possesses an extraordinary vitality.[3] Just like the dislocation of this great social energy to the sacred object in religion, the audience at home and at talent shows misread the social excitement as coming from the contestants and their performance and not from the social gathering itself. However perhaps an all-important addition to this account must look at the institution (not the object) that utilizes this social "energy" for its own purposes and the institution in this case is the Israeli media. Far from mainly being about talent or even fame, talent shows are really about the narcissistic, self-celebration, and self-valorization of media itself. It is as if the motto of "art for art's sake" has been transmuted into the motto of "media for media's sake." The main message of talent shows is precisely the power of the media to create the new "holy," and in a complimentary fashion to make everyday life profane. The show says in effect that everyday lives are hopeless and drab, that there is really no hope for those living them. One's enjoyment and meaning can only come through contact with the media that allows individuals to experience something of its charisma and glamour. Needless to say, there is little we can achieve together as a group of politically oriented people. One's only true hope is an act of grace by the media itself, that by its power will pluck you out as an individual, separate you from your drab surrounding, raise you to the heights where you will win success and fortune, but even more important recognition and love. This is not far removed from the truth of contemporary mediatized lives, as in fact one can say that public recognition and love have themselves been almost wholly monopolized by television. There is rarely a possibility of garnering public recognition or love outside of television and social media. Only television is able to bestow fame and celebrity status. Israeli psychoanalyst and social commentator Carlo Stranger analyzes the attractiveness of contemporary celebrity status as a fantasy of a return to Eden. One yearns to be loved like in early childhood just for being oneself. Being famous reinvents a person as immortal, masks the fear of the breaking down of the body, and acts as a defense against death and the meaninglessness of life.[4] While couched in classical psychoanalytical and religious terms of childhood yearnings, Eden and immortality of the self, this kind of explanation does not provide an account of why celebrity has become so important in Israel since the 1990s. The answer is perhaps more sociological than psychological and has to do with a deficit in recognition and a depreciation of regular forms of life in Israel. As we have seen this depreciation of regular forms of life has occurred hand in hand with global marketization. The material and ideological backing of everyday life disappeared with the decline of the welfare state and other collective institutions. Everyday life was left to its own. Without the symbolic support generated by ideology it has lost its political recognition.[5] Recognition has moved away from everyday life toward highly artificial, media-created spaces. Most reality shows provide much sought out recognition in special "arenas" like the stage of a talent show or the island of a show like *Survivor* or the location sites around the world of *Race to the Million*. Outside of these special arenas life itself is deemed unworthy of representation and empathy. Thus, celebrity status is perhaps a unique way in which young people yearn for validation in the special realm of reality television that cannot be sought in everyday spheres of reality. Ironically almost all reality television shows articulate a "reality" which is wholly separate from everyday reality and is in many senses not real. One show that stands out from this pattern is the show *Connected* (Mechoobarim/ Mechoobarot) that turned everyday life into a stage. Connected is a docu-reality featuring five women (the second series depicted five men). The program follows five participates from different socio-economic backgrounds who document and narrate their lives in video diaries. Every participant receives a video camera, and was instructed to film at least one hour of their daily routine for a year without a pause. Participants were allowed to take the camera everywhere. Every two weeks they provided what they have documented to the production unit. After the episode is partially edited, the participants watch and discuss the episode with the production unit before the final editing. The first season was devoted to five women, of which two were the most noteworthy. The first is Dana Spector, a thirty-seven-year-old journalist, married, mother of a two-year-old daughter, who is going through a midlife crisis. On the surface everything seems fine. She is a successful journalist who authors a popular newspaper column, she is married to a handsome and considerate husband and has a lovely child. They live in a beautiful apartment in a quiet neighborhood in Tel-Aviv. However, she has doubts if this is the life she actually wanted. Through the series she has an affair with Ran Sarig, who is featured in the male series, and eventually divorces her husband. The series ultimately shows both of them leaving their families and moving in together. The first episodes of the series however are mostly devoted to her amorphous longing for a more exciting life. The second participant is a sixteen-year-old Hana Ratinov who lives in Holon. Her parents have emigrated from Russia in the early 1990s after the breakup of the Soviet Union. Her father left the family; her mother is a hairdresser who lives with a man who works as security guard in a supermarket. In contrast to all the other participants in the show who come from the upper-middle class, Hana and her family portray working class Israel. For the middle-class viewer, the show thus provides a peek into a world that is strange yet reminiscent of the struggles that previous generations who have immigrated to Israel had to go through. For the economically struggling or working-class viewer it provides identification. Hana's presentation of herself revolves around her need for love but simultaneously a pessimism regarding relationships, "they always end with a broken heart," she says. The series follows her attempts at love, her frustrating work experience in low-paid service jobs, and her overburdened working-class family. The series and Hana's self-narration allow us to interpret her romantic pessimism as ultimately stemming from her social position. Perceiving those around her in frustrating dead-end jobs she cannot imagine a viable, successful future for herself, a feeling that is then projected unto the romantic realm. While some of these themes can seem ordinary and can be traced back to 19th century realism, with its stress on both finding fulfillment and excitement outside the framework of marriage (e.g., Madame Bovary) or growing up in a working-class immigrant family, the mediation of the content is completely novel and permeates the overall meaning of the series. The series is produced for commercial Israeli television and is broadcast in prime time. Both the production of the series and its consumption are a far cry from anything that can be considered a personal diary. The periodic meetings with the production team are most likely to powerfully intervene in the way that the participants narrate their lives, but are also likely to suggest courses of action and strategies of representation for the future. Their intimate lives are thus constructed and "staged" by collaboration between themselves and the production team. Consequently we are preview to a sort of mediated subjectivity sold for prime time television that nonetheless takes as input the reality of people's lives. Perhaps more than the production of the series its reception is what distances it completely from any kind of personal documentation. Participants know that their lives will be broadcast on national television and from the very beginning are looking to become public persona or celebrities. It is this fact that is definitive for the show. In order to understand the way in which it contributes to the show one needs to reflect on the culture of celebrity and its globalization. In addition to the psychological rewards cited above of being loved simply for one's self, in contemporary Israel being famous gives one access to social capital that can then be "translated" into various other sorts of capital including economic and political. Thus, many young individuals are strongly incentivized by contemporary social structure to attempt to become celebrities. However as much as it might be appealing to look at the phenomena of the celebrity from the point of view of a wannabe celebrity, it makes perhaps more analytic sense to look into the enabling conditions of celebrity than to try and ascertain the characteristics of celebrity directly. Nick Couldry, for example, has argued that the media creates a symbolic hierarchy between itself and the ordinary world. It thus presents itself as a privileged "frame" from which to access social reality.[6] Couldry does not go into the ways that the media succeeds in building this site that presents itself as hegemonic in relation to the other sites, but we can extrapolate from his basic framework. Israeli media succeeds in presenting reality television and celebrities as a privileged site of charisma because it builds on the general anomie, social atomism, and lack of organization surrounding culture and society. It is the weakening of political youth organizations, workers unions, and party organization that creates the kind of anomie that celebrity, as a kind of ersatz, compensates for. The dyed of fan-celebrity reveals an imagined relationship that is symptomatic of a new kind of psychological damage.[7] Neoliberalism severs real human relationships and then installs imaginary, mediated, ideological relationships instead. In the case of *Connected*, the media installs an imaginary, mediated relationship based on real people's lives. In contrast to other reality shows where competition ostensibly reveals talent, social skills, or cunning or sheer motivation; *Connected* is celebrity for celebrity's sake, epitomizing Daniel J. Boorstin definition of celebrity itself as "a person who is well-known for their well-knowness."[8] The show reveals a kind of pure marketization and commodification of personality and subjectivity itself without the need to provide this process with the "excuse" of talent or competition. While *Connected,* with relatively little self-reflection, commodifies the self, the Israeli drama *Very Important Man* based partially on the life of celebrity actor Yehuda Levi deals reflectively and makes commodification of the personality itself the very theme of the show. The series presents Yehuda Levi as himself, a celebrity actor who has just broken up with his famous girlfriend. In one of his paranoid moods he insults the rather plain and anonymous Ronna, his waitress, and then apologizes and develops a relationship with her. Throughout the series we bear witness to the strains and pleasures of having a marketable persona, and of the differences between celebrity status and everyday life. At one point in the series Yehuda complains about his life and the fact that he always feels conflicted and false regarding his charity work. Romi Aboulafia (another Israeli celebrity actress and model playing herself) offers the advice that her psychologist shared with her. She draws a pyramid and says that there are three kinds of people: At the bottom of the pyramid where most people are exist those who are good for nothing, stupid, and "basically garbage," she says in English. In the middle of the pyramid there are those who wake up in the morning and go to work, the "normal people." At the very top of the pyramid are the people who were meant to succeed, meant to go to the top; those who became rich and famous, the "Steve Jobs" of this world. It is precisely these people who are the most rich, famous, and successful; these are the ones who are most miserable and it is easiest to unsettle them. They continue the conversation on why this is so and the reasons to overcome their problems. However more important than the reasons for their problems is the naturalness in which this social ontology presents itself to them and to their audience. Hierarchy is presented as naturalized, with society rewarding those who are most demanding toward themselves. More importantly, however, this social ontology represents the majority of humanity as essentially valueless. It is a combination of a kind of competitive Nietzscheanism coupled with possessive individualism. It represents an image of individuals and society that is quite foreign to Israel's socialist as well as nationalist heritage. To gauge the change, in 1968 Uri Zohar typifies Israeli society as one in which "Every Bastard a King," and has the main protagonist be a car driver, while in 2014's *Very Important Man*, most people are "basically garbage." Though the show is ironic in the way it portrays the two celebrities, the very existence of this type of discourse was unimaginable even twenty years ago. It introduces an idea to Israel that has never been part of Israeli society. The idea that all that is good flows from individuals at the top of a pyramid.[9] This is literally the opposite of the labor-Zionist view that saw value as mainly created by those at the bottom of the pyramid.[10] Since the show focuses on Yehuda on the one hand, and on the other does so playfully and with irony, it reveals an interesting ideological ambiguity. We keep moving as an audience from identification with Yehuda as a talented likable actor, to our understanding of him as a celebrity: that is, as someone in which we and those around him invest in a kind of cycle of idealization and deidealization. Yehuda quite characteristically has no real friends or family closeness. He lacks autonomous judgment and is regularly and uncontrollably swayed by the opinions of his manager, new girlfriend, mother, serendipitous group of actors, and so on. The relationships that he has are always mediated by his public persona. There is no aspect of his life where his persona does not distort his interpersonal relationships including sexual expectations and relationship with regular people. A good example of the deprecation of regular life is a scene in the series were the hero goes out dancing with Romi Aboulafia. At one point the bartender displaces an ordinary couple on the bar to make place for the celebrity couple. Yehuda insists that the couple come back and two couples sit together. The ordinary couple is presented in the most unglamorous and provincial of ways. They start discussing their wedding plans, they relate that they will bring a great DJ and great food to their wedding. Yehuda and Romi start out warm and welcoming to the couple, they affirm their lives. Yehuda promises to come to their wedding. Soon the viewer feels impatience with the nerdish unattractive couple and would like to make them go away somehow. Later, Yehuda and Romi joke "who let such people into Tel-Aviv?" she asks, "they are such boring people, how did I get myself into this?" he replies. This and other scenes represent the devaluation of everyday life that the series both partakes in but also critically examines. At the end of the episode we learn that Romi initiated the date on the advice of her agent in order to get free publicity out of going out with Yehuda. This presents Yehuda's life, experience, and love as commodified experience. Feeling a lack of authenticity in his life, Yehuda seems to want the warmth of everyday life as he develops a relationship with Ronna, a waitress and an MA English student. However, the whole arc of the series reveals that everyday existence does not really make sense for Yehuda. That it will not resolve anxieties regarding authentic relationship, nor his difficulties in living up to his role today. At the end of the series he goes back to his celebrity self. During the show, we are called to both identify with Yehuda but also assume a kind of bemused critical distance from him. The series is a kind of meditation on what celebrity means in Israel, and reveals the desire for fame and celebrity status and yet the irony and ambivalence that Israeli society feels regarding this new phenomenon, that finds itself in an uneasy coexistence with older layers of Israeli society. *Very Important Man* is part of a novel wave of reflective and self-critical interrogations of commodification of life and reality in Israel. The selling of viewers for advertisements, the harvesting of attention, has necessitated the creation of figures of identification.[11] Identification itself, our distorted tendency to want to follow and "love" an idealized figure, a residual tendency stemming from childhood dependency, is used to draw and sustain our interest that is then sold to advertisers. Thus, the celebrity-fan dyad that is based on idealization, transference in psychoanalysis that seems to both celebrity and fan to be the center of attention, is actually an auxiliary, a supplement, an appendage to the main function of advertising products for sale. Celebrity culture is thus both necessary but at the same time really a kind of auxiliary side show that helps the business of selling products. When a fan, reader, or viewer encounters a story on a celebrity in a newspaper or television, the person falsely thinks that the situation is mainly about reporting something on another person. That is, that the situation is about the medium making certain claims about another person and relating them to an audience. The situation presents itself indeed as if this is the center of what is happening. However, the whole drama taking place before your eyes (a new separation, a new hookup, a divorce) is really a side show for the couple of seconds that will be paid for an advertisement. When consuming stories of celebrities our consciousness is structurally false from the outset, irrespective if the news report truths or falsehoods. This is because the motivation behind the representation and not its correspondence or lack of correspondence with reality is what makes communication distorted and ideological.[12] The figure of the celebrity is a well-rewarded tool for the media, a means for other ends. The "love" for the celebrity is thus false on several counts combined. It is false because it is based on transference, that is a kind of infantile idealization and intimacy but it is also false since this whole constellation is in fact decentered. Yehuda feels in general that the love for him is either inauthentic (since mediated or infantilized) or indeed from the very first episode that he is exploited by Romi. The series presents the relationship with Ronni, the plain everyday girl, as an attempted way out of an inauthentic predicament. However, at the end of the series, Yehuda flees back to Tel-Aviv from a vacation in the desert with Ronni, signaling that he cannot acclimatize himself to the "desert" of every life. He goes back to the attention and pleasures of his commodified career as a celebrity in Tel-Aviv. A direct and thought-provoking attempt to deal with Israeli capitalism itself has been exquisitely rendered by Nir Baram in his book *World Shadow*.

NIR BARAM'S *WORLD SHADOW* AND ZIPPI BRAND'S *GOOGLE BABY*

In his novel *World Shadow* Nir Baram examines life under contemporary global capitalism. The book transitions between three main settings: the Israeli business elite, a political consulting firm in the United States, and an anarchist group in the United Kingdom. The novel begins with Gabriel Mantzur a young Israeli who through his father's connections gets to know a Jewish American hedge fund manager, Michael Brockman who takes him under his wing and who then employs him as director for philanthropic activities in Israel. Due to these connections with the fund manager, Gabriel gets access to the milieu of Jerusalem's business elite that he then becomes part of. This Israeli business elite is depicted as being an integral part of the labor movement that ever seamlessly transitioned from representing labor to conducting business on a global scale often using their connections with government officials.[13] Gabriel succeeds in his investments, a success that culminates when he puts together the international business fair for a New Middle East. At a later point in the novel that is set in the economic crash of 2008, Michael asks him to put most of his investor's money in Michael's own hedge fund whose value is fast declining, the investments are then completely devalued. Aside from narrating a story of the rise and fall of an Israeli investor, Baram is interested in the morality and subjectivity of central players of global capitalism. Gabriel is a kind of capitalist everyman. Baram steers away from presenting Gabriel as a bad person, rather his protagonist exhibits a sort of personal emptiness. In a characteristic anecdote at the very beginning of his relationship with Michael, Michael asks him to suggest philanthropic causes in Israel that he (Michael Brockman) will then financially support. Gabriel looks online for favorite philanthropic causes among wealthy American Jewry and provides Michael with a list. Michael is disappointed with the lack of originality of the list, whose items appear every day on his desk as requests. Gabriel is at a loss as to what to suggest, and ultimately uses his father's idea of funding an American-Israeli summer camp that brings Jewish Israelis and Jewish-Americans together. The narrative reveals a kind of lack in the generation of emotional and intellectual productivity. Rather than representing a highly driven and ambitious young man, Baram represents someone moderate and rational. Rather than dramatizing success, Gabriel's rise is slow and gradual. When he loses other people's lifetime investments he is not represented as a bad person, but as someone with only a limited moral awareness. The other two settings of the novel are also characteristic of contemporary trends in Israeli culture, in that they do not take place in Israel and involve non-Jews. The first tells of a group of unemployed English anarchists who come from poor families and who have been withheld access to gainful employment and middle-class lives. Unlike the middle class, they did not receive an education that socializes them to believe in the norms and rules of society. They are looking to dismantle, not reform, the world; they fundamentally challenge liberal democracy and its relations with capitalism. One of them comes up with the idea of a global strike with a slogan, "Global Strike—One Billion Striking—11.11," which goes viral especially after the group engages in sabotaging and burning various places devoted to high culture (museums, art galleries, etc.). The third setting is devoted to a political consulting firm MSV, that behind the scenes has had a decisive influence on manipulating public opinion almost wherever an election is taking place in the world (Britain, Bolivia, Congo). The machinations of this firm reveal how hollow and empty democracy is, and how easily public opinion is manipulated. One of the main workers in the firm, Daniel Kay, develops strong feelings against what he is asked to do. For Baram, Kay represents another kind of everyman in a capitalistic system. In an interview to *Haaretz* Baram states:

> In our generation, there is sometimes complete separation between your profession and your ideology. You get up in the morning to serve forces that deep inside you don't believe are beneficial to the world, to put it mildly. And then in the evening you return home and write posts on Facebook against those forces and their ilk. In totalitarian regimes like those I wrote about in "Good People," they demand your total loyalty. They say: Work for us and believe in us—or at least pretend that you believe in us. Whereas, capitalism says: You can be a socialist or a Marxist, you can shout at demonstrations, but give me your talents, and, for example, invent apps that will make 14-year-olds press a button. That depicts a very large gap between the professional and ideological worlds, a gap inside the soul that is hard to repair.[14]

It is the gaps between what one knows explicitly but often times just implicitly is right and what one does that is one of the central interest of the book. This gap of subjectivity, this split self that capitalism enacts is the real hero of Baram's book. A self that is sometimes aware and sometimes represses, sometimes recognizes and sometimes dissembles the hard truths of his or her contribution to a system whose effects include covert and overt forms of dispossession, discrimination, exploitation of some, and the creation of a luxurious life style for others. What interests Baram are the machinations of subjectivity in this state of affairs, the way subjectivity adopts and reacts to the capitalist system. Using the narrative form of the novel Baram gives a nuanced dynamic answer to this. Gabriel Mantzur, Daniel Kay, and the anarchists occupy differential places within the system but also experience them differently. Mantzur is the one-dimensional man per excellence, he does not think deeply into what he is doing until it is too late, he rides along the wave of his success. Daniel Kay experiences self-deception and bad faith. From his perspective he lets himself be deceived by his generally genial, American liberal supervisor who stresses that they have always helped social democrats get elected around the world. However, self-deception does not last, Kay resigns from his position and helps and advises his former adversaries in the anarchist group. Rather than present us with stereotypes, Baram is always careful to show us the complex kinds of human beings that work within the system. Some like Gabriel fit well within the system, but they too are not presented as negative just as emptily self-interested. Others like Daniel Kay and some of the other professionals at the consulting firm feel that they are significantly compromised by their work or engaged in subtle forms of self-deception. While he may be critical and often judgmental of some of his characters he is very careful not to distort them. His characters are formed by the system that they live in but they are not wholly determined by that system.

Both internal mental and spiritual parts of themselves have been formatively affected by the system they were born in, and their contemporary situation is deeply affected by these same forces. Baram protagonists present almost kind of Greimsian semiotic square. The anarchists are autonomous heroes, wholly resistant to capitalism, Daniel Kay and Gabriel Manzur's bosses present their opposite, two different types of leaders of the system. Daniel Kay is a negation, a non-anarchist working within the system to replace it. Gabriel Manzur is a simple conformist; he does not lead capitalism he simply follows along.[15] Yet Baram does not represent them as just nodes in the system that they occupy, rather he skillfully brings us their interactions with one another and the moral dilemmas that they face. The book is perhaps the first book written by an Israeli author that has capitalism and its subjectivities as its main protagonist. It is hard to underestimate just how novel this development is. Both the protagonists, the relationship with the audience, as well as the entire dynamic are wholly novel to Israeli fiction.[16] Especially noteworthy is the novel's description of the British anarchists: twice distanced from Jewish middle-class protagonists that Israeli novel focuses on. As we have seen, protagonists in mainstream Israeli fiction are likeable Israelis that one can identify with. Gabriel precludes any such simple identification. The other characters are indeed non-Israeli and non-Jewish that is extremely rare in Israeli fiction, which was traditionally a kind of mirror held up to Israeli society. The classic themes of Israeli society—immigration, war, and the Holocaust—are also missing; they seem to be relegated to the irrelevant past. Zionism itself is relegated to the status of an ideology that serves as a good excuse for developing business connections and getting tax cuts for contributions. The Israeli state is a resource to use in a new kind of crony capitalism that enables businessmen to leverage their governmental connections in order to get preferential legal permits, tax breaks, or grants but especially advertise their governmental connections with foreign companies who will then cut deals with them. Baram's book is about today's global capitalism and shows its dynamics as they affect adult persons. Interestingly what Baram chooses to reveal about Israel is very different from works that deal with capitalism in the United States. Capitalism is relatively new to Israel and in its implementation creates new kinds of lives that are different from previous kinds of life in Israel and from capitalism in its European or American variety. In general terms the author attempts to view Israel from the position of the international anti-capitalist left. Though he is well aware of the particularities of Israel, Baram attempts to overcome Israel's left intellectual isolation by reconnecting it with global anti-capitalist left movements. In his statements to the press Baram claims that Israelis have suffered from a consciousness that views Jews as better than others. This isolated consciousness is due to the fact that the "political establishment has convinced everyone that Jews are better,

more moral, more special, and at the same time more miserable than any
other ethnic group. These were hollow words, of myths, fear and kitsch.
One needs to free oneself from all these mythical and ethnic viewpoints.
The Jews are human beings no much better and not much worse, and they live
with other human beings and they are not better nor worse, and they are not
more moral than anyone else."[17] In an attempt to free himself from what he
calls a mythical viewpoint, Baram provides us with cool dispassionate narratives on Israeli and world capitalism. Perhaps what is missing from Baram's
narrative is a more layered approach to socialization in Israel and how it
essentially creates identity and subjectivity. Israeli and Jewish nationalism
and familism are still in many respects the bedrock of socialization in Israel.
While nationalism may be on the decline, both Jewish identity politics and
familism are on the rise. Capitalism and commercial culture come as a second
layer on this "bedrock." Within the very strong structures of familial experience one receives a steady stream of capitalist socialization. In Israel parents
have only fairly recently become socialization agents for the job market.
Though such developments are recent, in many cases they are deep, in many
other cases familism and globalized capitalism intertwined are there from the
very beginning. A fascinating representation of this interaction is expressed
in Zippi Brand Frank's documentary *Google Baby* that narrates exactly these
interactions. *Google Baby* is a story that mainly follows Doron Mamet-
Meged as he starts up a business that coordinates the global production of
babies. After paying for surrogate services in the order 100,000 dollars he
decides to start a company Tammuz that will coordinate a lower cost option
for the global production of babies. In one of the options technically called
gestational surrogacy with egg donation, a surrogate is implanted with an
embryo created by in vitro fertilization using the intended father's sperm and
a donor egg. In the film Doron's company uses this method in order to "globally produce babies." Eggs are taken from white US donors, sperm is taken
from an Israeli gay couple who are paying for the baby, and the expensive
process of surrogacy is outsourced to India. At one point Doron says: "I have
a high tech background and outsourcing to India is very trendy now. Companies send programming work to India to cut costs. Because surrogacy is the
most expensive element in process of baby production, I thought that probably one could outsource the pregnancy to India, I assumed surrogacy would
be much cheaper there." In Doron's words there is no questioning either of
surrogacy or of the capitalist logic of globalization and outsourcing. However
what is motivating Doron's endeavor is as much rooted in Israeli culture as it
is rooted in global capitalism. It is not serendipity that has made an Israeli
company become the forefront of global production of babies. Israel is quite
exceptional for its pronatalist culture and practice. This policy is overdeter-
mined by Jewish religious culture that views fertility as a blessing, by the
post-trauma of the Holocaust that requires a restoration of the population as

well by the demographic "competition" with Palestinians. Zionist praxis and culture has also stressed children as embodying the fulfillment of ideals of the new Hebrew man and thus placed special stress on their growth. However, most analysis of this phenomenon describe a too simple, even unrealistic, causal connection between nationalism and the womb. No contemporary Israeli woman conceives in the name of the nation and there is strong reason to doubt whether this has taken place in the past. Zionism did indeed create a child-centered society where the joys of having many children and the altruistic "heroic" aspects of parenting are stressed.[18] However paradoxically there has probably been a slight increase in childrearing and child centeredness as national collective ideology declined.[19] In a society that is increasingly competitive and privatized, family and children become an important source of material support and emotional satisfaction. The area of Israel is small, and extended family regularly participates in events which only the nuclear family would participate in the United States. In contrast to previous generations of immigrants who were often alone in Israel or with children only, normative families in Israel include at least three generations, often four in more traditional communities. This means that for many the year is packed with family events such as birthdays, religious and national holidays, marriages, bris and baby naming ceremonies, and picnics and outings. Participation in family oriented religious ceremonies like the Friday night's dinner that was not part of the sought upon ideal type in the Kibbutzim has become a new standard for secular families. Parents who just a generation before used to conceive of their vacation as a well-deserved rest from work and parenting now take their children to almost every vacation. Families in Israel have also grown larger.[20] Social mimicry creates strong pressure on women to conceive and birth many children especially in orthodox communities. Even in Israel's most modern sector that does not partake in the religious injunction toward fertility, often financially lucrative employment is sought in the male dominated high-tech industry while many women find personal expression solely in childrearing. Israel's highly pronatalist commitments are also formally enshrined in Israeli law.[21] These different factors have created a child-centric society in which average birth rate is almost double than that of European countries but also well above countries such as India, Turkey, and Brazil. Israel's pronatalist social agenda expresses itself in a strong pressure to have children even if there are very difficult obstacles to rearing children. As one of the gay protagonists in *Google Baby* says jokingly "we tried and tried and we could simply could not conceive." The film however shows us the way in which global market economy is activated in order to further goals that have been strongly set by a national culture. Nir Baram's *Shadow World* and *Google Baby* both deal with the way in which Israel is implicated in the global production network of capitalism. Both reveal an interesting intermeshing of capitalism and ideological and cultural practices in Israel. Nir Baram's main protagonist works on behalf of the Zionist sentiment of an American Jewish philanthropist. In reality however he is neutral regarding those sentiments themselves. These sentiments do not animate him and just stand in the background of much of his economic activity. Nationalist sentiment is practically nonexistent in *Google Baby* and yet it expresses itself as a background that explains pronatalism. Both works, though very different, reveal a complex combination of older sentiments and convictions juxtaposed with the new global ways of doing things in the world. The novel and the documentary express an ambivalence regarding these new kinds of production, essentially an ambivalence regarding globalization itself and its corresponding creation of the life-world through work. The active participation and construction of global networks of services and production is seen in them as ethically problematic. This ambivalent stance can be understood as having at its backdrop a normative model of an autonomous and democratic national economy. However, these forces are also understood as those that animate and construct individuals to the greatest extent. For Baram these forces create distinct new types of subjectivities and new kinds of internal conflicts. These subjectivities can become defiant and insurrectionist, they can live for a certain time with bad faith or double-heartedness between work and the ideals that they hold, or they can numbingly or in a celebratory manner confirm or internalize what Baram thinks is a bad system. *Google Baby* provides a radical case of Israelis being actually produced from the beginning by a globally integrated market. Thus, in many ways it both carries the logic of globalization to its most radical conclusion, but it can also serve as a kind of extreme symbol to the fact that all Israelis reproduce themselves and their world in global ways. Though Israel has always depended on global forces the societal fabric itself has never been integrated to the same extent as today. The globally integrated production of everything including life itself has created new beings, new sensibilities as well as new ethical questions. Both *Shadow World* and *Google Baby* narrate typically Israeli protagonists within the circuits of world production. They thus share this book's premise that contemporary narration of Israel and Israelis needs to situate them within global developments. Indeed, narratives that lack being so situated increasingly sound provincial, distorting, and unreal.

ISRAELI CONDITION AND THE GLOBAL MARKET

The combined effects of integration into the globalized market have unleashed powerful forces in Israeli society. They have incorporated Israel into the world economy where an ever-growing stream of commodities, ideas, and people circulate at an increasingly fast pace. Many of these forces are felt as liberalizing, democratizing, and empowering. They have freed many from the physical and mental constraints of the nation-state and from dependence on patriarchal family structure. They entailed increases in freedom of movement, of consumption, of greater autonomy for woman, minorities, and the LGBT community. Such developments naturally lead to both actual, real world diversity in society, as well as to conceptions of society that are more inclusive. At the same time, many of these forces have been constraining, exclusionary and undemocratic. While many have been freed from the physical, economic, and mental confines of the nation-state and enforced patriarchy, they have been subjected to a new set of constraints associated with the global market economy, as well as a resurgence in racial hierarchies of all sorts. Short-term profitability at all costs has become a central consideration in actions, institutions, and projects that were relatively free from it in the past including health, defense, education but also scientific research and technological development. The global market itself became ranked or graded according to those who are central to its network of production of knowledge and services, those who are peripheral, and those who are wholly excluded. These different positions articulate distinct regimes of incentives and threats, diverse kinds of socialization, social habitus and worldviews. In many ways people in Israel are now doubly "coded" as they occupy a social ecological niche both in the nation-state and in world production. These two of course interact in complex ways, a Mizrachi woman software developer might be positioned globally more centrally than an Ashkenazi male army officer while being more peripheral in the hierarchy of the nation-state. Often dominance is reinforced as when soldiers who worked for signal intelligence unit in the IDF (Unit 8200), a unit that occupies a privileged position in Israel, use their knowledge in order to lead the high-tech field in Israel that is in turn the most dominant global field in Israel. They often adopt software and technology that is used in the army to gather information against Palestinian militants, terrorists, and Arab countries to multinational high-tech firms who are looking to manage and control various kinds of information on work, employees, and clients. The skills and software associated with control of information have become a key resource in the knowledge economy. While stratification and hierarchy as part of the economy and society of the nation-state is very familiar to us and has been amply represented and theorized from the middle of the 19th century until today, its contemporary global counterpart is more difficult to theorize and in many ways is less visible. Hierarchy and stratification have been theorized in the nation-state mainly using class and then gender and race. In a relatively recent analysis Pierre Bourdieu has conceptualized stratification using concepts of field and symbolic capital.[22] Both concepts are relatively static and their explanatory power is best fitted to a relatively autonomous nation-state. The political, economic, and cultural fields and their respective antagonism are all national, while symbolic capital is clearly tied to the national language. In an environment of increasing globalization recent theorists have looked to concepts of flows of people, money, goods, information, and ideas along networks rather than metaphor of "layers" which animated discussions of stratification according to class.[23] The metaphor of flows and networks also allows its own kinds of power inequalities according to centrality and the importance of positions within these networks. Networks that are both local and global at the same time are the ones that hold productive power in Israel. Such networks include business, technology, government, military, media, arts, and academia. Such networks are not self-contained either in the nation-state nor are they totally limited to the specific professional field.[24] For example, a person who is central in the media network will also often be implicated in academic networks abroad, governmental network, and business. Israel also abounds in people who have translated their capital in one professional field (media, high-tech, business, army, religious authority) into political capital or into monetary capital often in conjunction with various partners abroad. Just as characteristic to this state of affair are people and groups who fall outside of these major global networks that create wealth and knowledge. These groups have often been conceptualized as a local forces resisting globalization, increasingly it is clear that they articulate an alternative kind of globalization. Worldwide groups such anti-globalization activists and environmentalists all organize beyond the nation-state. In Israel/Palestine both Jewish and Muslim religious groups such as Chabad, religious Zionists, Hamas, the PLO, and Islamic Jihad are highly globalized. Though the first kind of globalization is the more powerful of the two, both kinds make their way deep into the landscape as well as to subjectivities. Silicon Wadi, for example, dots the coastal plain in Israel, and comprises high-tech parks in Herzlia, the diamond exchange district in Ramt Gan, Netanya, Ra'anana, and Rishon Le Zion. In like manner, certain places in Israel have become global centers of religious learning including "global" Yeshivot in Jerusalem, Safed, and Beni Brak as well as Muslim religious centers in Ramallah and Gaza. Thus, we have the ever increasingly powerful technocapitalist core of globalization and various peripheral or "superstructural-like" globalizations that accompany it. However these peripheral or superstructural globalizations are far from lacking in causal power in their relations to the core. Rather they influence the core in various ways. A good example is the way in which maintaining a state for the Jewish people, something which is surly likely to be viewed as relatively peripheral to the main engines of modernity and capitalism has led to a plethora of technological innovations in the defense industry, communications, and medical technology.[25] As we have seen, two good examples are the technologies of signal intelligence that is the covert gathering and protecting of information but also assistant reproductive technologies. Defending a Jewish state in the Middle East requires unceasing innovation in military and intelligence technology, while Jewish tradition and Judaism and the Holocaust have created a culture that favors innovation and use of reproductive technologies. It is for these reasons that Israel has become a leading exporter in both data security and in reproductive technology, a leader in bio/information economy.[26] Economy, culture, and politics interweave in complex ways, core economic-technological developments influence culture and politics, while developments in culture and politics often exert strong pressures on the kinds of technological developments that are pursued. As we can see particularities do matter and Israel globalizes along particular paths. It has been the argument of this book that an undistorted view of contemporary Israeli culture embeds the changes that it went through in its integration into the global production. Presentations of Israel whether in novels, journalism, or film that present it as unique or as predicated mostly on the Holocaust and art-Israeli conflict risk distorting Israeli society, culture, and its changes. An older generation of writers, such as Amos Oz, A. B. Yahushua, David Grossman though wholly integrated themselves into global culture, have tended to preclude or deny representations of this integration itself in the works. For the younger generation who came of age in 1990s presenting Israelis under the pressures of global capitalism is much more self-evident. Recent works like *Very Important Man*, *World Shadow*, and *Google Baby* each open a window to internal psychological conflicts regarding authenticity, bad faith, and relationships with others under global commodification. Though very different in what they relate, all three attempt to represent globalization as its effects Israel's secular elites. *Very Important Man* concentrates on the elite of the media, *World Shadow* on the political and business elite, while *Google Baby* concentrates on high-tech protagonist turned reproductive technology entrepreneur. Being at the power center of global networks they all largely benefit from commodification and globalization in various ways. As we have seen other groups who are less related directly to capitalism have globalized as well, however their globalization is an alter-globalization; a globalization that works itself in certain tension with the main global kind. Despite this characterization it is difficult to characterize succinctly the changes that Israel is going through due to globalization. Globalization and integration are happening on so many levels with different and conflicting social actors that it is often hard to offer a general picture or image of its effects. In the next chapter I will attempt to provide just such a picture. A picture of a society that is quickly moving away from the European model of social democratic secular nation-state.

NOTES

1. Aside from Pessach and Yom Kippur that are almost universally celebrated among the Jewish population, reality television is de facto the universal weekly cultural gathering. See, for example, Nati Tucker, "Television Ratings Rise, but Ad Revenues Decline."

2. "הטלוויזה החינוכית: הילדים משכונת חיים."

3. Emile Durkheim, Carol Cosman, and Mark Sydney Cladis, *The Elementary Forms of Religious Life* (Oxford; New York: Oxford University Press, 2001).

4. Carlo Strenger, *The Fear of Insignificance: Searching for Meaning in the Twenty-First Century* (New York: Palgrave Macmillan, 2011), 23–46.

5. I am extending the concept of political recognition theorized by Axel Honneth to recognition that nation-state realism gave to ordinary people, see Axel Honneth, *Das Ich Im Wir: Studien Zur Anerkennungstheorie,* 1. Aufl. Suhrkamp Taschenbüch Wissenschaft 1959 (Berlin: Suhrkamp, 2010); Axel Honneth, *Kampf Um Anerkennung: Zur Moralischen Grammatik Sozialer Konflikte,* 1. Aufl (Frankfurt am Main: Suhrkamp, 1992).

6. Nick Couldry, "Teaching us to fake it: the ritualized norms of television's "reality" games" see Susan Murray and Laurie Ouellette, *Reality TV: Remaking Television Culture*, 2nd ed. (New York: New York University Press, 2009), 57–74.

7. One can see this as a kind of regression to pre-oedipal reciprocal relationship of what Lacan calls the imaginary, see Jacques Lacan and Bruce Fink, *Écrits: The First Complete Edition in English* (W. W. Norton & Company, 2006).

8. Daniel J. Boorstin, *The Image: A Guide to Pseudo-Events in America,* 50th Anniversary ed. (New York: Vintage Books, a division of Random House, Inc, 2012), 271.

9. Highly unfamiliar for Israel such an ideology has first been articulated explicitly as a reaction to the October revolution by Ayan Rand in her first novel Fountainhead. See Ayn Rand and Leonard Peikoff, *The Fountainhead,* Anniversary ed. (New York: Signet, 1996).

10. It is interesting to note that Berl Katznelson, the ideological father of Labor Zionism, the hegemonic ideology in Israel for its first 40 years, talked of settling of Jews in Palestine as overturning the pyramid: that is, enabling Jewish people to work at productive labor near the base of the pyramid. Berl Katznelson, *Revolutionary Constructivism: Essays on the Jewish Labor Movement in Palestine* (Young Poale Zion Alliance, 1937).

11. For an overview of the commercialization of attention, see Tim Wu, *The Attention Merchants: How Our Time and Attention Are Gathered and Sold,* Export/Airside ed. (London: Atlantic Books, 2017).

12. Slavoj Žižek, *Mapping Ideology* (Verso Books, 2012), 1–34.

13. Perhaps Baram is relying here on his own experience and connections of being the son of labor politician Uzi Baram who belongs to a similar milieu.

14. Maya Sela, "Acclaimed Israeli Author Nir Baram Settles the Score with Globalization and the Israeli Left."

15. See Frederic Jameson introduction to Algirdas Julien Greimas, *On Meaning: Selected Writings in Semiotic Theory* (University of Minnesota Press, 1987).

16. While there has been several books that aim to represent the changes that Israel went through in the last forty years, critics such as Yaron Peleg have often concentrated on individualism or romance, and have not dealt with books that have capitalism as their subject. See Yaron Peleg, *Israeli Culture between the Two Intifadas: A Brief Romance* (University of Texas Press, 2009).

17. From Nir Baram's speech "(16) ניר ברעם נואם בהפגנת האלפים נגד חוק הלאום - YouTube."

18. For a review of the causes of pronatalism in Israel, see Jacqueline Portugese, *Fertility Policy in Israel: The Politics of Religion, Gender, and Nation* (Westport, CT: Praeger, 1998).

19. Israel is among the few countries in the world whose fertility rate has gone up since the 1990s, and has the highest fertility rate among the major countries in the world standing at 2.96 above countries such as India, Turkey, Brazil and of course high above any country in the European Union. See fertility rates at World Bank. Think tanks in Israel have explicitly dealt with the demographic "threat" of the Palestinian fertility. *2007-2020 ביסטרוב ישראל דמוגרפיה וצפיפות של ישראל*.

20. Paul Morland, "Israeli Woman Do It by the Numbers," *The Jewish Chronicle*, April 7, 2014.

21. See "Taxation, Labor and Welfare Policies" see Portugese, *Fertility Policy in Israel,* 91–117.

22. On concepts of taste and field see Pierre Bourdieu, *Distinction: A Social Critique of the Judgement of Taste* (Cambridge, MA: Harvard University Press, 1984); For symbolic capital see Bourdieu and Passeron, *La Reproduction; Éléments Pour Une Théorie Du Système D'enseignement.*

23. For statement on global networks see Manuel Castells and Manuel Castells, *The Rise of the Network Society,* 2nd ed., With a new pref. The Information Age: Economy, Society, and Culture, v. 1. (Chichester, West Sussex; Malden, MA: Wiley-Blackwell, 2010); For a more micro treatment of networks see Bruno Latour, *Reassembling the Social: An Introduction to Actor-Network-Theory*, Clarendon Lectures in Management Studies (Oxford; New York: Oxford University Press, 2005).

24. Higher education has tried to reflect these processes by a greater stress on inter and trans-disciplinarily in a sense trying to catch up to developments in society and inform them.

25. Dan Senor and Saul Singer, *Start-up Nation: The Story of Israel's Economic Miracle,* 1st ed. (New York: Twelve, 2009).

26. Susan Martha Kahn, *Reproducing Jews: A Cultural Account of Assisted Conception in Israel,* Body, Commodity, Text (Durham: Duke University Press, 2000).

Chapter 3

It Ain't Europe Here

On October 21, 2014, a new hit was launched by Margalit Zanani, a veteran and well respected Mizrachi singer and ARISA, a new Gay-Mizarchi line of music produced by Omer Yobi and Yotam Pepi, its name was "It Ain't Europe Here." The hit featuring a well-known drag artist wearing 17th century style clothes accompanied with Mizrachi male semi-nude models was filmed on location in Tel-Aviv's old Israeli bus station, home of Israel's poorest migrant workers. The semantically condensed yet popular lyrics are as follows:

It ain't Europe Here
Madam Rothschild, had enough of Tel Aviv?
Hilton was too full, you went off to Paris
Came home with the scent of Chanel
Back to Ben Yehuda St, don't get mixed up
Miss Hipster, nu, how's Berlin?
Fitting in easily with the Germans?
You don't want to hear any more Left/Right-wing
So Gute Nacht Aufwiedersehen

Hey, here it ain't Europe
Here it's Israel—get used to it
Kapara, hey, it's not Europe here
Here it's Balagan (a mess), the Old Middle East

Everywhere you feel like Miss Universe
And work hard with the non-Jews to assimilate
And you have a start-up thanks to a Jewish brain
You wish for a Spanish passport

In the beginning we're created Wild
Americans with an Arab sense of honor
It'll do you no good to keep cursing
You're addicted! To Israel!

Repeat*

Hands up! Hands up in the air!
I recognize you from afar
Deep in your heart you are still a child of God
You're not from London or from Amsterdam
Your look my dear ... is from Bat Yam![1]

The song and the video are joyous, funny, and celebratory. We are instantly called to affirm their vision. Here, in Israel, reigns a joyful *balagan* (mess, chaos) and we are called both to "get real" and to celebrate this at the same time. Though celebration of something messy and chaotic might seem contradictory, in fact it offers a kind of freedom from rules and strictures, a kind of childish enjoyment of disorder. In many senses this is a continuation of a classical topos and praxis of Israeli culture in which Israeli existence is seen as a kind of unshackling of desire, a throwing away of the yokes of fear, and European regimes of order and repression.[2] In fact many who have offered a comprehensive interpretation of Israeli culture have stressed its relative anomie, its lack of self-regulation.[3] The roots of this *balagan*, this chaos and lack of regulation are deep and simultaneously a result of the Zionist rebellion against several different sources of norms and rules. First and foremost, Zionism of the East European variety was a rebellion against the strictures of orthodox Judaism and often implied an actual rebellion in parental authority that embodies these orthodox norms. At the same time specifically socialist Zionism was a rebellion and negation of the norms of the European bourgeoisie middle class. Lastly following the rules has been tainted by what Zionists perceived as the compliance of Jews in their own destruction in the Holocaust. Thus, Zionists rebelled against the norms of orthodoxy in the name of nationalism. They rebelled against the norms of the middle class in the name of socialism, and, finally, following rules has been tainted in their eyes by the compliance of diaspora Jewry to Nazi rule in conquered Europe. These various rebellions were often articulated as a total negation of what Zionist thought of as the cowering lives of diaspora Jews. These rebellions and negations have created ambivalence toward rules and norms that had had a lasting effect on Israeli culture. On its surface the song might be read as a classic Israeli celebration of this resulting anomie and the freedom associated with it. On a deeper level the song reveals more than a new instance of the continued celebration of lack of norms. On this level the song reveals discontinuities, anxieties, and tensions along surprisingly numerous axes including east/west, heterosexuality/homosexuality, secularity/religion, social democracy/ capitalism, nation-state/globalization, identity/assimilation. While many of these tensions existed from the beginning of the state of Israel, in their specific articulation they are relatively new to Israeli society. The song is addressed to Madam Rothchild who symbolizes both the rich Rothschilds, the Jewish nobility of Europe, and Rothschild Boulevard in Tel-Aviv, perhaps the most expensive real estate in Israel. At the same time the video reveals a kind of cross dressing, gender bending, identification with this glamorous lady of Rothschild, revealed by the person miming the song dressed in 17th century royal clothes. The very use of the word "Madam" (גברת) has for Israeli ears something quaint about it, but it can also refer to the characteristic way that Mizrahi working-class men (auto mechanics, house repair men, plumbers, etc.) refer to well to do Ashkenazi married women, reinforcing the working-class Mizrahi perspective of the song. The song is ironic toward this Rothschild lady. The irony soon turns to criticism as the song moves from playful sarcasm to more serious critique. First the speaker pokes fun at her for buying and using the quintessential luxury item, French perfume, then at being a hipster in Berlin and "fitting in easily with Germans." Being a hipster is just adapting to fashionable international trends, however, "fitting in easily with Germans" already connotes a kind of a post-Holocaust betrayal. Finally the charge of working hard to assimilate with the Goyim, the non-Jews, using the Hebrew word *Lehitbolel* (להתבולל) has a harsher more negative ring in Hebrew. That is the accusation of willful negation of Jewish identity and then to add insult to injury looking for a Spanish passport, that is seeking to leave Israel with the implicit assumption that it is usually Ashkenazi Jews with a European ancestry who can attempt to get a European passport while Mizrachi Jews who originated from states in the Middle East can afford no such privilege. Perhaps another essential reference in the song is "this is the old Middle-East" which refers to Shimon Peres' book *The New Middle East* that was published in 1993. The book offered a vision for the Middle East that featured economic integration, liberal government, and prosperity along the lines of the European Union. The song slyly remarks that we are in the old Middle East. That is a Middle East ravaged by economic instability and war. Another key reference of the video is the singer who is eating a kind of chocolate pudding with whipped cream on top referred to with the trademark Milky in Israel. The speaker thus situates his critique of Miss Rothschild at a particular social context known as the Milky protest.

THE MILKY PROTEST

The Milky protest was one of a string of social justice events that protested to the high cost of living starting with the one million strong demonstrations in

2011.⁴ The Milky protest in particular started with a young Israeli man post-
ing a picture of his receipt of groceries bought in a store in Berlin. In it he
says "want to know how much I paid for this? This has cost 22.79 euros—
that is 107 shekels. How much would buying this cost in Israel? Twice
as much? Three times?" Then he posted Olyim LeBerlin (immigrating to
Berlin), but using the loaded word "olyim," ascending to Berlin a Zionist word used exclusively for immigrating to Israel that means spiritually
ascending. He also uploaded another receipt and wrote: "one of the things
that we most miss in Israel is Milky (chocolate pudding). Pay attention to
the picture of the price of the Berlin version of Milky (which is even bigger
in here) just 0.19 euro. 80 Israeli agorot. Milky in Israel … costs just above
3 shekels each."⁵

Yair Lapid the then minister of finance said "these young fellows are right,
the costs are intolerable" but then said that those who choose to immigrate
to Berlin are "a bunch of despicable of post-Zionists, the kind of disgusting
thing that needs to be stricken down."⁶ Several Holocaust survivors have
called the people calling to immigrate to Germany sinners and called the
protest a nightmare. The minister of agriculture said, "I pity those Israelis
who forget the Holocaust and immigrate (*yordim* - go down) to Germany
because of Milky. Anyone willing to sell his Jewishness for this let him be
healthy (שיהיה בריא)."⁷ There have also been claims that the media has tried
to silence the protest.⁸ Thus the context of the song is in actuality a string of
social justice protests initiated by young people of the professional middle
class usually of Ashkenazi background that has brought one million people
into the street at 2011, demanding social justice. These young people have
experienced a decline in their living standards and economic security relative to their parents. They, like other members of the increasingly influential
global creative class, are looking for a cosmopolitan tolerant city (in this case
Berlin), where they can find opportunities to engage in artistic, economic,
technological, or scientific creativity.⁹ They are also looking for an economically viable city for young people both in terms of rents and in terms of costs
of living. Specifically for Israel this class would like to experience the freedom of choosing its relationship with religious and ethnic traditions as well
as experience living in a cultural, ethnically diverse setting.¹⁰ Coming back
to "It Ain't Europe here," we see these aspirations are cast in a very negative
light. First, conspicuous consumption of a quintessentially superfluous luxury
item, French perfume, is derided, chocolate pudding is eaten ostentatiously,
then the economic problems of the middle class are undercut by juxtaposing
the greater need and suffering of African foreign workers. Finally, the need
for freedom from religious coercion and the ability to freely decide which
kinds of people you want to associate with is cast in the negative light of
assimilation. While the song celebrates gay freedom from heteronormative

repression and even a sort of Jewish liberation from the strictures and repressions of Europe, underneath its gay façade it slyly calls the creative class to abandon their liberal aspirations and share in the realities of the Middle East. It playfully expresses a resentment arising from the history of a dominated position in Israeli society that essentially figures in the song as a kind of "low" realism, a local patriotism that celebrates Bat Yam, a shabby part of the greater Tel-Aviv metropolitan era. The anger articulates itself specifically against the creative class of urban professionals who would like to see Israel follow the European model of a politically liberal social democracy. One can see the song more symptomatically as a comment on the distance that Israel is assuming from the European model, and consequently one would do well to question this new distance to Europe.

WHERE IS ISRAEL?

We might benefit at this point from zooming out from the song's expressions of distance from Europe, but still use its metaphorical and ideological sense of space and ask "where is Israel?" Where was it in the past and where is it now? The answer until quite recently was that Israel is somewhere between West Europe and Russia, or at least that it is where it wanted to be. The young state's ideology, its institutions, and many of the immigrants themselves came from that region. Its original worldview has been a mixture of East European romantic nationalism and socialism. Its stress on political organization of workers, on public ownership of means of production, its revival and creation of Hebrew culture all cannot be understood outside of this influence. Zionists who came from Germany stressed more liberal conceptions of the state such as equality before the law and various civil institutions. However, this mix of liberalism, nationalism, and socialism was not unique to people coming from East and central Europe. Most states that have their origin in the second half of the 20th century saw their model as some combination of European western nationalism and socialism. The model was quite compelling for almost the whole 20th century. Some kind of combination of nationalism and socialism was seen as an explosively potent force of economic and social development. It was observed by contemporaries to have unleashed unparalleled forces of production and power both in Nazi Germany and the Soviet Union. It was also perceived as the only way in which weak countries that have suffered under West European colonialism could "catch up" or even overtake the West as the Soviet Union seemed to do against seemingly impossible odds. At that historical period an economy significantly planned by the state was almost universality perceived to be the most effective and productive, even the United States engaged in economic planning through the

New Deal.[11] Technological development was seen as tied closely with state control. Almost all technological innovations in the second half of the twentieth century were due to governmental funding and organization including the computer, the internet, the discovery of DNA, and the space program. Planning in development, both economic and technological, was seen as the best strategy to ensure fundamental improvement.[12] Disagreement among policy makers and political leaders in these new countries centered around whether a state should have a mixed economy or a fully planned one. A mixed economy has considerable public ownership of the economy combined with small business ownership coupled with strong state intervention in boom and bust cycles of economy (Kayneanism of Western Europe). A full command economy of the communist variety has all property collectively owned and the state orchestrates and planes what needs to be produced and how. In terms of economic order most new states formed after World War II choose something along the spectrum from West European social democracy to Eastern European socialism. Thus, there was a consensus among postwar leaders that some kind of state planning of the economy was both positive and necessary. A relative consensus on how these new post world war two states should be built was not confined to economic and developmental issues. There was also a strong agreement among policy makers in these new nation states regarding conceptions of tradition, identity, and culture. Religious traditions in places as different as Algeria, India, and Israel, though providing cultural independence from the West, were understood to be largely symbolic underwriting of nationalism.[13] Leaders often used religious traditions as force of mobilization, but these leaders were projects of modernization. Those coming from the West in search of religious expression and spirituality were often dismayed at just how secular these national projects were. Leading culture was essentially local and unique national variants on European forms; a local social realism, a local modernism, and local popular culture. In Israel this included social realist or psychological realist novels (Yizhar Smilansky, Amos Oz, A. B. Yehoshua, Amaila Kahana Carmon), modernist theater of the absurd or fantastic realism (Hanoch Levin, Nissim Aloni), modernist poetry (Nathan Alterman, Leah Goldberg, Nathan Zach), Beatles-like rock music (Erik Einstein, Shalom Cahnoch), new wave cinema or Cinéma vérité (Uri Zohar, David Perlov). These developments were celebrated first as the creation of a new Hebrew culture and then transitioned almost seamlessly to the celebration of Israeliness. Cultural production itself was seen as an expression of citizenship, perhaps comparable to being in a political youth organization or a trade union, culture was a contribution to the public good. Culture was in many ways connected to the national project even when it was turning its back on the national project or critiquing it. This constellation of economy and culture was hegemonic in Israel for more than sixty years from the 1920s to the 1980s. In the last forty years Israel has transitioned away from this model in almost every respect. To characterize Israel and Israeli culture today it seems that all we need to do is negate all the assumptions of this comprehensive model. Instead of a partially planned economy and a welfare state, Israel transitioned to a thoroughly privatized hyper-capitalism. Classic secular nationalism the kind that created the state has really seen its demise, giving rise either to religious nationalism or to global post-nationalism. There is a wide spread reluctance to be bothered by the physical, financial, and emotional burdens and honors of citizenship specifically as they express themselves in military service. Israelis have partially moved away from articulating themselves as citizens, they now articulate themselves through a complex interaction of family, religion, and consumer and job market. Globalization and the weakening of citizenship has incentivized many segments of Israeli society to cooperate with people of "its kind" abroad rather than with fellow citizens who do not share their worldview. For instance, the sons and daughters of the former secular national service elites are now closely working together with professional middle-class Americans and Europeans on everything from software to films. The chances of them engaging with the ultra-orthodox, with Palestinians, or with foreign workers are negligible. However, it is not only they who are globalizing and moving away from their fellow neighbors and citizens. Chabad communities in Israel, for example, regularly participate in mass gatherings at Brooklyn Heights while Palestinians with Israeli citizenship are working for their national cause in such organizations as American Muslims for Palestine, Students for Justice in Palestine as well as participating in business opportunities in the greater Middle East, Europe, America, and elsewhere. The point is not that these groups have less and less in common. These groups were very distinct from each other from the very beginning, what is new is that in the age of globalization they have less and less incentive to work together or try to find some kind of workable overlapping consensus.[14] Rather than drawing together of these marginalized groups into efforts and benefits of a common project of building both a civil society and state, the state-building project has even been partially abandoned by the secular Zionists that initiated and lead it. Starting in the 1990s classical tasks of state building are not seen as generative, remunerating, or desirable in the way that global networking and collaboration on technological innovation, scientific research, finance, high-tech, and global religious practices are. The generative power of these collaborations in a growing global knowledge economy has outgrown anything that can be produced nationally. The only group that is fully committed to state building are the religious nationalists who make up about 10 percent of the Israeli population. Though they are very active, their state building project is often seen as antiquated by the global secular left, dangerously secularizing by the ultra-orthodox and politically

oppressive Palestinians. With the decline of commitment to state building and
citizenship, Israeli identity has been experiencing the forces of deterritorialization as a kind of disembedding from place. This process is happening in a
country that has "territorialized" itself only in the 20th century and that is still
in the process of settlement and building in the territories; a country whose
borders are still nonpermanent.[15] To be more precise in the last half the century Israel has been experiencing two territorial logics at the same time, both
originating in their contemporary form in the late 1960s and early 1970s.[16]
The first is the strange hybrid form of religious colonization initiated after the
war of 1967 by the settlement movement. This logic has entailed the rise of
Jewish population in the West Bank from 1,182 in 1972 to 534,224 in 2010.[17]
It is the most highly contentious project: that is, according to many commen-
tators, one of the main obstacles for democracy and normalization in Israel.[18]
The second territorial logic is almost an opposite process: that is, a process of
deterritorialization. This process of deterritorialization is achieved through
greater integration with global capitalist knowledge economy. The process of
deterritorialization has expressed itself in multiple ways in Israeli society and
culture. It has expressed itself in the adaptation of what can be typified as
world culture, the culture of Google and Hollywood. But perhaps a paradoxically particular characterization has been the transformation of travel and
tourism. In the early years of the state, Israelis put a premium on touring the
country on foot, in order to know the land intimately and develop a sense of
belonging to it. In the 1960s and 1970s the newly formed middle class went
on sightseeing trips to Europe. Since at least the 1980s walking trips in Israel
have been largely replaced by extended tracks all over the world. Young
people, after their army service, go overseas for long periods of time to India,
South America, Vietnam, and Cambodia. Essentially what started as a nationalist praxis has metamorphosed into a globalized coming of age ritual.[19]
Indeed several authors have used their protagonists' extended trips in order to
comment on Zionism itself from an exterritorial position, a good example
being Neuland by Eshkol Nevo.[20] The novel's protagonists leave Israel for
extended trips to South America and Germany. Though the trips are explicitly
about finding and reconnecting with family members who have left Israel,
their trips are an opportunity for both them and the author to reconfigure and
rethink their relationship with Israel.[21] This refiguring, rethinking of both
emotional and psychic ties to Israel can only be achieved in the novel through
an extraterritorial position. In Nevo's novel the deterritorilization of the family is what allows protagonists and readers to reflect in a new way on their
relationship with Israel itself. Another kind of deterritorialization of Israeli
literature are novels that are written on protagonists that are not Israelis and
do not live in Israel, often written by Israel's literary diaspora. These novels
mostly take place in major world cities and relate the life of the Jewish

diaspora. A good example is Reuven Namdar's *The Ruined House*.[22] The main character of the novel, set in contemporary Manhattan, is Andrew Cohen an American Jew and a sophisticated professor of comparative culture who experiences a midlife crisis. His midlife crisis expresses itself in visions of the holy temple in Jerusalem. The novel already shows an advanced kind of self-satisfied deterritorialization that is accompanied by urban sophistication that suddenly experiences a breakdown of its worldview and symbolic order and is saturated by visions and desires for *the* place: that is, the holy temple in Jerusalem. In a sense it reveals contemporary deterritorialized subjectivity as crisis ridden, in a way unsustainable, lacking in some deep sense, a place in the world. Another interesting example of the deterritorialization of Hebrew literature is Matan Hermoni whose *Hebrew Publishing Company*, mostly set in New York's Lower East Side, tells the story of Mordechai Schuster, an orphan who immigrated from Polin in the 1920s.[23] Mordechai first works as an apprentice printer at the Hebrew Publishing Company in New York and later becomes a best-selling author of popular Yiddish books. The book shows the fascination and perhaps even desire of Israeli audience to experience an alternative Jewish existence that does not have its center in Israel. Another major writer who has been very active in this trend is Maya Arad. Her book *Seven Moral Failings* takes place in an elite American research university where four post-doctoral fellows and one doctoral candidate via for a tenure track position.[24] The Israeli protagonist Yoav Evron, who has got the position of assistant professor for the history of ideas, is at first very happy with his new job, however his salary is low, his rent is high, and the university does not offer his wife who completed her doctoral work a position as well. He becomes tormented with jealousy when his childhood Israeli friend Ilay Bahat wins a tenured associate professor position in the same institute as well as a position for his wife and financial support for housing. His specific moral failing, that of jealously, represents his difficulty in accommodating to some aspects of American style academia. Instead of concentrating on himself he concentrates on others. He is also over demanding of the institution and voices his demands to a greater degree without realizing that articulating demands, using one's "voice" often has a limited efficacy within the university administration. That advancement often comes through "exit", through opportunities created at other institutions.[25] In general he overfamiliarizes and is too embedded and invested in the people and the place without fully internalizing that a career is a vocation ("Beruf"). A vocation as Max Weber articulated is an abstract calling, deterritorialized from the immediacy of the present.[26] In Marxian terms one can say that he has overly stressed his own use-value to the detriment of exchange value.[27] That is he has solely concentrated on his "use" and worth in the eyes of students and colleges, his value as a professor embedded in his university, and less on his name in the academic world, on "exchange" value in the academic job market. Both articulations of an abstract calling and of exchange value come under the sign of deterritorializaiton and seeming freedom, however they also entail new disciplinary measures. The protagonists are under intense competition to get a tenure track position, a competition that demands rational self-control and a high degree of reflectivity.[28] The sins of the protagonist can profitably be seen as a kind of resistance or difficulty with the new disciplinary measures. In the case of the Israeli protagonist Yoav Evron, his character relates the contradictions and problems that arise for someone who grew up in Israel who tries to succeed in the United States. The difficult transition from the privilege that arises from being male, Ashkenazi, Jewish-Israeli professional and upwardly mobile in Israel to being part of minority culture and a contracted employee within the United States, is compounded by the exacting demands and pressures of competitive academia. American academia is a wholly new setting for the Israeli novel. It is twice removed from previous milieus chosen for Hebrew literature, both in people and in place. In terms of protagonists, academics were relatively rarely featured in Israeli fiction, since they don't fit in either the social realism of the state generation, a social realism that featured soldiers and kibbutniks, nor late modernism that preferred extreme situations and characters often in situations of dramatic power inequality.[29] In terms of place, the novel is set in the United States; that is, it cannot directly reflect and comment on Israel as a national project. One can only get an indirect sense of it as the Israeli protagonist attempts or fails to fit in the American workplace. Another writer writing from a well thought out deterritorialized expat position is Shelly Oria. Her book *New York 1, Tel Aviv 0* portrays Israelis who live in New York and juggle national identities as well as sexual orientations. In a story called "The Disneyland of Albany" Avner, an Israeli artist, reunites with a young daughter that he has left behind in Israel in order to pursue a career in New York. His career in New York has been very much compromised due to his working for Jewish collectors who do not care for his artistic talent and buy his work as a representation of Israeli Zionism. The story reveals the compromises and losses associated with moving to the center of both the art world and of capitalism. It represents this move not as liberation from nationalist confinement but mostly as a loss of both authenticity and family. Oria's other stories explore new freedoms accorded to her protagonists through their life abroad, especially freedom from the traditional conceptions of family as the story relates a threesome living together. It represents an Americanization of Israeli fiction, as its main themes and its intended audience is US based. Its themes are the themes of contemporary American fiction of successful upwardly mobile immigrants. These themes include issues of dual-identity in a globalizing world, as well as the transgression of traditional sexual and familial norms.

Indeed, this novel, like the others above, partakes of a general trend in which Israeli culture increasingly adopts its themes as well as its form from American culture. *Ruined House* with its narrative of the upper-middle class in midlife crisis draws on rich tradition of such plots in American literature and film. Like popular novels such as the *Da Vinci Code*, it draws on the needs of urban professional audiences to experience an enchantment away from the exacting instrumental rationality of everyday life. Likewise, *Hebrew Publishing Company* is also probably influenced by books such as Michael Chabon's *The Amazing Adventures of Kavalier & Clay* that relates the story of two Jewish immigrant artists who try their hand at comics in New York City before World War II. Taken as a whole these novels represent the changing focus of Israeli culture. Up until the 1970s Israeli culture saw itself as using European cultural models, usually of appropriating folk culture, modernism, and realism in order to reterritorialize and adopt them to Israel. Since the 1990s literary models have shifted toward the United States and at the same time the process of territorialization among the literati has changed to that of deterritorialization. Though several groups partake in deterritorialization, Israel secular elites are especially active in this process. These secular elites embody the sense of Deleuze and Guattari use of the term "deterritorialization," the freeing of labor power from specific means of production. While in the past those culture producing elites have been largely embedded within what can be described as social means of cultural production of the state, through the process of deterritorialization their labor power becomes for the short term, virtual, preparing itself for local actualizations all over the globe. Though deterritorialization effects almost every aspect of Israeli cultural production little research has gone into examining its effects and unfolding. Among the few who have looked into it is Uri Ram in his book *The Globalization of Israel: McWorld in Tel Aviv, Jihad in Jerusalem* that relates the effects of globalization on Israel. Uri Ram has willingly put aside all the other rifts in Israeli society in order to adopt Benjamin Barber's thesis of *Jihad vs. McWorld* for Israel.[30] Barber's general thesis is that the world is split between forces of new kinds of tribalism and parochial hatreds and a universalizing market economy that offers fast music, fast computers, and fast food. For Barber the world is simultaneously falling apart and coming together. In Israel itself Ram posits Tel-Aviv as representing a McWorld, while Jerusalem represents Jihad. Ram's complex and persuasive book analyzes many aspects of Israeli society in support of his main thesis. The book follows several key issues in Israeli society and shows how they partake in the process of globalization. Ram analyzes the economic transition to neoliberalism, the resultant rise in inequality, the decline of effective and ideologically distinct political parties and the mediatization and commercialization of politics, the penetration of fast food, the ideological rise of post-Zionism and its counterpart neo-Zionism in the 1990s. As we saw above, Israel is an active participant as well as adopter of global trends in culture such as reality television, global art house films, and blockbuster books. This book is written and is in many ways indebted to Ram's book. It both extends his analysis but also reaches different conclusions, both because it concentrates mainly on literature and culture and because it is written more than ten years after Ram's book. A good place to start is with what I would like to call uneven Americanization. Ram illustrates Americanization through examples of the decline of ideological parties and rise of commercial politics, as well as through fast food. While both are certainly persuasive there are complications. The strength of parties and collective ideologies has been on the decline since World War II and certainly there has been an Americanization of the relationship between media and politics. However as one moves toward core commitments in worldview and ideology Americanization is on more difficult terrain. The decline of the state, globalization, and liberalization did not result in any simple adoption of an American style individualist liberalism with its stress on rights and religious toleration. While it is certainly true that collective solidarity as expressed in unions or collective endeavors such as the party, unions, the Kibbutz has declined, individualism as ideology and world view has never deeply caught on in Israel. The groups that people belong to exercise an inordinate amount of influence on identity and self-conception, on thinking and behavior. Different segments of Israeli society are very conscious of their differing interests, worldviews, histories, and treatment by the state. Many things tie members of these groups together, mutual interests, and histories. Jewish groups for instance both share narratives of how and from where they came to Israel, the degree and character of their Jewish, ethnic and national identity. Groups are also important since they are often in antagonistic relationship with other groups. The list is long and familiar but it is worth reiterating. The secular and religious are mutually threaten each other regarding secularization or religionization, Arabs and Jews are at odds regarding possession of the land. Mizrachi and Aschkenasi are often at odds regarding the treatment of the Mizrachi in the past but especially over class and social mobility in Israel today. The rich and poor are at odds regarding the distribution of wealth in society. One is born into a group that is in friction or open conflict with other groups. The group itself offers protection and identity, thus one is very early on acutely aware of one's group identity (e.g., Jewish, Arab, Religious, Secular). With such strong collective tensions it is often hard to articulate a classical individualist ideology. One is born into a group, thrown into it ("geworfen") as Heidegger would term it, but more importantly receives a socialization inside the group through the discourse and praxis that it uses. What can be described as sectarian discourse and praxis (rather than either individualist or universal discourse) has, if anything, intensified in the last thirty years. This is true both for basic socialization in family and schools that have come to stress religious, ethnic, and social group identity to a greater extent, but also through discourse in media and literature.[31] For example, since the 2000s there has been an increase in discourse on Jewish identity (among the secular), Mizrachi discourse, social justice discourse, and discourse advocating group rights of the Palestinians who live inside the green line in Israel. Interestingly in a series of articles in *Haaretz*, there have been calls by the Israeli WASP's the Shkenazi; the secular, Aschenazi, socialist, veteran, Zionist to start perceiving themselves as a special interest group rather than as "universal" citizens as they did in the past.[32] In fact one can say that the new Shkenazi alternate between articulating themselves as a distinct secular interest group, an hyperactive force of cultural and economic globalization, and a group that protests for social justice and against high cost of living. Discourse over various security threats from Iran to ISIS has also contributed to group cohesion. Thus, there is no simple implementation of American style individualism in Israel. Even wealthy political candidates like Naftali Benet stress classical conceptions of citizenship as expressed in military service, rather than their achievements as individual entrepreneurs as American politicians would. Americanization is indeed complex and uneven in Israel. In contrast to the burification espoused by Barber and Ram, it is perhaps more accurate to look at the ways that globalization and marketization effect different fields and groups often splitting them further into a myriad of identities, affinities, and classes that do not proceed as a kind of two way split of homogenizing McDonaldization or Jihadization of society.[33] This complex splitting is often conceived of in a rather impoverished way as multiculturalism. In fact people and groups in Israel are differentiating from each other on many levels most importantly in their typical patterns of accommodation and reaction to globalization. A good example of the way in which economic globalization does not strictly create burification is the way that immigrants from the former Soviet Union adopted to Israel, an adjustment that cannot be said to McDonaldize or Jihadize in any meaningful way. First, they are staunchly secular and are unlikely to "Jihadize." While they do accommodate to Western forms of capitalism they are also not "McDonaldizing" or even Americanizing, they often reproduce in their children what can be articulated as Russian or soviet traditions in areas such as classical music, gymnastics, Russian classical literature and theater, and an appreciation for pure intellectual culture (mathematics, chess). At the same time, however, they are often fiercely nationalistic. Another way that burification seems perhaps to be too schematic a way to conceptualize changes in Israeli culture and society is that it essentially both takes the extremes of religion/ethno-nationalism and of capitalism as its point of reference but also more importantly it views them as opposing forces. While there are certainly many tensions between religion and global capitalism especially around issues of cultural influence, gay marriage and intermarriage, equality between the sexes, there are a host of synergies and ways that they have complemented each other.[34] For example, religious communities are often called to overcome the individualism, the isolation, and the dislocations and lack of security that can often be associated with life on the market. In fact, rather than saying that society and culture are riveted apart by two opposing forces of capitalism and religion, it makes more sense to say that the whole of society in Israel finds itself in an environment in which both capitalism and religion are stronger forces. Rather than pulling things apart into two directions they are moving everything and everyone in a more globalized, capitalist, and religious direction. This type of analysis is in line with the concept of false contradiction between the disruptive force of the global economy and the attempt to return to traditional symbolization. While the conflict between McWorld and Jihad, between global capitalism and its reaction in fundamentalist religion or racial nationalism is often bloody and violent, it monopolizes the general interest, and seems to force a false choice between adhering to global market economy or to ethnic or religious nationalism.[35]

The second critique that can be leveled against Ram's model of globalization is that it follows a rather strictly historical materialist interpretation of history and does not provide sufficient place for the effects of discourse and ideology on culture and the economy. From Ram's perspective economic globalization is seen as prior, independent, and the cause of the discourse of globalization. What it discounts is the fact that it is discourse, with its socially contiguous characteristics, with its ability to 'explain' situations and create desires that often pervasively affect culture. Many of the actors cited above are discoursing on globalization, a discourse that exerts power on action and praxis. In fact, in a host of different organizations and institutions, globalization is seen as an active imperative, that must be followed vigorously if the institution is to survive and thrive. The discourse of globalization is propagated by a variety of different agents including the intellectual elite in the universities, at *Haaertz* newspaper, and at journals such as the Israeli journal *Theory and Criticism*. Globalizing discourse is highly prevalent at firms, governmental, and non-governmental organizations, and even in what we might think of as religious groups that mostly shun modernity such as Chabad. Post-national discourse among the cultural, religious, and economic opinion makers has pervasive effects on both life and culture. While the nation-state was strong it was unchallenged common sense that life and culture are articulated as an integral part of the nationalist project. Post-national discourse has broken this giveness. Its discourse has served as a way of "de-enlisting" the service of elites from their national responsibilities of chiseling away at national common sense and contributes to their looking and finding alternatives and at many times global avenues of self-expression. Groups that had a tenuous relationship with the nation-state from the beginning have increased their autonomy and power in the age of globalization. While this book will mainly be devoted to mainstream secular Israeli culture, it benefits to take a brief look at other kinds of globalization discourse in order to see how hegemonic it truly is. The Chabad globalization discourse that was certainly not driven by economic globalization and integration has led to a praxis in which Emissaries (*"Shluchim"*) as they are called are sent literally to every place on the globe. The list may be surprising to those who are used to think of Jewish life around the America-Europe-Israel triangle since it includes places like Kinshasa of the Congo, Noord of Aruba, Phnom Penh of Cambodia, and Montego Bay of Jamaica. At the Chabad site they write this about the Shluchim:

> They are a team. Husband and wife. Shliach and shlucha. They are the emissaries of the Rebbe, the representatives of Lubavitch, the messengers of Chabad.
> They are the shluchim.

Within the Lubavitch community, the title shliach evokes respect, perhaps even a tinge of envy. They are the chosen few, the elite. Children aspire to be shluchim, dreaming of manning a Chabad house in far-off exotic lands where strange languages are spoken: the product of childish minds, it is an idealized dream, free of the difficulties and traumas that beset the shliach in real life.

There are no trumpet sounded when they arrive in their new home city, no red carpets unrolled in their honor. They have few friends, no relatives, no familiar culture, atmosphere, or environment. Many commodities, such as kosher meat, dairy products and other basics, may have to be flown in, but here are certain staples, vitally essential to their mission, which they bring with them by the truckload: friendliness, affection for all Jews, compassion, tolerance, self-sacrifice, utter devotion, and selfless dedication.

Armed with these, they immediately begin their work of outreach-explaining, shedding light, dispelling myths, countering stereotypes. "What does it mean to be a Jew?" "Rabbi, how can I observe the Shabbat-when my store has its best sales on Saturday?" "How are mitzvot relevant today, in this community?" The shliach of Chabad does not insist; he suggests. He does not criticize; he encourages. He does not "preach down" at people; he acts as a genuine equal, a friend. And the revolution begins. It takes place without anyone realizing it. A few years fly by, and, "out of nowhere," it is a familiar and accepted sight to see families with sukot, observing Shabbat, kosher, and so on.

Among the many things that can be analyzed in this passage is the pride in those "holy soldiers" of Chabad who go off and do their Jewish duty in far away and difficult places. The mission is difficult but for that reason perhaps even more heroic. The childish "dreaming of manning a Chabad house in far-off exotic lands where strange languages are spoken" is simply another expression of the pride of Chabad that it is a truly global organization "conquering" places that know of no Jewish life before. The dilemmas that the Rabbi is called upon to solve are exactly typical tensions between religion and market activity like the "store has its best sales on Saturday" question. This type of globalization is instructive on several accounts. First, the discourse of globalization affects the practice of it as much as the other way around. The shluchim are not a result of economic globalization but are actually part of an explicit and planned policy of Chabad. Second, globalization is not "owned" nor is it solely pursued by the aforementioned secular Aschknazi elites. Chabad is globalizing as an ideology, the economic incentive, the "return on investment" from Chabad house in Phnom Penh is likely to be minimal. We can view both economic global integration but also importantly globalization discourse as creating certain pressures, possibilities, and incentives the response to which, actually splits a broad rainbow of praxis and identities well beyond McWorld and Jihad. In many ways globalization is as much a force of differentiation as it is homogenizing. Another segment of Israeli society that on deeper analysis reveals the problem with Ram's purely economic explanation that posits cultural bifurcation is the success and empowerment of religious Zionism. At first the quite plausible economic explanation goes as follows. The Ashkenazi secular elite has abdicated its role as state builder in favor of economic and cultural globalization and Americanization. In this void, religious nationalism has taken the lead in what can be seen as an outdated project of state building, wholly out of touch and in fact antagonistic to globalization. It has often been remarked that the settler movement repeat in vision and action, in dress and speech what the secular Zionist have left behind. While undoubtedly there is much to commend to this account of religious nationalism, it misses the fact that it too is a global phenomenon that articulates itself as a new kind of global religious nationalism often with explicit awareness and recognition of similar movements all over the world (e.g., India) and especially in the United States. Some institutions of religious nationalism in Israel are just as Americanized and globalized as the secular elite. For example, religious nationalists have engaged in the none trivial task of translating American conservatisms as an ideology and culture into an acceptable local idiom.[36] A good example is the work of Yoram Hazony. He has founded the American style conservative think tank, the Shalem Center. In 2013 Shalem Center has been approved by the Israeli government to grant a BA degree and Shalem College has been added. The center and college are intended to confront what Hazony sees as the dangers of post-Zionism and to strengthen both Judaism and Zionism.

The center running on a budget of ten million dollars a year is financed by donations by Jewish philanthropists such as Ronald Lauder, Sheldon Adelson, and Sanford C. Bernstein.[37] In many ways the global biographical and intellectual trajectory of Yoram Hazony is typical. Hazony was born in Rehovot, Israel, in 1964, but graduated from Princeton University and Rutgers University. In Princeton he has experienced a personal turn toward Judaism and Zionism. From that time onward both his writing and his organization skills are devoted to strengthen both Zionism and Jewish identity in the face eroding modernity. After putting together the Shalem Center he turned to a new project, the Herzl Institute. Their mission statement states "The Herzl Institute aims to contribute to a revitalization of the Jewish people, the State of Israel, and the family of nations through a renewed encounter with the foundational ideas of Judaism." This global route is quite typical of the new religious national intellectual elite. Another good example of a new kind of intellectual is Prof. Yedidah Stern, He earned master's degree (1984) and doctorate (1986) from Harvard Law School on corporate law, he then worked at a leading Manhattan law firm and went on to direct the Israeli Democarcy Institute as well as various other think tanks and centers in Israel. Stern uses sophisticated theories of post-modernism and multiculturalism to argue persuasively for converging on middle ground between secular law and religious law in Israel. These intellectual's lives and trajectories show globalization as an all-encompassing phenomena that touches and transforms what are often thought of as "local" orthodox and national-religious segments of society.[38] In restructuring and transforming how all things are done in a way that disembeds people and institutions from local and national space (even in the case of religious-nationalist nation building!) globalization has effected all cultural production and identity formation in Israel. It had both homogenizing as well as differentiating effects on subjectivities as well as cultural practices, in many ways it's the new medium in which every type of social action takes place. A medium that encourages deterritorialization, global integration through hyper-connectivity, that promotes disembeddedness from locality. The ways in which it has effected identities, subjectivities, and cultural praxis are complex and subtle and yet all pervasive.

Globalization in Israel is not wholly new. Israel has always been something of a postwar Western global project: heavily supported by France in nuclear technology, Germany in reparations, and indispensable US diplomatic, financial, and military support. Its culture was heavily influenced by European culture, directly by early East European migrants, but generally in terms of the global influence of Europe in the first half of the 20th century. In the 1960s and 1970s immigrations have also brought with them the cultures of the Middle East. What is new however is the global integration of economic production and cultural reproduction for a significant majority of the population and the resultant deterritorialization of identities and subjectivities that find themselves in a new "place." McWorld vs. Jihad would like to articulate this new place as between America and the fundamentalist Middle East. The song "It ain't Europe here" concurs and says that Israelis are "Americans with an Arab sense of honor." As I hope I have shown both characterizations though striking cannot adequately provide a nuanced picture of where contemporary Israel, ideologically, culturally is. In the next chapters, I hope to provide a better articulation of contemporary Israel, one that sees not globalization as a McWorld with its reaction in "Jihad," but much more a new totalizing context that includes the dominance of the knowledge economy, informational individualism, hyper connectivity, and global integration of cultural production: the total reach of popular culture and the return of religion. All segments and all cultural players in society are both active in producing this new context and are reacting to the opportunities and challenges that it offers. It is a new global environment that strongly structures mentalities, socializes toward certain worldviews and habits, schedules rewards and punishments, and steers toward certain kinds of cultural production. All producers of culture though they may occupy different cultural fields (international art films, religion, etc.) have found themselves under this new global context especially those that deal with national identity. It is specifically to national identity as it is articulated by mainstream culture in this context that I shall turn to in the next chapter.

NOTES

1. The song is translated by Han Keat Lim, a native Chinese translator on the internet site Lyrics Translate. The fact that a native Chinese who resides in China is translating a Hebrew song into English is symptomatic of how pervasive the effects of globalization are.

2. Transgression, lawlessness, and lack of boundaries have been a pervasive theme in Hebrew culture, from iconoclastic poetry of modernist poet Abraham Shlonsky of the 1920s through to the films of Uri Zohar and Assi Dyan that thematize the Israeli condition as one of lack of norms. In many senses this is built into the very fabric of Israeli culture. On a more general level former colonies while engaging in mimicry of European state building often have articulated themselves and have been articulated by others as having those things that Europe often either imagines or feels it misses: Indian spirituality, African "happy earthiness," Middle Eastern homosexual practice, and so on.

3. Sociologist Gad Yair in his book the *Code of Israeliness* characterizes Israeli culture as a set of injunctions or commandments. Often these injunctions relate to an active negation of rules and regulations as they express themselves in an ethic of improvisation and lack of respect toward authority see Gad Ya'ir, *Tsofen Ha-Yiśre'eliyut: 'aśeret Ha-Dibrot Shel Shenot Ha-Alpayim* (Yerushalayim: Keter, 2011).

4. For an overview of the economic situation leading to the protest see Michael Shalev "The Economic Background of the Social Protest of Summer 2011" in Dan Ben-David, *The State of the Nation Report.*

5. For the organizers statement see "זה לא המילקי טמבל."

6. "לפיד."

7. מרחם על ישראלים ששכחו את השואה וירדו בגלל מילקי, "באתר מעריב השבוע" 13.10.14 http://www.maariv.co.il/news/new.aspx?pn6Vq=J&0r9VQ=GGIJD.

8. נתי טוקר , "יש כלי תקשורת שבהם מקבלים הוראות להשתיק את מחאת המילקי", באתר The Marker, 25 2014 באוקטובר http://www.themarker.com/markerweek/1.2466532

9. For an analysis of the creative class see Richard L. Florida, *The Flight of the Creative Class: The New Global Competition for Talent,* 1st ed. (New York: Harper-Business, 2005); For its mobility see Florida, *The Rise of the Creative Class.*

10. Oz Almog and Tamar Almog *"The Y generation in Israel" Samuel Neaman Institute for National Policy Research* (Hebrew). http://www.peopleil.org/details.aspx?itemID=30362.

11. As much as neo-liberalism has played a key ideological and practical role in the last forty years, in the first third of the 20th century it was both minority opinion (the economic school of Hayek) which needed to be rehabilitated in the 1970s against both Kaynesian and socialist theory and praxis which ascribed great importance to the state. David Harvey, *A Brief History of Neoliberalism* (Oxford; New York: Oxford University Press, 2005); For their minor status of neoliberal thinkers and their ultimate success see Philip Mirowski and Dieter Plehwe, *The Road from Mont Pèlerin: The Making of the Neoliberal Thought Collective* (Cambridge, MA: Harvard University Press, 2009).

12. Audra J. Wolfe, *Competing with the Soviets: Science, Technology, and the State in Cold War America* (JHU Press, 2012).

13. The use of tradition was indeed decried by traditionalists who saw this as a dangerous innovation see E. J. Hobsbawm and T. O. Ranger, *The Invention of Tradition*, Past and Present Publications (Cambridge [Cambridgeshire]; New York: Cambridge University Press, 1983); also E. J. Hobsbawm, *Nations and Nationalism since 1780: Programme, Myth, Reality,* (Cambridge [England]; New York: Cambridge University Press, 1990); Most recently Hobsawm has commented that "in the first instance 'Westernization' was the only form in which backward economies could be modernized and weak states strengthened" Causing cultural dependence at the same time "Paradoxically, an official Indian national song was written by a senior native member of the Indian Civil Service of the British Raj." On this process see E. J. Hobsbawm, *On Empire: America, War, and Global Supremacy*, 1st ed. (New York: Pantheon Books, 2008); More recently Michael Walzer has commented on the way in which religion that served as background in national liberation movements has moved to the forefront of articulating national projects see Michael Walzer, *The Paradox of Liberation: Secular Revolutions and Religious Counterrevolutions* (New Haven, CT: Yale University Press, 2015).

14. The term "overlapping consensus" was formulated by the political philosophy of John Rawls see John Rawls, *Political Liberalism*, The John Dewey Essays in Philosophy, no. 4. (New York: Columbia University Press, 1993), 134–49.

15. Regarding contrasts and antagonism over borders see Matt Evans, "Reterritorialization or Deterritorialization? Israel's Gaza Withdrawal," 42 (2014).

16. I am using territorial logic in the way in which Gills Delueze has used the terms of deterritorialization that was then extended to discussions of globalization. Gilles Deleuze and Félix Guattari, *Anti-Oedipus: Capitalism and Schizophrenia* (Minneapolis: University of Minnesota Press, 1983); For use in Globalization see Ajun Appadurai, "Disjuncture and Difference in the Global Cultural Economy," *Public Culture* 2, no. 2 (1990), 295–310.

17. "Housing Minister Sees 50% More Settlers in West Bank by 2019," The Jerusalem Post | JPost.com, accessed October 13, 2016, http://www.jpost.com/National-News/Housing-minister-sees-50-percent-more-settlers-in-West-Bank-by-2019-352501.

18. This has been the basic position of the left Zionism inside Israel as well as the position of a broad international consensus that supports the two state solution.

19. Chaim Noy and Erik Cohen, *Israeli Backpackers From Tourism to Rite of Passage* (Ithaca: State University of New York Press, 2014).

20. Eshkol Nevo and Sondra Silverston, *Neuland*, 2014.

21. According to Rachel Harris Eshkol, Nevo's novels use travel in Israel and abroad as a metaphor for reconfiguring identity first as part of a multi-ethic (no purely Jewish Israel) as well as reconnecting with Jewish history. Rachel S. Harris, "Between the Backpack and the Tent: Home, Zionism, and a New Generation in Eshkol Nevo's Novels Homesick and Neuland," *Shofar: An Interdisciplinary Journal of Jewish Studies* 33, no. 4 (2015), 36–59.

22. Ruby author Namdar, *ha-Bayit asher neḥrav* (Or Yehudah: Kineret, 2013).

23. Matan Hermoni, *Hibru poblishing ḳompani: roman* (Or Yehudah: Kineret : Zemorah-Bitan, 2011).

24. Maya Arad, *Shevaʻ midot raʻot*, Ḥargol plus (Tel-Aviv: Ḥargol : ʻAm ʻoved, 2006).

25. I am using Albert O. Hirschman's concepts of voice and exit that he posits as two fundamental responses to a perceived grievance from a member of an institution. Either "exit" that is withdraw from the relationship or "voice" improve their position through communication of complaint. Hirschman posits "exit" as associated with an economic logic of Adam Smith's invisible hand, while "voice" is often political and confrontational. As institutions are increasingly being governed by the market, "voice" becomes penalized while exit becomes the default action. Albert O. Hirschman, *Exit, Voice, and Loyalty: Responses to Decline in Firms, Organizations, and States* (Cambridge, MA: Harvard University Press, 1981).

26. Otherworldliness was indeed a central characteristic of the Protestant ethic. See Max Weber, *The Protestant Ethic and the Spirit of Capitalism*, Routledge Classics (London; New York: Routledge, 2001).

27. For original formulation see Karl Marx, *Capital, a Critique of Political Economy*, Modern Library of the World's Best Books (New York: The Modern library, 1936).

28. For reflexivity as a sign of contemporary modernization see Beck, Giddens, and Lash, *Reflexive Modernization*.

29. One important exception to this lack of regard for Academia has been S.Y. Agnon who has a major novel devoted to an academic protagonist. See Shmuel Yosef Agnon, *Shirah* (Jerusalem: Shoḵen), 731.

30. Benjamin R. Barber, *Jihad vs. McWorld*, 1st ed. (New York: Times Books, 1995).

31. For new school subject see Kashti "There's a New Subject on the Curriculum." For campaign aimed at keeping of the Shabbat see Mazya "The 'Israeli Friday' Campaign."

32. Kashti, "No Longer Mamlachtim."

33. One is likely to forget that nationalism itself was a dynamic global movement that articulated itself differently in different nationalist movements Hobsbawm, *Nations and Nationalism since 1780*.

34. Such convergences would be evident even without going as far as Max Weber did in seeing the very origin of capitalism itself as having roots in Protestantism. Weber, *The Protestant Ethic and the Spirit of Capitalism*.

35. See "Alain Badiou."

36. This task is difficult because the relationship toward the state in Israel is radically different. There is no tradition of night watchmen state, and the right is as enthusiastic with using the state as the left was.

37. Lanski, "Storm in Neo-con Teapot."

38. It is instructive to compare this to the situation in contemporary Islam. Political theorist Olivier Roy claims "secularization and globalization have forced religions to break away from culture, to think of themselves as autonomous and to reconstruct themselves in a space that is no longer territorial and is therefore no longer subject to politics. The failure of political religion (Islamism as a theocracy) comes from the fact that it tried to compete with secularization on its own ground: the political sphere (nation, state, citizen, constitution, legal system). Attempts to politicize religion in this way always end up secularizing it, because it becomes mixed up with day-to-day politics and because it presupposes both allegiance from each person and individual freedom," while this book agrees with Olivier Roy's first claim that religions, but also culture itself, have become more autonomous and unrelated to space, his claim that political religion failed is yet to be born out in Israel where political religion is gaining momentum. See Olivier Roy and Ros Schwartz, *Holy Ignorance* (2013), 2.

Chapter 4

Refiguring National Identity under Globalization

Modern nationalism as a culture and ideology corresponds best with a society that shares not only a common past heritage, language, and land but also sovereignty and a sense of shared political and economic future. The ideals and norms of nationalism encourage equality and solidarity of the people within the nation-state, as nationalism usually highlights the citizen as well as ethnic identity which most the inhabitants are said to share equally. Of course, nation-states have always used ethnicity, race, and citizenship to create new hierarchies within the nation-state. These hierarchies are both internal to the nation-state as well as relate to those that the nation may temporarily or permanently occupy. Nevertheless, in contrast to other ideologies that stress hierarchy from the onset like monarchism, nationalism has had an egalitarian imaginary. On the economic plane nationalism in the 20th century has been articulated by a relatively autonomous national economy much of it owned by the public or the state. As we saw globalization has eroded the conditions that support the nation-state as an autonomous unit. Global production has outstripped the national unit. Due to modern media, members of the nation-state are at very close proximity to the world at large, while the nation-state increasingly has more "others" who come from all over the word as workers, refugees, and foreign professionals. Marketization creates economic inequality and various ideologies have come to rationalize and justify this inequality. Finally both consumer capitalism and liberalism focus on the individual and not the nation. In such a context classical secular ethnic national culture becomes less convincing and much more vulnerable to critiques for its parochialism, exclusionary forces, and use of violence. Only under conditions of economic globalization and marketization has the critique of nationalism taken center stage. Such an argument is not as self-evident as one would think, since many feel that the critique of nationalism is objective and has little to do with its underlining conditions, in fact widespread discontent with nationalism is only prevalent either under military defeat (Japan, Germany, etc.) or under the weakening of its agency and institutions due to globalization.[1] It is due to marketization and globalization that mainstream Israeli culture of the 1980s and 1990s has taken a more critical look at the nation and some of the violence of its actions. In the realm of culture and narrative such critical interventions were articulated through a hero who ostensibly stands for the nation. This could be a solider, a state secret agent, a politically committed writer, or a nationalist mother. Many narratives take the hero as a national emblem and use therapeutic discourse and understanding to attempt to treat rigid, compulsive, unproductive, or violent national behaviors. Such narratives present the violence of the protagoinst as ultimatly resulting from trauma, are optimistic regarding therapeutic change, and would have audience identify and sympathize with the main character. Other kinds of narrative aim at satire. They exaggerate or distort the behavior of the main character with the hope that audiences will draw conclusions regarding the unsustainability of many aspects of nationalist identity. In this chapter I will analyze five ideal types of narratives that challenge behavior and identity.[2] I will analyze Amos Oz's novel *A Tale of Love and Darkness*, Eitan Fox's film *Walk on Water*, Yoram Kaniuk's novella *Bastards*, Orly Castle-Bloom's novel *Dolly City*, and Sayed Kashua television series *Arab Labor*. I would like to start with Amos Oz's therapeutic intervention in the identity of the new Jew, the pioneer, and the nationalist persona of the writer.

THE NEW JEW: THE ISRAELI IMAGINARY

Amos Oz occupies a special place in Hebrew literature. Oz is the most prominent living Hebrew writer in Israel and the best-selling Israeli author abroad. He is also a dominant political essayist and commentator both in Israel and around the world. Alongside his considerable talent, Oz's initial domestic success was partially also due to the way that he embodied classical Zionist ideals of the masculine committed writer. A good-looking Kibbutznik and soldier, tough and masculine on the outside with a Chekov-like humanist sensitivity, his public image functions like Lacan's register of the imaginary.[3] Just as the child uses his mirror image in order to create a pleasing and coherent sense of self out of chaotic self-perceptions, the image of Amos Oz provides a likeable idealized mirror image that can tie together the very chaotic mutually warring attributes of Israeli identity, its humanism and military masculinity, into one coherent and attractive picture.[4] Oz's autobiography *Tale of Love and Darkness* transcends his public image, undermines it, and engages in a reworking and reinterpretation of the meaning of Zionist national identity. Oz deconstructs the traditional Zionist narrative prevalent until the 1980s. This narrative has diaspora Jewry immigrating-ascending to Palestine where they are quickly transformed into productive and pragmatic pioneers and soldiers. Oz ironically describes the image of the pioneer he had as a child:

> I pictured these pioneers as strong, serious, self-contained people … . They were capable of loneliness and introspection, of living outdoors, sleeping in tents, doing hard labor … they could ride wild horses or wide tracked tractors; they spoke Arabic, knew every cave and wadi, had a way with pistols and grenades, yet read poetry and philosophy; they were large men with inquiring minds and hidden feelings. … They are stamping their mark on the landscape and on history, they are plowing fields and vineyards, they are writing a new song, they pick up their guns, mount their horses, and shoot back at the Arab marauders: they take our miserable human clay and mold it into a fighting nation.[5]

Though he is committed to the defense and protection of Israel, Oz wants to effect a change in identity. He implicitly sees the heroic masculine ideal as rigid and non-productive—compulsively and impotently discharging violence with no end in sight.[6] In reaction, Oz strives to revise traditional narratives of Israeli nation building. The conventional story of heroic transformation becomes instead one of immigration and dislocation, where Oz's parents and acquaintances are portrayed as displaced persons and refugees. The Jerusalem of his childhood is filled with a heterogeneity of different religions and races, with most people in the lower-middle classes: "Most of our neighbors were petty clerks, small retailer, bank tellers, cinema ticket sellers, schoolteachers, dispensers of private lessons, or dentists."[7] His father is a weak, effeminate Jewish intellectual-turned-librarian who makes revisionist speeches about how a new, muscled Judaism will materialize in Palestine. His mother is not Zionist at all, and remains so hostile to her surroundings that she eventually commits suicide. Amos himself almost perfectly displays the characteristics of the new Jew. After his mother's suicide, he leaves Jerusalem and his father at fifteen, moving to a Kibbutz. This Oedipal rebellion constitutes an implicit fulfillment of his father's Zionist ideal, since, in rebelling against his father, he is acting out his father's Zionist wishes. However, in the Kibbutz itself, Oz represents himself as marginal—still the weak Jewish intellectual among the boys. Oz, who took an important part in the construction of the classical image of masculine Zionism, thus decenters himself in his autobiography, suggesting that the image of the Tzabar—the ideal native born Israeli—was an idea constructed by his parents' generation that subsequent daughters and especially sons were asked to embody.

More concretely, by presenting both the ideological image and the reality underneath the image, Oz's representation of both himself and his family deconstructs the dichotomy between the old and new Jew, the opposition between diaspora and homeland. Interestingly, this split is affirmed both by classical Zionism and by more recent critiques of Zionism inside and outside Israel, ones that either uphold diaspora culture (e.g., Daniel Boyarin) or nostalgically yearn for the moral innocence of Jews before they had a state. In short, both classical Zionists and recent critics recognize the split between the old and new Jew, but disagree in how they evaluate the two categories. However, Oz challenges this dichotomy while moving beyond classic Zionism. He shows both the continuity of the new Jew with the old Jew and the hybridity inherent in the new Jew himself.

It is important to underline how this dichotomy has deep roots not only in the history of Zionism, but also in individual psychology. For instance, Malenie Klein's psychoanalytic theory interrogated the psychological dimensions of splitting—that is, of dividing whole objects of desire (usually the mother) into two fictional objects, one that are exclusively good, and the other that is exclusively bad in a kind of psychological defense. Frustration or rejection by the object of desire leads to an attempt to safeguard the wholesome pure goodness of a desired object by projecting its negative attributes onto a separate, often nonexistent object.[8] One can use this theory to illuminate not only individual psychology, but also many of the ideological tensions that characterize Jewish history. One can hypothesize that the frustration stemming from years of social exclusion from Gentile society created a variety of good/bad splits within Jewish culture (enlightened/unenlightened, assimilated/unassimilated, socialist/bourgeoisie, Zionist/diasporic, etc.). In short, a multiplicity of "good" and "bad" Jews emerged, with the division between Zionist and diasporic Jews being but one variety.

Interestingly, according to Klein's theory, it is regressive for adults to insist on such divisions. Eventually, the young child should transition to a mature "depressive" stage, where the desired object becomes whole, where the bad mixes with the good (which somehow survives in diminished form). This, I suggest, is the mature nationalist position of Oz's *Tale of Love and Darkness*.[9] As stated, Oz most forcefully depicts this position by making his parents' story one of immigration and displacement rather than Aliya.[10] In the text, Oz's family history is not the story of heroic pioneers transforming themselves, but instead that of poor migrants. The new Jew becomes a fantastic projection not dissimilar to the wishes of immigrants to other areas, who hope that their children will embody ideals and success of the new country. Oz thus works to free his readers from an ideologically rigid identity, enabling them to see themselves as a nation of dislocated immigrants.

Moreover, Oz also challenges the way that his audience may perceive his own persona.[11] He does not lead the audience to believe that there was some authentic "real" self beneath his projection as the quintessential new Jew. There is no heroism of the boy as a young man or artist. In contrast to Hebrew modernists of the earlier generation, there is no self-aggrandizement, no cult of the writer as a unique individual. Oz ironically discusses the way in which his family situation has "constructed" his personality. Indeed, he often presents himself as an over-socialized young boy, relating in detail the powerful ideological inculcation he received as a child—the way he was interpolated as part bookworm, part masculine Zionist, was politicized and made to be a representative of the nation. In this way, Oz's autobiography enables us to see how the author and political persona are socially constructed.

As we have seen, Oz is a representative of Zionist discourse, but also works to revise key aspects of the discourse, altering what Zionism means from under the noses of his classic readership. I would like to further examine this revision. To reiterate, Oz attempts to rethink historical splits and accept fragility, finitude, and compassion. It is the portrayal of his parents as displaced persons in Palestine (rather than as pioneers) that opens up a progressive space to reinterpret the historical origins of the nation, to soften the rigid compulsiveness of the mythic Zionist fantasy, and to make discursive room within the literary imaginary for other displaced persons (that may then perhaps, make real room for them as well). As a refuge for the displaced, the Israeli state becomes something both less and more. On the one hand, the state loses its ideological and almost messianic furor, since it no longer promises transformation and total self-fulfillment. On the other hand, it comes to offer shelter and a provisional home for the displaced. The ecstatic response to the book—a response, that essentially was a kind of affirmation "Yes, this is me and these are my parents"—only verifies that the latter depiction resonated with its audience at a deeply personal level.[12]

The very ambiguity of the new figure the combined Old/New Jew precludes just one interpretation. One approach will surely claim that presenting the New Jew as displaced and victimized just continues a classic strand of Zionism that seeks the support and legitimization through victimhood. This approach will posit the continuity with the old Jew as a way of distancing Israeli identity from its increasingly strong association with the Arab-Israeli conflict. It attempts to recreate legitimization, at a time of growing delegitimization and critique. Essentially Oz is saying to both his domestic and European readers that he himself is a displaced cosmopolitan, a European Jew, a persona preferable to that of the Israeli citizen whose image has been tarnished by its involvement in occupation and war. Although such an image seeks to create legitimization on the global stage, it contradicts the classical values of Zionism that stress an active, autonomous rootedness.

Globalization, the weakening of the state, and the continuation of the Arab-Israeli conflict conflate to distance the writer from portraying himself and his characters as active citizens. Oz is a very global writer in a country with a small domestic market; most of his readers are not Israelis. His writing is increasingly geared toward the international market and, as such, it internalizes the perspective of the international reader. In Oz's writing the implied global reader is no less important and perhaps more important than the domestic reader.[13] This creates a text that is essentially a double text, a text that is designed almost like a hologram to be looked at from two different points of view: domestic and the global. Domestically it is designed to provide positive mirroring while dismantling national excess, while globally it is aimed at mediating a somewhat apologetic national narrative to a global audience. Both demands have led to a rejection of a citizen-solider persona and the adoption of a kind of diaspora Jewish identity. Indeed Oz's current writing typifies a third cultural phase in Israeli culture. If the first phase is marked by a culture geared toward state building usually by assuming the style of socialist realism, and the second expresses statehood normalcy with high modernism or a kind of psychological realism, than the third phase is marked by a distinctly Jewish cosmopolitanism and globalism. Thus diaspora-cosmopolitan discourse prepares subjects for globalization that reveals itself negatively as lacking agency and autonomy on the domestic plane with a heightened opportunity on the global plane. Oz's intervention in the acceptance and valorization of displaced and uprooted Jewish identity has had as its positive surplus the affirmation of a culture based on a cosmopolitan ethos.[14] To summarize, one can say that the proximity, reliance, and internalization of the global reader ultimately result in a transformation of identity. A displaced/cosmopolitan Jewish identity is constructed and affirmed under the internalization of the gaze of the other. A fascinating variation between self-transformation of identity and its relations with the other can be analyzed in recent Israeli films that intervene in the present rather than rewriting the past. A highly illuminating example is the film *Walk on Water.*

WALK ON WATER: REWRITING THE
SOUL WITH THE NEW BIG OTHER

Walk on Water is the story of Eyal, an intelligence agent/hit man whose wife has recently committed suicide. As a result of her suicide the agency decides to give him a less challenging assignment: to find an aging Nazi war criminal and kill him "before God does." Eyal's assignment is to pose as a tour guide and befriend Axel and Pia, the former Nazi's adult grandchildren, who are on a visit to Israel. Axel is a gay schoolteacher: warm-hearted, friendly, and spiritual. Eyal takes him around Israel: they visit a Kibbutz and the Sea of Galilee. They bathe in the Dead Sea, shower, and make a fire together and visit Jerusalem. Eyal who is very emotionally repressed and unable to cry opens up to Axel. However, he is also frustrated by the assignment that he deems a waste of time when he could be assassinating terrorists. Axel flies back home to Germany. Eyal's boss insists that Eyal finish the job and assassinate the Nazi, and thus he too flies to Germany for Axel's father's birthday party. At the party the aging, Nazi grandfather is suddenly introduced (flown in from South America). Eyal attempts to kill him, but he is unable to go through with it, he breaks down crying and hugging Axel and says "I cannot kill anymore." Two years later we see Eyal married to Axel's sister Pia, a happy new father living in the Kibbutz.

Similar to Oz's autobiography, the basic narrative can be productively interpreted as a kind of therapeutic intervention in Israeli identity. In its own way this intervention also tries to recreate continuity with the past that comes about through a meeting with the other, this time the German other. While for Oz this other is internalized as the implicit global reader, in *Walk on Water* it is projected into the narrative itself. The film in actuality represents the nation to the gaze of the other both in terms of its actual distribution, audience, and its narrative. The film thus responds to economic-psychic compression and proximity that globalization entails. The "other" of the nation (in this case Germany) is involved in all aspects of cultural production from funding the film to its premiere not in Israel, but in the Berlin International Film Festival. This intimate involvement with the other cannot sustain an isolated national identity partially based on the othering of the German and the Arab. The film thus represents a therapeutic intervention in a problematic, psycho-national orientation whose etiological source is explicitly presented as a reaction to anti-Semitism, essentially an "abusive" relationship.

The therapeutic intervention entails revisiting this relationship with an empathic other. In fact the relationship between Eyal and Axel works very much like a queer variant of the therapeutic process described in Freud's "Remembering, Repeating, and Working-through."[15] Although exhibiting resistance to his therapy most markedly as a result of his repressed homosexual urging and resultant homophobia, Eyal starts confiding with Axel about his relationship with his now dead wife, and about his experience as a child of Holocaust survivors. He gets to know a sensitive young German with whom he speaks quite openly about homosexuality and he visits a new Germany. Meeting Axel is made plausible by globalization but it is also, like all films, a wish fulfillment, a fantasy of being cured and taken care of by the other. Axel allows Eyal to transform himself from the embodiment of a certain kind of warring, national ethic to a more open and progressive national ideal. He goes from being hyper-masculine, defensive, isolationist, and violent to a soft, maternal fatherhood, a communality marked by living in the Kibbutz and a transnational openness signaled by his hybrid German-Israeli family. From a certain kind of masculinist, security-oriented "closed" Zionist he is transformed into one of its "open" and "out" (the queer connotation intended), left-wing conceptions. The film in short espouses a new relationship with the big, German other. Although the film ends with a heteronormative couple it is clear that Eyal's real relationship was with Axel. A clenched and violent national identity is represented as heteronormative, after all Eyal sticks a poisonous phallic needle in the people he assassinates; he has a phallus that kills. His cure conversely involves being penetrated psychically by the German other, with the viewers positing an implicit sexual encounter.

Characteristically for Israeli film since the 1990s this refiguring of national identity is achieved using the global formula of a Hollywood film, in this case the American, buddy film in which two people of the same sex with contrasting personality are paired. This American genre is then fused and transformed "glocally" to arrive at this new hybrid form: an Israeli national-identity-buddy-film thriller. Indeed various hybrid formats have the working out of trauma as their narrative core and prove highly successful in the international film market. Examples include *Waltz with Bashir*, a film that deals with the massacre at Sabra and Shatila refugee camps in Beirut in 1982. The television series *Chatufim* that narrates the homecoming of prisoners of war, a series that was bought by the 21th Century Fox and became *Homeland*, as well the series *BeTipul* which became *In Treatment*. The therapeutic national narrative formula achieves not only glocal creativity, transforming global forms to suit local tastes but fascinatingly has been recreated at the very center, signaling that Israeli writers and filmmakers are not only rewriting the nation using global forms but their productions have a global appeal.

The therapeutic national narrative source of strength is, as I have claimed, double; it mirrors as it explains, it gives an intelligible narrative of trauma and its symptoms, and a coherent personification of the nation as person. As we have seen the narrative usually unfolds as a national Oedipal conflict. In this story, the first generation is the Holocaust generation or the displaced generation with attendant symptoms, the second is the macho, Zionist generation explicitly rejecting the first generation's way of life while internalizing their wish for empowerment. This narrative of course is a highly revisionist perspective on historical truth since the soldierly, masculine, Zionist generation and the displaced generations were often two discreet groups. There is something too tidy about this narrative. It often brings together family experiences that do not really belong together. More often than not, the survivors' displaced family did not generate the masculine solider in the next generation, while the ideal soldier's family never felt displaced or victimized.[16] Less conservative narratives, that I shall turn to now, display dissociation between victimization and violence, between the Holocaust and Arab-Israeli conflict. The first does not directly "explain" the second, but provides an ominous background for the contemporary narrative. Narratives of parody and madness reside not in a coherent explanation but rather in the gaps and dissociations inherent in the national story.

NARRATIVES OF PARODY, MADNESS, AND DISINTEGRATION

In his analysis of the Field of Literary Production, Pierre Bourdieu sets an important place for parody:

> It is significant that breaks with the most orthodox works of the past, i.e., with the belief they impose on newcomers, often take the form of parody, which presupposes and confirms emancipation. In this case, the newcomers "get beyond" the dominant mode of thought and expression not by explicitly denouncing it, but by repeating and reproducing it in a sociologically non-congruent content, with the effect of rending it incongruous or even absurd, simply by making it perceptible as the arbitrary convention it is.[17]

Indeed such narratives do not seek to explain what exists or intervene therapeutically, but rather to effect a transformation in identity through parody, critique, and shock.

An excellent representative of this genre is Yoram Kaniuk's work. Kaniuk was born in Tel-Aviv in 1930. At the age of seventeen he joined the paramilitary unit Palmach, fought and was wounded during the 1948 war. Kaniuk is known for his iconoclastic, grotesque, and morbidly humorous novels humor, that were for the longest time perceived as marginal in the national consciousness, only recently has he received acclaim by the general public. The work that I would like to examine here is a novel called *Nevelot* a word that literally designates corpse or cadaver but is used colloquially to mean bastards.[18] *Nevelot* is a story of a retired group of aging men who have been friends since their joint service in the Palmach in the war of 1948. They congregate around at the same café for the last thirty years, watching today's youth parading in front of them in a gentrified trendy street in Tel-Aviv. They envy and resent the youths' over-sexualized appearance, their thoroughly narcissistic, selfish, commercialized existence, and their lack of respect and knowledge of the achievements and sacrifices that went into creating the state. One morning one of them utters the word *Nevelot* (bastards) and their resentment congeals into action. They start a killing spree of youths, snuffing the life out of what they consider an overly hedonistic Tel-Avivian nightlife. Rather than explaining violence and masculinity as a response to the trauma of the past, it is explained through resentment, in this case resentment toward liberal, post-nationalist youth. Rather than taking on a compassionate, generative stance in old age, they choose to reaffirm an almost Nietzschian will to power, a "might makes right." There is nothing apologetic, nothing that tries to justify or explain. As the narrator explicitly says "only the winners get to tell their story." The novel's protagonist thus presents the spirit of the classical solider-citizen of the past that comes to haunt the commercial present. The reaffirmation of masculinist-nationalist violence and the virtues that went along with it such as male bonding, courage, and sacrifice are fleshed out as sheer madness in the commercial-civil, society atmosphere of Tel-Aviv. There has been a transfiguration of values from a kind of warrior tribe mentality to a kind of urban hedonistic commerciality. The novel shows that there is no real option to reinstate the original principles that accompanied the state's foundation. Kaniuk's narrative can be fruitfully contrasted with films like *Walk on Water*. Instead of touching the traumatic past in order to cure the present, to make it more amendable to reality, it reaches back to a warring past in order to show its irrelevance, its sheer craziness. With a first person narrator who uses paramilitary army slang from the 1950s, who is rough, violent, and ill mannered, Kaniuk undermines idealized versions of the 1948 war and the Israeli elite who participated in that war. In a way Kaniuk highlights the two very different subjectivities that Israel constructs, the commercial code that stresses self-expression, sexual desire and fashion, an easy affection coupled with lack of true attachment to other people versus the military code of warring citizenship that stresses true loyalty, courage, and violence. Like *Walk on Water*, masculine soldierly identity is seen as needing in revision, but the very way in which this subjectivity is articulated is different. *Walk on Water* does not view the citizen-solider (a Mossad agent) as an illusionary projection of displaced Jews (the way *Tale of Love and Darkness* does) but it does take the pains to explain and justify this persona. First, by the suicide bombings that form the background of Axel's visit to Israel and, of course, by Eyal's being himself a son of Holocaust survivors. With Kaniuk, the citizen-solider is not explained away as an illusion or necessary evil, it is affirmed and negated at the same time. Affirmed, since this persona exhibits values that otherwise have no place in contemporary civil society, values such as sacrifice, true friendship, and courage but at the same time there is something indiscriminately evil and violent about these same values, values that entail something demonic and necessarily create a violent dehumanization of the other. The extreme lack of control and violent behavior of the protagonist arouses various effects, among them the sudden (comic) release of (comic) tension.[19] There is something ridiculous about the lack of control of a person in a fit of rage, like other comical effects it is the result of something "low" or repressed suddenly being revealed.[20] However when this violence has its origins in state building, then its presentation as something uncontrollable has a critical element as well.

Kaniuk's representation of the Palmach generation is complex in its affirmation of solidarity and bravery but in the last instance it makes the viewer face
uncomfortable facts regarding the national use of violence.

DOLLY, CITY CRITIQUE, AND PARODY
OF NATIONAL PARENTING

The narratives dealt with up until this point treat national identity as a
given, an end product that can then be therapeutically transformed or parodied. Both therapeutic narratives as well as Kaniuk's novel do not aim to
transform national identity at the site where national identity is constructed.
Walk on Water, for instance, offers the most prosaic narrative of Eyal's
identity as the combined result of the Holocaust and the Arab-Israeli conflict. Amos Oz provides a more in depth description of his socialization as
a national subject; the way in which he was interpolated as a good, smart,
Jewish boy whenever he said something vaguely political. He tells of the
way his father told him with tears in his eyes that Jews will not have to be
beaten up anymore during the night of the declaration of independence.
However these descriptions are not critical, and do not aim to be transformed. There is a sense that the author is rather pleased with the results of
his socialization, his displaced parents projected an empowered, essentially
fictional, Zionist identity on him that he then took up and that has, in many
ways, served him well. His "line of flight" from his father was also set by
the father himself; in order to fulfill the Zionist ideal, he had to leave the
right-wing version of Zionism he grew up on and move to the Kibbutz where
he attempted to join mainstream labor Zionism. Thus, Oz's more detailed
description of socialization is not done in the name of transformation but in
order to understand and empathize. A very different picture emerges when
we move from therapeutic narratives that involve the Oedipal son and father
conflict to narratives that concentrate on the mother. While the Zionist
father interpolates politically, giving the illusion of political agency, sometimes paradoxically by being critical of the state, it is mothers and teachers
who speak the nationalism directly. It is their business to educate, form, and
construct the national subject. They regulate discourse minutely and have
the tasking job of constructing the national subject on a day-by-day basis.
Historically it was their task to quickly create a common language (from
the babel of linguistic diversity that came with immigration), they speak the
dominant official language as it relates to the socialization of the national
subjects and they have the job of monitoring deviant uses.[21] It is the teachers
who are supposed to create the Hebrew speaking man out of a multiplicity
of languages. There is an element of ventriloquism in the tone and language

of the socializing agent that creates a distinct feeling of someone talking in a discourse that comes from beyond real social circumstances.[22] It is against this normalizing background of the mother as a socializing agent that we must analyze Orly Castle-Bloom's novel *Dolly City*.

First published in 1993, it is a story of an extremely abusive mother named Dolly. Told in first person and set in a future dystopian Israel, the novel concentrates on Dolly's violent anxiety regarding the health of her adopted son. She worries that he might be suffering from various medical conditions ranging from cancer to missing an internal organ. In response to her worries she repeatedly and needlessly operates on him. She cuts him open and holds a "role call" of his organs, checking and rechecking that they are all there. Dolly is obviously both psychotic and paranoid and the reader might come to think that this is a purely personal madness, but both Jewish and Israeli motives in her madness continually make an appearance. Through the novel, we come to realize that Dolly is a sinister parody of the Israeli mother and the way this figure "socializes," Dolly's incessant worry can be seen as an exaggerated manifestation of the Yiddishe Mame overprotection: an overprotection that translates into a manipulative intrusiveness, an almost total domination on the life that is in her care. But this is not only a controlling Yiddishe Mame, she is also a very psychotic, nationalist, right-wing, Israeli mother. At one point in the story she goes to Germany where, like *Walk on Water*, she meets the "new" German, this time a saintly woman who takes care of orphans. She uses the woman in order to extract the kidneys out of the children who are there. This episode signals the exact opposite of the progression that *Walk on Water* takes. Rather than normalization or even self-transformation with the German other, we get a fantasy of revenge. Above all, however, the parody of the mother as a coercive socializing agent reveals itself in the homage to Kafka's *In the Penal Colony* where Dolly etches the map of Israel on her son's back.

> I took a knife and began cutting here and there. I drew a map of the Land of Israel during the Biblical period on his back, just as I remember it from school, and marked in all those Philistine towns like Gath and Ashkelon, and with the blade of the knife I etched the Sea of Galilee and the Jordan River, which empties out into the Dead Sea that goes on evaporating nonstop.
>
> Drops of blood began welling up in the river beds cutting across the country. The sight of the map of the Land of Israel, amateurishly sketched on my son's back, gave me a shiver of delight. At long last I felt that I was cutting into living flesh. My baby screamed in pain—but I stood firm.[23]

The passage parodies and makes explicit both in terms of the image and the way in which it is related, the arbitrary and violent nature of socialization. This violence and arbitrariness reveal themselves both in what she does and the way in which these actions are given to us in the paragraph. Sentences that start casually are often derailed and finish arbitrarily, such as the second long winding sentence that finishes abruptly and therefore arbitrarily with the "Dead Sea goes evaporating non-stop." The language of the passage joins the image of drawing a map, forming a figure, an identity on her son's back.

Her son is ultimately taken to a children's home under the ministrations of Dolly's kindly sister. Dolly, however, meets up with him six years later. Her son is surprisingly a vibrant flourishing thirteen year old, energetically swimming in a pool, she can hardly recognize him and so she wants to make sure, she asks him to show her his back.

> "Get out of the Water, that's and order!" I shouted "Turn around," I said. He obeyed, and I saw the map of the Land of Israel on his back. The map was amazingly accurate and up-to-date; someone had gone over all the lines and expanded them as the child had grown. I examined the map carefully, and one thing stood out: He had returned the 67' borders! Beyond belief! Yes, that's the generation gap for you, I reflected. My mother spits on Arabs, I look them straight in the eye, and one day my son will lick their assholes.[24]

Dolly City, written around the time of the Oslo accords, exhibits an optimism regarding the secession of the Arab-Israeli hostilities and a real expectation that Israel would withdraw to the 67' line, with a two-state solution and mutual recognition resulting in the process. The novel critiques of the violent, over-controlling mother who literally painfully writes, etches an identity of a greater Israel on her son's back. A critique, that is made possible precisely at a time of real optimism regarding the peace process. It is only at a time of change and basic hopefulness that enables a critique and parody of the way in which the national subject is socialized. Castle-Bloom pokes fun at the way in which national identity is created and reproduced; she represents this socialization as a violent imposition. At the same time, however, national socialization and national identity create an in-group and an out-group. As the image of the map entails, socializing toward an identity is always an active process of creating borders that form a hierarchical regime of inclusion and exclusion. While unavoidably imposing itself on the subject it also "raises" this subject to a position that is seen as above other subjects, in the same way in which foreground is more "elevated" than background. It is this aspect of national practices of exclusion and "back grounding" that form the main thrust of our next author, Sayed Kashua.

CHALLENGING NATIONAL IDENTITY: ASSIMILATION AND MIMICRY

Sayed Kashua was born on 1975 in Tira, an Arab village that lays about a quarter of an hour's drive west of Jerusalem inside the 67' line. As a young boy, he was sent by his father to a prestigious, Jewish-Israeli, boarding school in Jerusalem. Thus, he was socialized as a Jewish-Israeli and integrated into Jewish-Israeli society. Kashua writes in Hebrew. His works include three novels *Dancing Arabs*,[25] *Let It Be Morning*,[26] and more recently *Second Person Singular*.[27] He is also known for his satiric columns for *Haaretz* newspaper, where he addresses in a humorous, ironic, tongue-in-cheek style the problems faced by the Arab minority in Israel: that is, those Palestinians who live inside the 67' border and possess an Israeli citizenship. Kashua has also scripted a television series now in its third season. Most of his work is loosely autobiographical. Taken as a whole his corpus can be quite usefully compared to Oz's massive *A Tale of Love and Darkness*. I would like to concentrate here on the television series since it has had the most effect on public discourse in Israel.

Avoda Aravit, or *Arab Labor*, is a satiric sitcom written by Kashua that is broadcast on prime time Israeli television. It is the first Israeli television series devoted to the ordinary life of the Arab-Israeli minority in Israel. Amjad and Bushra, and their two young children live in an Arab village on the outskirts of Jerusalem. Bushra is a social worker, pragmatic in terms of economic integration in Israeli society but holds firmly to her Arab identity. Amjad, loosely based on Kashua himself, is a journalist working for a liberal, Israeli newspaper, much like *Haaretz* that Kashua works for. Amjad desperately seeks to assimilate into the Jewish-Israeli elite with mixed and often comical results. He might for instance ask his colleagues at the newspaper which car he should buy so as to appear Israeli and not get stooped at road blocks, or how to pronounce certain letters in Hebrew with an Israeli accent. The way in which Israeli culture excludes the Arab is revealed in small incidents in an otherwise integrated lifestyle. In one episode, Amjad and his family are invited to celebrate Passover by a mother from the mixed Arab-Jewish kindergarten his daughter goes to. Amjad considers this the pinnacle of his attempts at assimilation and social integration into what he considers Ashkenazi high society. Because Passover is the national ritual par excellence, where the nation is narrated and indeed imagined together, it makes for a dramatic and fitting occasion for the show to critically examine the regime of inclusion and exclusion that socialization entails. In the Passover scene Amjad does his utmost to be the ideal participant in the Seder, he puts on a yarmulke and reads in the traditional liturgical intonation. Like the wise son of the Seder, he asks all the right questions: why do we eat hard boiled eggs; or what is the Charoset to which he is offered either totally arbitrary answers or paternal ones. For example, the Charoset is supposed to represent mortar since the Israelites worked in construction (e.g., like today's Arab Israelis).

For the viewers, the Passover Seder changes its meaning completely in the presence of an excluded minority. Some of the statements of the Passover meal that in a diaspora context are interpreted as fantasies of revenge of a prosecuted minority like "Pour you wrath on the Goyim," and so on become sinister when enunciated by a majority with its own minority. The very presence of Amjad and his family at the Passover meal signals the need to reinterpret, to refigure Jewish-Israeli identity in a new way, as if to say culture has to be revised when it turns from a minority culture to essentially a state culture.

However, far from solely expressing critique, Sayed points to those aspects of the Jewish tradition that provide an exceptional resource for dealing with the new political situation. Kashua's writing is in fact very familiar to Hebrew readers; his heroes are very similar to the protagonists of Jewish literature from the turn of the century, a literature filled with comic-tragic Jews who wanted to be Gentile. In some of its classical manifestations, Zionist culture is built on the failure to assimilate so there is something ironic about trying to assimilate to it, in turn. In contrast to cultures that flaunt their supposed universality, Zionist culture is based on a bitter experience of a failed assimilation. In trying to assimilate and to mimic this culture, one is constantly being reminded of one's own minority status, assimilating to Israeli Jewish culture is an attempt to adopt a culture of minority by a minority. Instead of assimilation being a metaphor of losing particularism and being swallowed, homogenized by the greater whole, one is necessarily bounced back to one's original identity, the identity that one tried to get rid of. A complex web of references and ironies manifests itself in the show. After coming home from Passover and while getting ready to go to bed, Amjad tells his wife:

> *Amjad:* From now on, no more blood, no sheep, no grill. From now on, new rules. For your information that's why they always win.
> *Bushra:* What's that got to do with it?
> *Amjad:* I'll tell you. These things start with little things. No, big things. On holidays they all sit together sing the same songs, recite the same prayers read the same stories. If we ever want to be human beings we should learn from them. Can't we sit quietly together? Just family, without blood, or grill, no smell of roasting and dirt? (season 1, episode 5)

In this scene and in strict congruence with all minor literature,[28] politics is inserted painfully into everyday life. Amjad projects material and military power relations unto culture. He idealizes Passover as exhibiting a spiritualized and textual unity that he sees as the basis for Jewish success in getting hold of Palestine. In his idealization we can read self-critique and Arab self-hatred that results whenever a dominated culture or class exists under a dominating socialization system.[29] Arab self-hatred, of course, harks back to Jewish self-hatred that in turns points to the tragic dynamic of overcoming self-hatred by becoming a major culture that then creates self-hatred in others. Amjad's foolish valorization of unity and disembodiedness is ironic in several respects since it, too, is a direct and exceedingly rich allusion to Jewish existence as a minor culture and especially to its relationship with Christianity that conceived of itself as more united and more spiritual. Paul's founding statements on unity and spirituality that "sublate" Judaism are very instructive here. On unity Paul says: "There is neither Jew nor Greek, there is neither bond nor free, there is neither male nor female: for ye are all one in Christ Jesus." (Galatians 3:28), and regarding disembodied spirituality: "A man is not a Jew if he is only one outwardly, nor is circumcision merely outward and physical. No, a man is a Jew if he is one inwardly; and circumcision is circumcision of the heart, by the Spirit, not by the written code." (Romans 2:28–29). These sentiments reverberate through the centuries and have set the way in which Christianity as a major culture perceived Judaism. Kashua makes use of this background in order to make a complex statement on minority culture which is bound to project unity and spirituality unto the major culture even if that same major culture is "known" for its values of embodiment and multiplicity. Amjad's foolishness makes us negate what he affirms, but this does not make us negate Judaism, but only a Judaism that becomes a tool of the state.

Ultimately this critique is not about religion or culture but about power. It is about the way in which a dominating culture has the ability to present itself as more persuasive, natural, unified, strong, and spiritual in the face of a fractured minority culture wholly unsure of itself. In a sense Kashua makes his viewers rearticulate and split contemporary Jewish culture into two: a major state culture and a minor diaspora culture. In fact, he presents for us in the Pesach scene, a diaspora Judaism that has taken the inappropriate garb of the power of state culture. Implicitly he calls for the diasporaization of Jewish culture, essentially its deterritorialization and globalization.[30]

In another sophisticated episode Kashua points his critique not to the relationship between power and culture per se but toward actual coexistence: the living together of Arabs and Jews. In the first episode of the third season Amjad decides he wants to participate in the Israeli version of *Big Brother*, in order to demonstrate that Arabs and Jews can live together, coexist in the same house.

BIG BROTHER AND ITS NEW POLITICAL USES

Big Brother of course forms an exceptional political metaphor, not in the original totalitarian sense which Orwell intended it, but in a way which is related to the television show's main dramatic motor: the periodic evictions of certain members from the house, a process that resonates strongly both with the Jewish national story—being evicted from Europe, being under the threat of being evicted "to the sea" in their new homeland, and of course with the Palestinian national story that is essentially a story of evictions, that is the evictions of 48' and 67' and the threat of transfer.

Before Amjad, our hero, meets the other housemates, he is asked by Big Brother to conceal his identity as an Arab, and impersonate a Jewish-Israeli, to which he is at first taken aback but then enthusiastically responds, perfectly mimicking the classical core of a past Israeli identity, in fact acting as the son of Palmach members that Kaniuk satirized. At the end of the series he is, of course, comically evicted. Such is the basic plot of Arab Labor, Amjad enthusiastically tries to assimilate, to mimic, to belong to the "house" usually by adopting some aspect of high Jewish-Israeli culture, either past or present, with results that reveal the fault lines in Israeli society its complex mix of acceptance and exclusion of the Arab-Israeli. The dynamic of mimicry, of acceptance and rejection, of reversals of success and failure at belonging are effective both as comedy and as political intervention. Amjad gestures to the powers that construct him as one of "us," and not one of "us" at the same time. As Homi Bhabha comments:

Mimicry is the desire for a reformed, recognizable Other, as a subject of a difference that is almost the same, but not quite. Which is to say, that the discourse of mimicry is constructed around an ambivalence; in order to be effective, mimicry must continually produce its slippage, its excess, its difference.[31]

Arab labor indeed comments on the societal forces that would like the Arab-Israeli to be completely like the Jewish-Israeli but that at the same time insist on Arab difference.

The themes of mimicry, assimilation, inclusion, and exclusion based on race and identity are both familiar and sensitive subjects in the Jewish national narrative; the attempt to assimilate in Europe and its violent end is always in mind while watching the series. Indeed many have commented that Sayed Kashua is the most classically Jewish-Zionist author writing in Israel, comparing him with Theodore Herzl the founder of political Zionism.[32] Herzl wrote theater drama, such as "Das Neue Ghetto" (The New Ghetto) that utilizes some of the same ploys as Arab Labor: the attempted mimicry of the Jews to their gentile surrounding, pride on assimilation, rejection of society, shame and nationalist reactions to shame. Kashua appeals to Jewish and Zionist tradition in order to critique the exclusion of today. In biblical terms one can say that Arab Labor episodes remind the audience "Thou shalt neither vex a stranger, nor oppress him: for ye were strangers in the land of Egypt" (King James Bible, Exodus 22:21). To conclude let us step back and look at the effects of all of these transformation narratives together.

REFIGURING NATIONAL IDENTITY
IN GLOBALIZING WORLD

These and other novels and films engage in a sustained reusing of the past and successfully transform the way people articulate their identity. They do this with an empathic retelling of the national story like Oz, with the German or Arab-Israeli other as in the film *Walk on Water* and *Arab Labor*, or with a crazed narrator like Kaniuk's and Castel-Bloom. Therapeutic interventions end with a working through of displacement and immigration, a heightened awareness of the effects of the Holocaust, and a new appreciation of the creative potential of Jewish identity and culture. Self-critical satire breaks open a monolithic national identity, exposing its constructed nature and call for creative transformations. We can now ask why these two narratives are so central to the way literature and film reimagine national identity in contemporary times? I think that the answer lies most prominently in globalization. International flows of culture, goods, and people help strengthen civil society in its critique and parody of state violence and state agents. Somewhat paradoxically, globalization also leads to a demand for specifically national narratives in the international market. In a recent talk, Salman Rushdie pointed out that contemporary writers are increasingly asked to mediate the story of a nation for an international audience.[33] Indeed that is what he himself did in *Midnight's Children* for India, J. M. Cotzee's *Disgrace* for South Africa, Toni Morrison's novels for the United States, and Oz and Grossman for Israel. Thus we get narratives that are called to represent the nation on an international market but heal, critique, or poke fun at it at the same time. The system in which Hebrew literature finds itself has radically changed; previously this system or field was constructed as a national field. Now the field is constituted as semi-global, some actors achieve international success while others remain domestic. Some mediate and explain the national story on the global stage while others parody the nation in order to change it.

Israeli national-cultural discourse is not a sole expression of some underlying economic forces that determine its content. However, its expression is a result of creative adaptation to economic and political pressures and opportunities that have become more and more global. Mainstream literature and culture have responded by articulating narratives that simultaneously reflect feelings of lack of political agency and an empathic apologetic self-representation for the global other. Minor literature in Israel saw an opportunity in the weakening of the state to articulate a critique in the form of parody that attempts to reconfigure national identity.

The reconfiguration of national identity is essentially a liberal project; it is the cultural "face" of the process of globalization. In many senses its ideology of inclusive humanism supports on the level of culture, the integration of

Israel into worldwide networks of production and consumption. However this same integration into a global market economy has brought with it other not necessarily liberal reactions. One such kind of cultural reaction that we saw before is the articulation of a religious counter-globalization in which religious culture articulates a global alternative to commercial culture. Another kind of reaction has tried to reinstate and essentially to reinvent the solidarity of the nation along classically republican lines. It is to these later attempts, to this neo-republicanism of the often called National Left that I turn to now.

NOTES

1. Most Post-Zionist critiques of Zionism often lack self-awareness of the enabling conditions of this critique. They often do not ask why self-critique over events which were known since 1948 receive wide spread circulation in Israel only since the late 1980s.

2. I am using Max Weber's account of "Idealtypus" Weber, *Methodology of Social Sciences*, 90.

3. Jacques Lacan and Jacques-Alain Miller, *The Seminar of Jacques Lacan*, 1988, 122–23.

4. Many different cultures have articulated a similar persona as a point of imaginary identification. Soviet Russia had hero of labor Alexey Stakhanov, while popular American culture expressed this kind of efficacy embodied in the usually white hero of popular films embodied by a series of actors such as John Wayne, Paul Newman, Clint Eastwood, Tom Cruise, and so on. Amos Oz adds to this kind of hero a dash of Jewish intellectuality as well.

5. Oz, *A Tale of Love and Darkness*, 5–6.

6. Many contemporary narrations of Israel in literature and film include this theme, among them *Munich*, *Waltz with Bashir*, *Walk on Water*, and *Nevelot*.

7. Ibid., 16.

8. In Melanie Klein's psychoanalytic theory, the breast-feeding baby is often frustrated at the way in which nursing occurs. In a defensive reaction to this frustration, the baby splits the breast to "good" and "bad" manifestations. In creating the "bad" breast the baby protects the wholeness and goodness of the breast that feeds her from frustration, aggression, and disappointment. According to Klein, this distinction underlies dichotomies of good and bad from which much thinking proceeds. See Melanie Klein, *The Writings of Melanie Klein. Love, Guilt and Reparation and Other Works 1921–1945 Vol. 1 Vol. 1* (London: Hogarth Press and the Institute of Psycho-Analysis, 1975).

9. One can compare this position to the one still being articulated by A.B Yehushua, who insists on the classical Zionist position of negating the Diaspora. See Blumenfled "A. B. Yehoshua."

10. While I argue for the disenchantment (or "deflation") of the Aylia narrative to an immigration narrative, Mendelson-Maoz, in contrast, argues for a dialectical relationship between the two using Foucault's distinction between utopian and heterotopian spaces. Mendelson-Maoz, "Amos Oz Tale of Love and Darkness."

11. Eran Kaplan reads the novel as deconstructing the Sabra in order to tell the specific story of Oz's own group—the secular Ashkenazim, which has moved from being a dominant group in Israel to being one among many competing factions. While seemingly persuasive, this argument underemphasizes the fact the Oz is also writing for a global audience that does not differentiate between different "tribes" of Israel and is more familiar with a "general" Jewishness see Eran Kaplan, "Amos Oz's 'A Tale of Love and Darkness' and the Sabra Myth," *Jewish Social Studies* 14, no. 1 (2007), 119–143.

12. See Yigal Schwarz "You Entered an Enchanted Palace and Released it From the Spell": A Tale of Love and Darkness as a Cult-Novel," *Israel: Studies in Zionism and the State of Israel: History, Society, Culture*, no. 7 (2005), 173–211.

13. For a similar analysis of this phenomena for another global writer see Miura "On the Globalization of Literature: Haruki Murakami, Tim Brien, and Raymond Carver | Electronic Book Review."

14. Most recently Oz has coauthored a book with his daughter Fania Oz-Slazberger whose main thrust is to conceive of Jewish identity neither in religious terms nor in territorial terms but as a culture dependent on an essentially diasporic secular culture and pedagogy. See Amos Oz and Fania Oz-Salzberger, *Jews and Words* (Yale University Press).

15. Freud, "Remembering, Repeating, and Working-through," 47–156.

16. For a literary representation of the first option, the "failed" socialization of the second generation Grossman, *See under—Love*; For Masculine Zionist generation see Michael Gluzman , *The Politics of Canonicity: Lines of Resistance in Modernist Hebrew Poetry* (Stanford, CA: Stanford Univ. Press, 2003).

17. Pierre Bourdieu and Randal Johnson, *The Field of Cultural Production: Essays on Art and Literature* (New York: Columbia University Press, 1993), 31.

18. Kaniuk, *Villany and Vultures* (Tel Aviv: Yedioth Books, 2006).

19. Herbert Spencer, *Progress: Its Law and Cause: With Other Disquisitions, Viz.: The Physiology of Laughter: Origin and Function of Music: The Social Organism: Use and Beauty: The Use of Anthropomorphism* (New York: J. Fitzgerald & Co., 1881), 395–402.

20. Sigmund Freud et al., *The Standard Edition of the Complete Psychological Works of Sigmund Freud. Volume VIII, 1905, Volume VIII, 1905* (London: Hogarth Press: Institute of Psycho-analysis, 1960).

21. This characterization uses Bourdieu's analysis of the role of language in education. Pierre Bourdieu, *Reproduction in Education, Society and Culture*, Sage Studies in Social and Educational Change; v. 5. (London; Beverly Hills, CA: Sage Publications, 1977), 71–107.

22. For ventriloquist aspects of the voice see Slavoj Žižek in Sophie Fiennes, *The Pervert's Guide to Cinema*; The ventriloquist aspects of official language are the staple of Israeli comedy especially when parodying school teachers, military personals, and politicians. An excellent example of such comedy at the height of the post-Zionist era was the *Chamber Quintet (Ha-Hamishia Hakamerit)* a weekly Israeli satirical sketch comedy television program created by Asaf Tzipor and Eitan Tzur which aired between 1993 and 1997. See *The Cameric Five*, Comedy, 1999.

23. *Dolly City* was first published in Hebrew by Zemora Bitan in 1992, all citations are from Orly Castel-Bloom and Dalya Bilu, *Dolly City*, 2010, 31, http://public.eblib.com/choice/publicfullrecord.aspx?p=1754293.

24. Ibid., 114.

25. Sayed Kashua and Miriam Shlesinger, *Dancing Arabs* (New York: Grove Press, 2004).

26. Kashua and Shlesinger, *Let It Be Morning*.

27. Kashua and Ginsburg, *Second Person Singular*.

28. Again I am using Deleuze's concept of minor literature that fulfills the thoroughly political nature of a "minor literature"; "its cramped space forces each individual intrigue to connect immediately to politics. The individual concern thus becomes all the more necessary, indispensable, magnified, because a whole other story is vibrating in it." Deleuze et al., "What Is a Minor Literature?" *Mississippi Review* 11, no. 3 (1983), 13–33.

29. For the Jewish analogy see Sander L. Gilman, *Jewish Self-Hatred: Anti-Semitism and the Hidden Language of the Jews* (Baltimore, MD: Johns Hopkins University Press, 1986).

30. For a theoretical take on the same call from a Jewish Perspective Daniel Boyarin and Jonathan Boyarin, "Diaspora: Generation and the Ground of Jewish Identity," *Critical Inquiry* 19, no. 4 (1993), 693–725.

31. Homi K. Bhabha, *The Location of Culture* (London; New York: Routledge, 1994), 122.

32. For a typical example of Sayed as Herzel see Modi Bar On's Television Owls in which he interviews Sayed Kashua.

33. "Salman Rushdie Delivers Convocation Address – The Source – Oberlin College," accessed October 12, 2016, https://oncampus.oberlin.edu/source/articles/2011/10/18/salman-rushdie-delivers-convocation-address.

Chapter 5

The New Discourses or the Culture of the Left

Among the most prominent effects of liberalization is multiculturalism and individualism both as normative ideals and as practice. Once the state partially withdrew from projects of identity building, alternate horizons and practices are foregrounded. As a predominantly immigrant society Israel, has experienced the 1980s and 1990s as a meltdown of the melting pot. From that point forward there is no longer a model of citizenship and culture that is seen as worthy of assimilating to; immigrants and their children creatively attempt to reproduce many aspects of their country of origin. As discussed in other chapters in this book, the late 1980s and early 1990s mark a profound change in Israeli society: from a society that thinks of itself as a revolutionary, secular nation-state with centripetal forces creating a new culture for itself, to a society under strong centrifugal forces where different ethnic groups and religious groups are strongly affiliated with groups abroad and are enmeshed in global production.

Israel is now best conceived of as a cultural mosaic or salad bowl in which cultures are juxtaposed to one another but do not tend toward merging into a single homogeneous culture. Israel, as a successful economy existing in an unstable world, has seen its population becoming ever more diversified. On top of its existing diversity, Israel has had an increase of population of documented and undocumented workers and since the mid-1990s political refugees who have come for reasons of economic survival or seeking refuge from war torn Eritrea and Sudan. Such populations are not expected in the foreseeable future to be part of the mainstream. Nor are the orthodox Jews or Palestinians expected to fully integrate. Jewish orthodoxy has engaged in long-term and highly successful resistance to modernity and is perhaps the most adamant sector in having total control over education and culture. Lastly, the Palestinian population has never been truly incorporated into a

97

state that conceives of itself as the state of the Jewish people. Not only do different groups keep to themselves along ethnicity, religion, and country of origins, individuals and families are increasingly autonomous. While in the past there was an implicit expectation among those who lead state and society that most of the different groups will converge around a secular kind of Israeliness, this is no longer the case. In the span of thirty years a society with a strong collective ideology articulating a new kind of person has become highly sectoralized and individualized. These radical changes necessarily create a break in the prevalent ideological self-understanding of citizenship and identity that was predicated on a vision of a future that combined secular nationalism and various characteristics of socialism. This chapter would like to examine how mainstream secular Zionist ideology responded to this break.

CITIZENSHIP AND DISCOURSE

In order to chart the changes in self-understanding and ideology of the secular left it would be best to begin with Shafir and Peled's analysis of citizens incorporation regimes. In their book *Being Israeli: The Dynamics of Multiple Citizenship* Shafir and Peled have characterized three prevalent citizenship discourses that compete in Israel: Liberal, Republican, and the Ethno-nationalist.[1] Liberal discourse designates freedom from the state and its demands, and asserts the rights and values of pursuing potentially infinite and unknown multiplicities of the good. The individual is a "sovereign author of her life who pursues her private rational advantage or conception of the good, and is not beholden to the community. The role of politics in this approach is to guarantee negative liberty that is freedom from coercion. This entails aiding and protecting individuals from interference by governments, and by other people, in the exercise of the rights they inalienably possess."[2] Though Shafir and Peled deal exclusively with political discourse and not with culture, it is precisely through culture that such abstract principles become part of the everyday self-understanding of the people. Liberal culture in Israel went through two distinct phases. As we saw (in the first chapter), in the late 1960s through the 1980s, poets, musicians, film makers and writers valorized and extolled personal autonomy and indeed the right of the individual to live and enjoy their private good and private sufferings in the face of the "enlisting" demands of the state. In literature this discourse was exemplified by Yehuda Amichai, Natan Zach, and Amos Oz, in film by Uri Zohar, in music by Israeli rock of the early 1970s. The late 1980s and early 1990s saw a distinct new kind of cultural embodiment of liberal discourse make its appearance in Israel—multiculturalism. While Israel was always a "multicultural" nation this was seen as something that needs to be surmounted in the creation of a new type of person (a new Hebrew man and new Hebrew woman) rather than as something to be appreciated or celebrated. Indeed all the various cultures, traditional East European, traditional Middle Eastern, and bourgeoisie European, were all seen as in need of radical transformation not affirmation and celebration. Multiculturalism and identity politics as an ideology and worldview made its way into Israel through the liberal west (especially Canada) in the late 1980s. Though it exists in certain tensions with classical liberalism it shares many fundamental values.[3] Cultural diversity and pluralism naturally seem to attest to the multiplicities of the articulation of the good. Liberals often point to culture in order to show the extreme diversity of human goals, desires, and wants. If one social group, let's say the ultra-orthodox, devotes a significant amount of its resources and time to interpretation of religious law, while secular Russians devote significant amount of energy to playing musical instruments and math, their interests and passions are diverse and thus they are not to be coerced to follow a unitary conception of the common good. Thus liberal discourse in Israel converges with multiculturalism.[4] Republican discourse in contrast fosters positive civic virtue as a common good. Citizens participate in the political community, and identify with its purposes. "Members of such a community experience their citizenship not intermittently, as merely protective of individual rights, but rather as active participation in the pursuit of the common good … . Active participation is the core of the citizens' civic virtue and the criterion entitling them to a larger share of the community's material and moral resources."[5] Political ideology however is not actualized solely on this level of philosophical abstraction that lacks emotional engagement. Society usually embodies republican ideals through culture and social praxis broadly conceived. Films, television and literature are among the many experiences and institutions such as school, youth groups that are responsible for articulating republican ideals. Republican culture usually has an ideal worker/soldier as hero at its center. This selfless figure is tireless in thinking and acting on behalf of the collective while the whole nation identifies with this figure in return. Group norms and rituals, narrative and ideology between the 1930s and the 1960s celebrate pioneering, physical labor, and, increasingly as time goes by, heroic male soldiering. Literature (reading being an essentially a private pastime) and film (a collective but not interactive pastime) were never traditionally the center of the cult of the soldier. This cult was traditionally sustained by wanting to measure up to one's peers and by collective rituals such as army parades and Remembrance Day rituals in schools. Nevertheless the role of media such as film and especially television has increased significantly in the last thirty years. These changes were accompanied by a transformation in the very conception and imagination regarding the figure of the soldier himself. Soldiers were first understood quit abstractly as ideal and manly heroic figures that were commemorated in various ways in memorials and public rituals.[6] In the last twenty years, discourse has shifted to view soldiers as vulnerable beings in need of care. Literature, film, and television follow their exploits, their living conditions, and the effects of war on families in minute details. Even though they are no longer perceived as heroic, nevertheless soldiers and their experience have been at the very center of republican discourse in Israel. Indeed, service in the army has been at the heart of citizenship and republican virtue going back at least to the founding of the state. However while service in the army has been the main articulation of citizenship for many years, a new kind of neo-republican discourse was seeking articulation after the second intifada and the withdrawal from Gaza that found its culmination in the social justice protests of 2011. I will go into detail and interpret these developments below. Yet before articulating this new republican ethos, it would be beneficial to introduce Shafir and Peled's third kind of discourse, perhaps the most historically rooted and "thickest" among the three discourses, ethno-nationalist discourse. Ethno-nationalist discourse does not look to protecting private articulations of the good like liberalism or to a projected common political good like republicanism, rather it conceives of society as having a mutual descent. The state is an expression of a preexisting group whose existence takes precedence over the state. "This discourse integrates nonpolitical, cultural elements into the concepts of citizenship. It portrays nations as radically different from one another because their members possess distinct cultural markers, such as language, religion, and history."[7] Ethno-national discourse sees the state of Israel as the political expression of the Jewish people. In many ways this has been the most dominant political articulation. Shafir and Peled's book narrates the vicissitudes of these three different discourses and incorporation regimes from the states foundation until the early 1990s. It essentially charts the decline of the republican discourse and the twin rise of liberalism, ethno-nationalism and the conflict between the two. Though offering a deep and insightful account, I would like to extend their findings in two major ways and more minutely examine attempts at revivals of republican discourse. First, chronologically this study takes off where their narrative finishes. Their study essentially ends with what looks like a trajectory toward liberalization and peace of the early 1990s. Liberalization and liberalism seemed to have wholly benign effects for the authors at that time, including the acceptance and even cultivation of a pluralistic civil society that is independent from the state, an attempt at peace with the Palestinians, and a liberal constitutional revolution that has legislated two basic laws that will form part of a future Constitution for Israel. One law approved in 1992 called "Freedom of Employment" whose spirit indeed dovetails with liberalization of the workplace. The other basic law, "Human Dignity and Liberty" also enacted in 1992, articulates basic rights concerning the dignity of man and freedom of employment. Since the 1990s liberalization has had a complex trajectory with multifaceted results. This book makes the argument that the early 1990s are a pivotal moment for Israeli society. Liberalization has entailed new mobility, opportunity, and reflectivity for individuals in areas of work, religion, and lifestyle, while at the same time created new inequalities. For many Israelis it has also meant a fragmentation and individualization of society along ethnic and religious lines. The analysis here also differs from Shafir and Peled's in that it concentrates on the dynamic and minute ways in which citizenship discourse skillfully adopts to political events and changes in the ideological field itself, most importantly to marketization and its attendant globalization as the most important structural change affecting all of the social field. Globalization has fundamentally changed the way that citizenship discourses have sought to reproduce, reconstruct, and reinvent themselves. While this book has mainly dealt with liberal interventions into culture before I will devote this chapter specifically to reactions to liberalization and globalization in the form of neo-republican discourse that seeks to revitalize secular nationalism.

NEO-REPUBLICAN DISCOURSE: MYTH AND REALITY

It may be asked why I use the term *neo*-republican and not simply republican? Precisely because old classical republicanism in its Israeli guise, that is Labor Zionism, had to rearticulate itself anew after the great liberalization wave of the late 1980s and 1990s. It is precisely the argument of this book that all value orientations and ideologies have had to rearticulate themselves after the cultural liberalization that took place in the late 1980s and early 1990s. Traditionally republican nationalism that has expressed itself mainly in Labor Zionism, has been the most prominent and successful ideology in Israel's history, essentially hegemonic from 1920s until the election of the Likud party in 1977. In many ways this ideology formed the core of Israeli identity. It is this ideology that has suffered the sharpest decline since the advent of globalization and neoliberalism and thus it provides the sharpest perspective on the changes that have taken place due to these processes. Looking at the way in which it has tried to adjust itself to this decline and its attempts at reformulation and rejuvenation is itself highly instructive. It is important to stress however that although this discourse has experienced a sharp decline, it is still in many ways hegemonic in the realm of cultural production. Literature, film, and television still largely reflect the interests and perspectives of the milieu that traditionally belonged to Labor Zionism. Israel has also experienced sudden peaks of use of republican discourse since the second intifada. The second reason is that since the second intifada, there has been a resurgence of republican ethos on several fronts from the call to social justice culminating in the one million demonstration in 2011, to the 2013 election whose key word phrase was "carrying the burden" that signaled the demand from the secular that the mandatory and universal draft be extended to the orthodox Jewish minority who were exempt from army service. Thus there is ample evidence of periodical resurgences in a republican ethos that is often incorporated into the discourse of many parties far from the traditional Zionist left. The vicissitudes of the Zionist left and its responses to globalization and neoliberalism can be differentiated into two phases. The first lasting roughly from 1980s until the end of the second intifada in 2004, in which the Left saw itself as the major agent of liberalism both in economics and in politics while making attempts at resolving the Arab-Israeli conflict. The second phase from 2004 until at least the middle 2010s essentially sees the Arab-Israeli conflict as nearly intractable and thus concentrates on trying to rectify the growing economic disparity in Israeli society. During the first phase Labor-Zionist leaders have been at the very forefront of a liberal transition with all that this entails: the privatization of government and collectively owned enterprise, the weakening of the unions, deregulation of financial transactions, the encouragement and opening up toward export, privatization, and commercialization of the media and in general the decoupling of society from the state. Politically the high point of this phase were the Oslo peace accords, it was to be the lasting legacy of Labor Zionism to resolve the Arab-Israeli conflict. During this first phase there was relatively little discourse on social issues nor any concern regarding economic disparities and the concentration of extreme wealth and power in the hands of the few. The second phase is marked by a pessimistic outlook regarding the Arab-Israeli conflict simultaneously with a call for involvement in social issues. This has culminated in political figures like labor member of parliament Shelly Yachimoviz who has ignored, almost bracketed the occupation and conflict in order to concentrate on social justice issues. But also in writers and ideologues such as Gadi Taub, Sheumel Haspari, and Aledad Yaniv who have tried to recreate the discourse of what they call the National Left. In many ways Gadi Taub's literary and ideological project is the most interesting and complex formulation of this new National Left. A well-known author, television celebrity, and professor for communication studies, Taub started expressing his views on Israeli culture of the 1980s and 1990s in a book called *The Dispirited Rebellion*.[8] His book provides a critically comprehensive interpretation of the then contemporary 1990s Israeli literature, music, and television and literature under the sign of postmodernism, multiculturalism, and political correctness. This rebellion is dispirited since those participating in culture making are rebelling by withdrawing from real political problems facing Israel (the occupation and the fragmentation of Israeli society). Instead of dealing with the political issues, Taub claims that cultural makers as diverse as Etgar Keret, Orly Castle-Bloom through to Israeli literary theory and post-Zionist thinkers articulate an escape from the intractable Arab-Israeli conflict and from a commitment to real political change. Writers withdraw from the problems facing Israel as a whole into the bubble of Tel-Aviv. Cultural theorists take flight by using antiseptic and abstract theoretical language rather than calling and engaging in real political change. Taub calls for a return to activity, pragmatism, and realism of classic Zionism. As mentioned, Taub is also a successful writer of fiction. Yaron Peleg in his book *Israeli Culture between Two Intifadas: A Brief Romance* analyzes Taub's and his generation's reaction to what was conceived of as the political impasse of Zionism after the first intifada, as a retreat to "romance." According to Peleg the pronoun "we" that has always articulated the nation comes to articulate the romantic couple, and romantic love is seen as offering personal redemption once the political has soured.[9] While this argument is certainly strong in regards to Taub's generation, especially in regards to Etgar Keret, Uzi Weill, and Gafi Amir, the main authors that Peled deals with. I would like to argue that Taub's main literary contribution and greatest achievement is to point the literary imagination to milieus and people that Israeli literature has not portrayed before. By contextualizing Taub's writing relative to the writers that have dominated the literary field we can better see this refocus. The three most successful contemporary Hebrew writers Amos Oz, A. B. Yehushua, and David Grossman have not significantly veered away from representing middle class usually Ashkenazi milieu that they have mostly rendered in highly complementary humanist light, in this way they have served the purpose of positive mirroring for their past core readership, as well as a familiar liberal figure of identification for their readers in Europe and the United States. Their aspirations, fears, and relations to the nation are often articulated through the prism of a learned, cultured, and thoughtful humanistic speaker who uses a heightened Hebrew. Taub in contrast has provided these same readers not with a better humanistic and better articulated version of themselves but a scopophilic access to "lower" worlds especially the seedy world of night clubs where immigrants from the former Soviet Union, Ethiopians, immigrant workers from Thailand, lap dancers all congregate. Taub's rendering of Israeli underworld reached its apotheosis in his novel *Allenbi* that Taub then remade into a highly successful television series. *Allenbi*'s story is comprised of several narratives around the famous dance club Allenbi 58 that was active in Tel-Aviv from 1994 to 2000 and in many ways symbolized Tel-Avivian hedonistic and optimistic culture of the 1990s. The narrative of the book and the series revolves around two couples. The first is a relationship between Arik an Israeli of Mizrachi origins who is a night club owner and formerly religious Mika, a strip dancer who got beaten up in his club. The second is between Eren, an Aschkenazi upwardly mobile reporter for a daily newspaper, and Noki, a lap and strip-tease dancer. The plot revolves around Mika being beaten in a nightclub by her brother (of which we later learn she had an incestuous relationship with) and Eren who takes her under his protection and patronage. Mika's boyfriend Dima, a bouncer from the former Soviet Union, beats the brother unconscious by kicking him in the head. Through the characters and their doings, Taub subtly lets the readers perceive that nihilistic violence, drug taking, and sexual transgression are predicated upon the disintegration of the national project. Mika's character reveals the way in which the traditional religious Mizrachi family oppresses its female members and how the "outside" world of dance bars and various forms of prostitution receive them, it is also a family in which a brother has sex with his own sister and beats her up in a club. Immigrants from the former Soviet Union are represented by the ultra-violent bouncers and bodyguards; they value violent masculinity in itself and act threateningly toward everyone. The well-integrated Ashkenazi reporter (probably an alter ego of Taub himself), who starts idealistically as an investigative reporter examining the case of an Arab bodyguard beaten up by his Jewish collogues, ends up following his sexual desires destructively in his relationship with the lap dancer Noki. This relationship, while exciting sexually, humiliates and degrades him, both for the fact that she continues lap dancing and giving oral sex services to men, but more painfully, she starts engaging in online dating while he is her boyfriend. Ultimately all of Taub's characters are victims of what he sees as disintegrating society in the process of active fragmentation, in which social cohesion and national purpose have been lost. In his programmatic writings Taub articulates his general critique of today's Israel that he puts under the rubric of post-Zionism and multiculturalism:

Today "multi-culturalism" is the problem not the solution. What separates is much and what is common is lacking: not a common culture, not a common language, not a common family structure and no common habits. It was clear for anyone who considered himself a Zionist that only a consolidated (*megobeshet*) society that has a stable sense of identity and a strong central focus of identification would be able to stand in the enormous collective effort of striving for political independence and the founding (*bisosa*) of the state. The founding of the economy, the building of political institutions and the enormous sacrifice needed in the war for independence, one cannot imagine without the feeling of shared fate. A state is the political institutionalization of a society, without there being a society with a resilient focus of identity—a society not a collection of individuals and groups—the political will stands on shifting sand. In other words, without an "hegemonic narrative" a state would not have been founded. (Gadi Taub, 2007)

It is important to note that the lack of strong communal ethos is not decried mainly in the name of inequality but for its lack of resilience and cohesion. The hegemonic narrative, though problematic for a variety of reasons, functions almost like the Plato's noble lie. Essentially Taub is adopting Leo Strauss's doctrine from *City and Man* where he discusses the myths required of all governments to create cohesion.[10] For example, the myth that the land of the state belongs to the state in a natural way, though it was likely acquired in war, and that citizenship is rooted in more than accidents of birth.[11] Taub's doctrine is very much influenced by the student of Leo Strauss Alan Bloom. Bloom sees relativism, deconstruction, postmodernism, and popular culture as a "closing of the American mind," while Taub sees it as a "bent over/depressed rebellion."[12] While Bloom concentrates on education/culture in the setting of the university, Taub looks to popular culture but more importantly society at large as it is represented in nightlife. According to Taub the celebrated liberation from the hegemonic grand narrative does not lead to diversity and freedom but to an atomistic unleashing of aggressive and sexual urges. Taub's fascination with the depiction of nightclubs serves two purposes: it allows us a preview of the forefront of liberal revolution, clubs being essentially the place where new sexual freedoms assert themselves; and at the same time it allows us to see the inherent fragmentation that multiculturalism and relativism entail. In a story called "Ingathering of Exiles: Outside the Circle of Consolation" that appears in Taub's *Against Solitude: Impressions*, Taub relates an upperwordly mobile young man who goes to a club where he meets a dancer, an immigrant from the former Soviet Union, the girl has taken drugs and alternates between acting promiscuously and standoffishly.[13] Finally the sexually aroused young man is able to take her back to her bleak apartment where her daughter is laying on a bare mattress in a room with no furniture. The young man ruminates about saving her from these surrounding, they had sex, the condom is torn, and the young man is worried about being infected with HIV. He wants to get tested but also to help the woman out of her squalid conditions. Directly after their sexual encounter he thinks:

> Mother of a girl! Mother of an eight-year-old girl! Does she even take care of itself? What is all this? Who are all these people in this apartment anyway? Is this their life? This way? Without a bottom? Without a floor? Without a net? That's how people are lying around in this country? Alone with a child, with fragments of a foreign language, without earth to grow her roots, without people to connect them, or attach them to something?

Ultimately the hero goes back to his world. This narrative enables Taub to provide a glimpse of a seedy sexual world but also to critique the lack of solidarity in today's Israel, the fact that thousands are "out of a net" as he calls it: that is, out of social support networks that can lift them out of a dejected existence at the edge of society. In this state of affairs people fall back on simple and unproductive hedonism. Relating a sexual act taking place in the back of a taxi the narrator comments:

> If you have a network that extends to everything beyond this traffic jam, into the morning, into the day the week the year, a network that comes out of the time that has passed into the time that will come, from 2003 to 2004, a network that spreads itself into the city and the land and the state and the world then it's disgusting what they are doing in the back seat over there. But if there isn't, if there isn't, all that is outside is one giant junkyard, wreckage after the tornado. Then you can just retreat to your body, block all the outside that if it is indeed a network, it is there to remind you that you are not part of the network, it is there, as if to mock you. Hence, from inside the bubble the outside, not inside, the outside is disgusting. Melting pot? What Melting? Did not melt anything, did not connect nothing, not even with masking tape. If there is no constant heat, stable, if there is no connection or relationship, then there is passion, a flaring up here and there, and it warms for a moment. Just so. One can at least withdraw to the groin, and to hell with the driver, and Stacy sticks my hand into her jeans.[14]

Thus Taub sees today's sexualized ethos as a direct result of lack of solidarity and direction, a need for a quick connection with other people. In response to this state of affairs, Taub can articulate in his programmatic writing a return to republican values of mutual solidarity and reaffirmation of original Zionist values.[15] Taub sees these worrying trends as being furthered by intellectual discourse in Israel. He thus criticizes the intellectual trends of 1990s Israeli academia especially post-Zionism and postmodernism. Taub has gotten to know these intellectual trends well but rejected them. While writing a dissertation on intellectual history in the United States he claims he uncovered their roots in the 1960s culture in the United States. Taub critiques Israeli academic discourse as an elitist, empty, and antiseptic reaction to a basic disgust with Israeli reality. By viewing postmodernism, multicultural- ism, and post-Zionism as a forces that break society apart, by going against "difference," he reaffirms a kind of renewed social realism, the new-old position of a committed intellectual, a modernist hero who truly cares for his society. Taub's argument thus rests on an overlap between post-Zionism, postmodernism, multiculturalism and neoliberal individualism. What consists in this overlap? According to Taub all of the above partake in an essential process of taking apart, of deconstruction of the solidarity that inheres in the nation-state. According to Taub, post-Zionist discourse uses postmodernism to distance itself from reality, to celebrate abstract freedoms while ignoring the real social existence of the people of Israel. It uses multiculturalism to critique the mythic glue that holds the people together, and to encourage particularistic viewpoints and grievances of first and foremost the Palestinians, but also Mizrhachim, the orthodox, women, diaspora Jews, Yiddishits, Bundists, Communists, LGBT, Holocaust survivors, and so on, all of which have a real or potential grievances with mainstream Zionism. Post-Zionism can be seen as utilizing liberal discourse in its call to de-enlist, to focus private life on personal romance, and to free the personal from collective demands. While this overlap between postmodernism, liberalism, and post-Zionism seems persuasive there are problems with wholly identifying between them. Though it is highly plausible to see the wave of critique of Zionism, starting in the 1980s and peaking in the 1990s, as having as a proximate cause the global weakening of grand narratives, the increasing role of both civil society, global capitalism, and the weakening of secular nationalism and the state, the actual contents of post-Zionism predate these processes. It is first noticeable that post-Zionism and its controversies were not inaugurated by texts that can be considered postmodern or multicultural. As is well established, post-Zionism begins with the new historians account of the war of 1948. At least the most influential of them Benni Morris is not critical of Zionism at all, but merely wanted to establish the historical truths regarding the war of 1948 and the refugee problem that the war created. His kind of historical writing has little postmodern about it, and follows a fact-based attitude. Morris writes his book from a positivist perspective always stressing that he is the first historian to use archive government sources in telling the historiography of the war of 1948. Another seminal contribution to post-Zionism was Baruch Kimmerling's two books *Zionism and Territory: The Socio-Territorial Dimensions of Zionist Politics* and *Zionism and Economy*, both gave a materialist account of Zionism.[16] The first looks at political economy of the acquisition and control of land in order to interpret Zionist collective ideology, the second extends this analysis to the whole of Israel. Kimmerling's perspective is historical materialist and neo-Marxian and thus too cannot be presented as participating in postmodernism in any meaningful way. More plausibly Taub is not referring to the original impulses of post-Zionism but to its later expression. Indeed post-Zionist critique expanded as it moved from the "real" objects of history and sociology to less positivist objects: that is, the critique of Zionist ideology, "hegemonic narrative," and discourse. Ultimately however post-Zionism rehearses various critiques of nationalism articulated either from a religious orthodox perspective or from international socialism, both predate postmodernism. Their criticism ultimately has less to do with some process of deconstructing discourse or undoing seemingly positivist truths and much more to do with alternative and competing value systems and mobilizations. Such alternative affinities and ideologies have simply survived alongside Zionism. Many Israeli scholars have indeed recognized that post-Zionism has long roots. Indeed, some Zionist intellectuals have approached this continuity as a critique of post-Zionism itself viewing little new to fuss about. In his article "There Is no Post-Zionism" Sholomo Avineri who like Taub vehemently opposes post-Zionism from a Zionist perspective has the following to say about post-Zionist claims:

> However, in their claims they are identical to those of the old-style anti-Zionists. These were, for example, the classical arguments of Communists and to some extent also those of the Bundists: that there is no Jewish people (see, for example, Stalin's doctrine), that Zionism is an ally of imperialism and that the Palestinian Arabs are victims of Zionist aggression. Not all of these arguments are entirely baseless, and those who disagreed with them also knew that the debate was a legitimate one.
>
> There is no reason not to repeat these arguments today, if one considers them to be correct. The intellectual dishonesty is in the attempt to create a sense of something new, supposedly "post" and fashionable: This is simply an old car they are trying to sell as though it has just this minute come off the production line of the latest intellectual innovations.
>
> Some of those who call themselves "post-Zionists" also come from the former communist camp. There is something pathetic that 20 years ago they believed in a new, just world that was to emerge from Moscow or Cuba, and the only thing that is left to them of that lofty vision today is anti-Zionism. Not the brotherhood of nations, not the liberation of the proletariat, not universal social justice—all of this has collapsed in a tragic way; the only thing that remains is the hatred of Zionism.[17]

Coming from an older European tradition, Avineri is willing to both recognize the existence and engage with leftist critique of Zionism. However, many Israeli intellectuals, Taub among them, interpret the critique of Zionism as necessarily post-Zionist. That is, they see it as necessarily "postmodern" or neoliberal.[18] Intellectuals like Taub make a strong point that the critique of Zionism is today very much integrated within a neoliberal worldview. Since liberalism is the dominant ideology of our time it stands to reason that contemporary critiques of nationalism would attach themselves to this point of view. However, one simply needs to look at the history of the critique of Zionism to clarify its relationship with various ideologies. First and due to the fact that Zionism was a late nationalism in Europe, leftist critique of Zionism reaches back not even to the beginning of Zionism but to proto-Zionism.[19] In the late 19th century and early 20th century Zionism contended in an open ideological "battle" with many other ideological orientations including orthodoxy, Bundism, Marxism, liberalism, and Reform Judaism. It is only natural that many of the fundamental critiques from these other ideological perspectives were already formulated early on. This battle of ideas was cut short by World War II and the Holocaust.

The age of extreme nationalism and the Holocaust seemed to many to have vindicated Zionism as an ideology while many of those holding rival ideologies have simply perished. However, collectivism in the form of extreme nationalism was also defeated with the Nazis themselves, and most countries moved away from communism since the 1960s. In many respects globalization, neoliberalism, and the rise of individualism saw the further erosion of milder forms of nationalism. Taub indeed shows persuasively that it is these forces that have enabled the critique of Zionism to become part of intellectual discourse in Israel. However, the content of the critique predates these forces. What is indeed new about post-Zionism was the weakening of the national ethos that allowed specifically Jewish-Israeli historians and sociologists to examine and analyze Israel in a way that was simply not possible for nationally committed historians and sociologists to do before. In terms of their substantive content, in terms of their critique, the first post-Zionist critiques had little to do with postmodernism or neoliberalism. They aimed at a factual historiography and materialist explanation for the crucial period of the Zionist endeavor, roughly from the 1920s to the 1950s. Only subsequent kinds of post-Zionism in the 1990s had anything to do with postmodernism, and it is this kind of post-Zionism that we must turn to in order to deal deeply with Taub's claims. In the 1990s post-Zionist critique has indeed made use of the kind of discourse analysis pioneered by Michel Foucault in his writings on the mentally ill and the incarcerated.[20] His mode of analysis that was later developed and utilized by Edward Said in his analysis of Western orientalist discourse and by Judith Butler in her analysis of the praxis and discourse of gender construction and policing.[21] It was also used and developed successfully by Jewish studies scholars such a Jonathan Boyrain in his descriptions of the split between Christianity and Judaism. Can we link post-Zionism to this type of postmodern discourse analysis? Arguably yes, and here one must deal carefully with Taub's argument that becomes much stronger. While there is a definite difference between the core of postmodernisms celebration of the free play of signs and Foucault's highly pessimistic analysis of discourse, both, like many other philosophical currents originating in France in the 1960s and 1970s, have sought to creatively fuse Marxist and psychoanalytical insights and interests with a stress on language and structure. This stress on analyzing discourse has been criticized as leading to depolitization and lack of action aimed at changing social reality directly. Thus, while we can argue that Taub ignores the contribution of post-Zionism that are "materialist" or "factual" and deal with historical happenings, one can quite plausibly argue that a critique of what can be called discourse-centric postmodernism is de facto a critique of some strands of post-Zionism, let us call these strands discourse-based post-Zionism. If one is persuaded that the critique of discourse is ineffectual and distracts from achieving real political ends, then Taub's critique of discourse-based post-Zionism is certainly more convincing. What about the claim that discourse-based post-Zionism is complicit with individualism and neoliberalism? It might seem that such a critique is warranted. Foucault inspired discourse-based post-Zionism seems to imply the undermining of the objectivity of the sciences and with them the grand narratives of enlightenment and progress, grand narratives that some forms of nationalism have appropriated for themselves. According to Taub this postmodern dismantling leads to individualism and multiculturalism. This is not a trivial claim. Foucault himself for instance was strongly committed to anti-individualism and talked about the death of Man. In fact all theoretical positions of the 1960s (Lacan, Derrida, Althusser, Deuluze, etc.) were strongly anti-individualist since their main inspiration was structuralism and Marxism. Even when they have been inspired by seemingly more individualist psychoanalysis they have stressed, like Lacan, that one's desire is the desire of the other and that the person is merely a juncture between the symbolic (discourse), the imaginary and the real. In explicit Marxist versions (Althusser), they claim that being a "responsible" individual with a sense of difference and autonomy is in fact an ideological result of social practices of the ideological state apparatus, of the family, media, religious organizations and most importantly the educational system. The very gist of such theories cannot be claimed to support or lend themselves to any kind of neoliberal individualist vision that sees individuals as existing prior to society and in coming together to pursue personal interests in markets and organizations. Nor are the American versions of French theory any more individualistic then the French. Edward Said deals with orientalist discourse that had a massive collective effect on both Europeans and their Others, while for Judith Butler gender identity is constructed by social performances that the subject *is made* to go through. In Butler's case as well, there is no pre-existing individual identity before society. Taub thus weaves an intellectual opponent from neoliberalism, postmodernism, Americanization, the Marxism of Althusser, gender theory, Foucault's critique of discourses and responds to this opponent with a reassertion of the committed and engaged nationalist intellectual. Behind the underlining progressiveness it seems that Taub is against many of the developments that have taken place beyond or after statist Labor Zionism that is deemed by him to be the authentic version of Zionism. This articulation is indeed based on both history and sentiment. Labor Zionism was certainly the most powerful force right before and for twenty years after the foundation of the state. In cultural and often in economic terms as well, its former adherents are still the leading sector of Israeli society. However, Zionism, like many other nationalisms, frequently "takes on" socialism, religion, republicanism, liberalism, conservatism with relative ease. Zionism is always being constructed, contested, and put to new uses. For example, in recent years both liberal Zionism and religious Zionism articulate and construct alternate histories to the "labor centric" ones, in which these movements' values and their achievements are stressed. In Israel, like in other places, different ideological orientations elaborate or keep silent, valorize or demonize different events and people. Perhaps most importantly they also contest the origins of ideological and political movements. Indeed, there are no pure origins; there is always a heterogeneity and conflict at the place that is posited as a pure source.[22] The conception of an autonomous Labor Zionism is problematic. Labor Zionism itself borrowed freely from various Russian and Western European models (Tolstoyian, Bundist, Leninist, Social Democratic, etc.) of state building, and the creation of a new culture and new identity. The type of nationalism that articulated itself in Israel shares a strong family resemblance with similar projects in East Europe and South America. While Israel certainly possessed many unique characteristics, it has shared with other nationalisms the heroic ideals of the self-sacrificing worker, farmer, and soldier, experimented in collective labor and collective ownership, shared a culture of social realism and modernism, and more. This way of collective being included both economic and cultural praxis, and was a comprehensive life form in the middle of 20th century, that was in fact global in its dissemination. While many view this life form as wholly unique, it is in fact global. Taub's nostalgia to what is deemed authentic exhibits a certain historical amnesia or willful distortion, often built into national point of view. Nationalism itself often willfully represses or denies its generic qualities or more precisely misreads what is in fact standard and generic as original, authentic and particular. Perhaps more than authenticity, Taub is after something that is largely cultural and emotional, an ethos that can serve as a basis for integration. Although often generic, social nationalism[23] has provided people with strong feelings and often practices of solidarity, meaning and telos. What Taub longs for are the emotional valences associated, and the meanings generated by a national socialist project, meanings, and affects that arise from collective political action. However, this commitment to Labor Zionism fails to recognize the hybridist, flowing, never repeating multiplicity of the political and the historical. There is never going back to a previous time. Taub's reassertion of leftist Zionism is paradoxically influenced from the conservative thinking of Leo Strauss. Like Strauss he wants an ethos, an ideology to deal with the disintegration and the individualism that comes with capitalism. This similarity is not a coincidence, Strauss claims:

> Political Zionism is problematic for obvious reasons. But I can never forget what it achieved as a moral force in an era of complete dissolution. It helped to stem the tide of "progressive" leveling of venerable, ancestral differences; it fulfilled a conservative function.[24]

This quote is quite remarkable; it is likely to shock left Zionists who would have never conceived of themselves a part of a conservative stemming of "the tide of 'progressive' leveling of venerable ancestral differences." Like Leo Strauss, Taub would like to remythize the people, make them more cohesive around Zionist ideology. Indeed, in another book Taub quotes approvingly from Allan Bloom, Leo Strauss's student:

> Alan Bloom has related in "The Closing of the American Mind," that while he was four he got to know a child that insisted on telling him that Santa Claus does not exist. "He wanted," writes Bloom, "that I will bath in the shining light of the truth." But the boy who brought Bloom the gospel of truth, did not understand Bloom's need as a boy in things to believe in before he can disassemble them. He did not understand the fundamental need for beliefs and myths, heroes and the exemplary stories so that we can build a picture of a world that has order. A picture that will allow through childish means, to establish the abstract concepts of "good" and "bad" and understand the very idea of morality.

In criticizing post-Zionism, Taub claims that Israeli intellectuals have borrowed "foreign" American and French intellectual fashions like postmodernism into Israeli discourse. We can note that however "foreign" these views are, they ultimately stem from the international Left and were an organic part of Jewish politics in the past. Taub claims, however, should not preclude us from seeing Taub's very own importing of what is in fact a very foreign ideology to the Israeli scene: Anglo-American conservatism, an ideology traditionally held by white upper class men, usually Christian Western Europeans after the French Revolution. A worldview that, for reasons both historical and sociological, has had until quite recently very little support in the Jewish world. While believing in Santa Claus might look harmless, the 20th century has taught us that myths that are politicized can be dangerous indeed. More broadly myths are often the stuff that buttress and indeed justifies hierarchies such as between Jew and Arab, Mizrachi and Ashkenazi, man and woman. Another question that may be asked pretains to the universalization of myth. Would Taub want to support nationalist myths of other countries? Would he want to universalize them? It is very likely that for other countries Taub would recommend an inclusive, culturally "thin" state that is neutral regarding citizens' origin and religion. Taub's political position is to counter tendencies that aim at a liberalization of society, but it is not mainly economic liberalization that is privatization or economic inequality that bothers him, but "personal" liberalization, the new state of loneliness where individuals have nothing greater than himself or herself to connect to. What troubles him is the liberalization of culture, liberalization of the heart and mind, the fact that groups of people do not believe in the same myths, that they are resisting against their culture and identity being dissolved in the melting pot, and that they do not share a common net. The critique of the increasingly global neoliberal order is done in the name of the golden age of Labor Zionism (1930–1967), the thirty glorious years of successful state building before the 1967 conquest and seizure of the territories. In looking at this age Taub is overlooking other ages in which Zionism was liberal and even more importantly he is discounting the hundred years in which Zionism was purely discursive, the stuff of books, plays, and newspapers. While presenting himself as duly returning to Labor Zionism, in the current context, traditional Labor Zionism might be seen as articulating a somewhat conservative agenda vis-à-vis Arab Israelis, Mizrachi Jews, women and the environment. Interestingly Taub's Labor Zionism is not seen as an answer for anti-Semitism nor as a utopian socialist project, but as an antidote, a counter to the disintegrative aspects of liberalism. Instead of looking toward future possibilities of a more democratic pluralistic social order, his political project is likely to result in the imposition of some of the same hierarchies that come with Labor Zionism, Jew over Arab, Ashkenazi over Mizrachi, man over woman and straight over gay. Taub recreates Zionism not as project aimed at the future, but Labor Zionism as a project aimed at the past—a conservative project. A project that seeks to defend against the threat of globalization and neoliberalism, and the lack of integration they create, but also a project that is likely to recreate cultural and ethos related hierarchies that are being dismantled. We can see in Taub a new kind of ideology being articulated in Israel that attempts to reuse the past. In the face of various "posts," Taub asserts a new kind of conservative "neo," a neo-republican discourse that itself can be seen as a mixture between two very different elements. An American conservative stress on restoration of the past and a European neo-republican ethos of "holding the forces of cultural tribalism and economic globalization in check."[25]

THE OLD-NEW AXIS OR THE
NATION-STATE IN A TIME OF GLOBALIZATION

It seems that Taub's position is a variation on the axis that will probably become the main axis that Israeli politics and culture will increasingly revolve around—the axis of globalization. Taub expresses his critique of the culture and theory of multiculturalism, post-Zionism, and postmodernism and though he is wrong to think that the contents of these theories are necessarily aligned to neoliberalism, in another sense Taub is right. From the point of view of the nation-state these are all forces that weaken and relativize it. This relativization happens on two simultaneous fronts: from within society and from without. From within, multiculturalism relativizes the nation-state to the communities from which it is comprised. Specifically, for Israel two communities do not share the basic premises that Taub posits for Israel: that is, Palestinians (with or without Israeli citizenship) and the orthodox. From without the universal norms of liberal democracy projected both from the United States and even more forcefully from the European Union threaten the Jewishness of the state in its particular mission. Taub is trying to reinstate the cohesiveness of the nation-state as a response to the very heterogonous but global set of ideological and material forces operating on Israeli society. In this sense Taub's point of view is one of the various complex ways that local politics responds to globalization, or to put it differently, the way in which globalization and market economy are forcing the refiguration of politics and ideology. Both Taub's writing and intellectual trajectory show how complex reactions toward globalization and neoliberalism have become. Much intricate than positions of simple affirmation like Fukuyama's end of history, that claim universal acceptance of liberal-capitalist democracy or Benjamin Barber's *Jihad vs. McWorld*, that posits two major trends of globalization, a capitalist American globalization, pitted against a neo-fundamentalist return to religion; in fact, globalization has not reduced the variety of political orientations and ideologies but has changed their character fundamentally. Taub's is but one of a variety of ideological positions that are articulated in a globalizing world. It is the argument of this book that all the ideological and political positions of today can be traced back to various reactions to the liberal cultural "revolution" that took place in the early 1990s. It is in a new neoliberal climate that they have had to contend for themselves. Taub's nationalism, though seems to reiterate the old Labor-Zionist ideology, is in fact a reactionary ideology in today's Israel in a very precise sense. It is a direct reaction to globalization and liberalization of the 1990s. Fore-shadowing both Brexit and the election of Donald Trump, Taub articulates a defensive nationalism that is fundamentally new. Commenting on this kind of ideology in the United States, Europe, and Latin America, Michael Hardt and Antonio Negri write:

> Right-wing thought and practice are in general not really conservative but reactionary: they seek not to preserve or protect what now exists but instead to restore a previous order. Those who have recently lost social power and prestige—such as white men in the United States, white working-class Europeans, or oligarchies in Latin America—constitute a core of right-wing mass mobilizations, with race, religion, and national identity most frequently the key unifying factors.[26]

Like its European and American counterparts, it is a nationalism intent on valorizing identity, that is seen as a kind of asset. It is this identity that unifies the people, and defends them against encroachment of leftists who are said to simply suffer from distorted self-hate and lack of realism, and the Palestinians who will not compromise for peace. In a way Taub straddles a mid-point between ethno-national or religious concerns for unity and continuity and more leftists concerns regarding solidarity. In the early 2000s Taub concentrated on the Russian and Mizrachi underclass in Israel and pictured them as being outside the supporting social net. Concerns over solidarity and cohesiveness in the age of globalization have definitely taken an economic turn in 2011, when the social justice protests exploded at the very center of Israel. It is also interesting to note that it was seemingly a privileged middle class that initiated the protest. It is this class that called for a return to the welfare state. These demonstrations for social justice reveal that the former Israeli Left and mainstream have stopped essentially to articulate themselves solely around differences regarding security and foreign policy, but essentially have regrouped around issues of economic globalization. For the protesters, Tel-Aviv has become just another metropolis that is to be judged in comparison to the affordability of comparable metropolises (e.g., Berlin). Some of those who participated in the social protests have explicitly stated that if Tel-Aviv does not become more affordable they will simply immigrate. Many of these protestors lead lives that are both national and global. In Israel itself this milieu are typically situated between "national" places: the school and the army and relatively cosmopolitan places of the university, the urban café, restaurants, pubs, modern office buildings, the airport, and metropolitan cities around the world. It is this class that feels the global pull the most. At the same time and precisely against liberal globalization, a neo-republican discourse surrounding army service articulated itself in which the same protesters were judged and evaluated on the scale of their military contribution to the state. Thus, the discourse around army service itself, a service that is described as "a burden" and that in the age of drones, robots, and cyberwarfare is indeed an economic burden on society and has less and less to offer in terms of real defense, is symbolically used to affirm the antithesis of the global liberal pole.[27] Thus mainstream politics accommodates itself to globalization on several fronts usually by "mixing" ideological ingredients whose commonality is that they either support or resist global marketization. Among the elements that generally resist the logic of global marketization are military service, economic redistribution, religion, and Zionism itself. Among facilitators include first and foremost the formidable forces of globalization itself: the high-tech economy, communication, global American culture, English language, and so on, but also liberal rights and indeed multiculturalism and post-Zionism itself. How than does Taub's main argument in which post-Zionism and multiculturalism are part of the same process, that is responsible for the weakening and dismantling of the welfare state and are inadvertent agents of global liberalism stand? Although much of post-Zionism repeats leftist anti-Zionist critique and is written from perspectives that does not necessarily espouse liberalism, taken as a whole in its contemporary context, it is aligned with globalizing internationalizing forces. Then in what resides the problem with Taub's formulation? I think that the main problem is in the belief that one can reinstate a truly autonomous nation-state in our time. Globalization and internationalization are an almost inevitable process of modernity itself. Technological development from the compass and sailing ship that enabled the integration of the old and new worlds to virtual shared reality that eradicates space completely have been eroding cultural and economic autonomy of any particular society. This process was well underway toward the end of the 19th century. The classic age of the modern state can now be seen as a step toward world integration. The conception of an autonomous nation-state of the first half of the 20th century, though clearly a modernization project in the relation to traditional societies, could only offset the integration and interconnectedness on a global scale for a certain period of time. Virulent nationalism of the mid-20th century already saw its enemies as the forces of globalization. For examle Nazi discourse and practice has already seen its enemies as Jewish capitalism and Bolshevism, that is as forces of globalization that undermine the autonomy of the nation. The last forty years has seen the creation of many supra-national economic free trading units including the European Union, the North American Free Trade Agreement, and the Trans-Pacific Partnership that includes the United States, Australia, Canada, Japan, Malaysia, Mexico, Peru, and Vietnam. In the works are the Transatlantic Trade and Investment Partnership between the EU and the United States, the biggest trade agreement the world has ever seen. Anti-global forces, among them neo-nationalists, religious fundamentalists, environmentalists, anarchists, and various kinds of leftists do not have a common agenda, are reactive to global forces and are also mismatched in terms of their military and economic power. The basic trend of greater and greater political and social integration has been constant in human history. Though there might be temporary reactions to this general movement toard integration there is very little chance of this trend significantly reversing itself and states and cultures becoming more rather than less autonomous. The difficulty with Taub's political orientation as it express itself in both his programmatic and literary endeavors is that he would like to reinstate the model of state and society of the first half of the 20th century for the 21st century. While it is reasonable to expect the state to buffer, attenuate, and compensate for many of the deleterious effects of globalization, it is less plausible to assume that both state and national ideology can have a similar role to the one they had in the first forty years of Israel's existence, when state and ideology shaped economy, culture, and a collective ethos. Under current conditions of globalization to imagine a people of a certain territory articulating a strong national and ethnic "we" can be misleading since it is unlikely that such a "we" will articulate itself again. It is questionable if in Israel with its Palestinians, orthodox Jews, Mizrachi this "we" ever existed in the first place. In any case societies all over the world are becoming more rather than less heterogeneous, more rather than less mobile. As political theorists have noted progressive politics today is increasingly arranged around global coalitions, an overlapping consensus of different groups. These groups have different interests and agendas that nevertheless articulate "overlapping communities of fate" that share both interconnectedness and common agenda regarding the adverse aspects of globalization itself.[28] This kind of collective political action simply follows the way in which most other kinds of work are done. The fastest growing and most influential sector of Israeli society are indeed those working in the global knowledge economy. They include various professionals in transnational conglomerates, engineers and high-tech workers working closely with clients abroad, financial and other service providers, scientists and scholars, workers in international NGOs, creative artists whose major funding and audience is European, and even many public officials in education and the defense industry who work closely with colleagues abroad. To imagine all these people as having an exclusive commitment to the national group rather than having a complex multiplicity of interests, global, national, and local is reductive and anachronistic. Indeed Taub's intellectual work itself is a result of globalization, his perspective on Israel is a complex adaptation of the American conservative response to the 1960s that Taub researched in his PhD at Rutgers University, which he later adopted to the Israeli scene. He also writes and draws insights from his frequent visits to Berlin.[29] His very own international scene of intellectual work is denied in his ideal for a nation-state or perhaps he sees this kind of international work as only fit for elite. Today many kinds of work interweave the global and the local, especially knowledge, service, and affective work. These kinds of globalizations create cultural communities and networks of producers and consumers who just as much belong to the nation as they belong to the extra-national. Almost every possible grouping in Israeli society has strong connections with networks outside of Israel, sometimes more than one kind. Thus a feminist, academic from the former Soviet Union married to a Mizrachi computer programmer might have commitments to Russian society and culture, American feminist academics, multinational software developers, and religious pilgrimage groups in East Europe. All of these connections and global networks are elective and voluntary, need constant maintenance and are essentially insecure. What Taub would suggest is to reinstate a kind of default network predicated on an active ethos of the melting pot and the nation-state. As I hope I demonstrated such a vision is unlikely to materialize in a rapidly globalizing world in which productive activity always takes place in both global and local networks and therefore an ethos that relies on both must be articulated. Rather than looking solely to the nation-state to secure viable support networks, political and literary imagination must look for both more local and more global alternatives. This includes reinventing kinds of local communal and egalitarian production and consumption as well as participating in global movements that aim to provide universal social rights. The fact that Taub has chosen to represent those who are "out of the net" is an innovative and truly important choice in Israeli writing that was for long time lacking this kind of realism. His concern for this social milieu is a creative, artistic, and moral force, however, the solution to these problems can no longer lay in a stronger articulation of the nation-state.

NOTES

1. Gershon Shafir and Yoav Peled, *Being Israeli: The Dynamics of Multiple Citizenship* (Cambridge; New York: Cambridge University Press, 2002).

2. Ibid., 4.

3. Will Kymlicka, *Multicultural Citizenship: A Liberal Theory of Minority Rights* (Oxford; New York: Clarendon Press; Oxford University Press, 1995).

4. Yael Tamir, *Liberal Nationalism* (Princeton, NJ: Princeton University Press, 1995).

5. Shafir and Peled, *Being Israeli*, 5.

6. Meira Weiss, "Bereavement, Commemoration, and Collective Identity in Contemporary Israeli Society," *Anthropological Quarterly* 70, no. 2 (1997), 91–101.

7. Shafir and Peled, *Being Israeli*, 6.

8. Taub, *ha-Mered ha-shafuf: 'al tarbut tse'irah be-Yiśra'el.* (Tel Aviv: ha-Ḳibuts ha-me'uḥad, 1997).

9. Peleg, *Israeli Culture between the Two Intifadas.*

10. For religious myth in the form of Political Theology see Rechnitzer, *Nevu'ah yeha-seder ha-medini ha-mushlam,* (Jerusalem: Mosad Bialik, 2012).

11. Leo Strauss, *The City and Man* (Chicago: University of Chicago Press, 1978).

12. A. Bloom, *The Closing of the American Mind: How Higher Education Has Failed Democracy and Impoverished the Souls of Today's Students* (New York: Simon and Schuster, 1987).

13. Gadi Taub, *Neged bedidut*, Liriḳah (Tel-Aviv: Yedi'ot aḥaronot: Sifre ḥemed, 2011), 123–49.

14. Ibid., 139.

15. "Jewish and Democratic: Zionism and its Critiques" טאוב, נגד בדידות *135-220* (Yedioth Books 2016).

16. Kimmerling, *Zionism and Territory*, Zionism and Economy.

17. Shlomo Avineri, "Post-Zionism Doesn't Exist," *Haaretz*, July 06, 2007.

18. A good recent example has been Danni Gottwien. See his "Post-Zionism, privatization revolution and the social left" in פרילינג, *ציוני-פוסט לעמית תשובה.*

19. The date of socialist critique of Zionism is very early indeed and predates Zionism as a political movement. Moses Hess, collaborator of Karl Marx and Friedrich Engels, a universalist internationalist who fought for Jewish emancipation in

Europe, wrote in 1862 the proto Zionist book called *Rome and Jerusalem: The Last National Question*. The fact that it is the last national question signals the awareness that Jewish nationalism appears very late on the European scene, after the powerful articulation of internationalist socialism. His book was ill received by Hess's socialist friends who viewed it as sentimental and deviating regressively back to nationalism from the universal workers movement.

20. Foucault, *The Order of Things: An Archaeology of the Human Sciences* (New York: Vintage Books, 1994).

21. Edward Said *Orientalism* (New York: Vintage Books 1979); Judith Butler *Gender Trouble* (New York: Routledge, 1990).

22. Edward Said argued for this powerfully when commenting on Freud's *Moses and Monotheism*. See Edward W. Said and Jacqueline Rose, *Freud and the Non-European* (London; New York: Verso, 2003).

23. I am using social nationalism as a generic label that combines practices of the nation and of socialism together. Such practices have have exhibited great variety from Nazism to British socialism. But all different conceptions entail a cohesive nation (which necessarily excludes others) and some form of solidarity and redistribution.

24. Leo Strauss and Kenneth Hart Green, *Jewish Philosophy and the Crisis of Modernity Essays and Lectures in Modern Jewish Thought* (Albany: State University of New York Press, 1997), 413–14.

25. For the French example of neo-republican theory see Michael F. Leruth, "The Neorepublican Discourse on French National Identity," *French Politics and Society* 16, no. 4 (1998), 46–61.

26. Micahel Hardt and Antonio Negri *Assembly*, (Oxford: Oxford University Press, 2017), 47.

27. There have been numerous suggestions coming from the IDF itself of reducing the amount of conscripts and ultimately turning the IDF to a professional army, these suggestions however are blocked for political and symbolic reasons see המגש והכסף, שלח.

28. For overlapping consensus in the tradition of liberalism John Rawls, *A Theory of Justice* (Cambridge, MA: Belknap Press of Harvard University Press, 1971), 340; Rawls, *Political Liberalism*, 134–49; For 'overlapping communities of fate' David Held, *Global Covenant: The Social Democratic Alternative to the Washington Consensus* (Cambridge: Polity, 2004).

29. Gadi Taub, "Killing the Pig" in טאוב נגד בדידות, 2011, 13–81.

Chapter 6

New Dystopias in Israeli Fiction

In the 2000s Israel has seen a surge of literary representations of dystopian future worlds. There were political, social, and environmental reasons that compel writers to use this genre. Key features of reality lend themselves to the dystopian imagination. The second intifada, started in September 2000 and roughly ended in 2004 with the disengagement from Gaza, inaugurated a new period in Israeli politics. Since that time many have had to revise their expectations regarding the future. From expectations of normalization and a future peace in a New Middle East, the intifada has created an anxious-filled horizon in which a clear trajectory toward a better future is lacking. Coupled with this diminished horizon of normalization with the Palestinians, the destabilization of Iraq and later of Syria has had profound effects on the way that the future is imagined. In the social realm, privatizations and the erosion of the welfare state have been in progress since the 1980s, their effects were at first largely offset by the dramatic increases in standard of living and con-sumerism from the 1960s to the 1990s.

However, it is important to understate that it is not really the objective difficulties that Israel faced in those years that have sparked the dystopian imagination. Israel and its population has objectively weathered much more difficult problems in its past. It is precisely the liberal intervention and atten-dant globalization of the 1990s that has undermined the symbolic imagination of a kind of strong nation-state developmentalism. It is precisely multicultur-alism and individualism as background ideology that make historical events, that in the past might be registered as tolerable sacrifices of nation building into events that lack in intelligibility. Such events and changes are then exag-gerated and projected into the near future as dystopian fiction. Starting in the 1990s the combination of increased consumption and precarious existence and employment has created an uneasy mix that made society itself seem out of joint.

In these years a new ethos of consumerist enjoyment has developed among the middle class. It had almost become a social imperative to enjoy oneself and to tell others about it, particularly in the realm of travel and food. Middle-class Israelis who in the past have contented themselves with a humble and local existence have made it a norm to travel all over the world for extended periods of time to places as far flung as Southeast Asia, South America, and India.[1] In the realm of consumption of food, the Tel-Aviv era has become the site of one of the finest and most sophisticated restaurants in the world, comparable only to truly global cities.[2] The consumption of entertainment as we saw before has also presented a new vision of plenty. Countless television channels, live music, dance clubs, theater, Hollywood, and world cinema are on regular offer for those who live within the Gush Dan era, that is essentially most Israelis.

However, this festive atmosphere of consumption has obscured the erosion in the fulfillment of more basic needs: among them are job security, affordable housing, adequate and timely health care, suitable pensions, open spaces and clean air and water, lack of noise pollution and natural habitat. As we saw before, concerns regarding cost of living have erupted in the 2011 protests for social justice. Though definitely taking a backstage to both concerns with war and economic security, more and more Israelis have become aware of the ongoing degradation of the environment, especially to several environmental catastrophes. In 2000 the area around the Dead Sea has experienced the creation numerous sinkholes due to a dramatic lowing of the sea level. Several extreme wild fires mainly due to dry heat have decimated large eras of forest in the 1990s and 2000s. While these were peripheral to the concerns of most Israelis, they have contributed to the general feeling of a precarious and unpredictably dangerous environment. The 1990s has also inaugurated a discourse of fear of religionization (*Hadata*) of Israel society among the secular. Key institutes in Israeli society including the IDF and the education system have increasingly been under the influence of institutional religious authorities rather than under forms of democratic deliberation. One of the roots of all these destabilizing influences is the marketization of Israel society and its integration in global capitalism that as we saw before has caused much creative destruction. Revolutionary in its own way, it has quickly devalued what can be called the three "olds" (though these "olds" were only sixty years old). Old ways of production: agriculture, textile, and light industrial production. Old ways of thinking: nationalist, and Zionist socialism. Old ways of culture: state television, realism, and secular Zionist culture. In general, the marketization of Israeli society has devalued and even destroyed previous forms of making sense of reality. It is both an expression of this state of affairs as well as an attempt to rectify contemporary trends that the Israeli dystopian novel comes to the fore. The dystopian novel in Israel comes to articulate both intellectually and emotionally a chaotic present lacking a clear progressive future horizon and implicitly calls for political change from the present trajectory. It is not a coincidence that dystopian fiction deals with the future since the past and its ways of thinking and world making have themselves been devalued. A series of novels have been concerned with natural catastrophe such as the submersion of Tel-Aviv under the sea (*The Sea above Us*) or the breaking off of Israel into an island due to an earthquake along the Great Rift Valley (*The Holy Land Sets Sail*). Other novels deal with environmental degradation especially around the issue of water and overpopulation (*Hydromania*). More social catastrophes are portrayed in Jonathan Geffen's *Temporary Crown* where government is subordinated to real estate agents and in which violence has been privatized in the form of private police and armies. In Shimon Adaf's *Kfor* religion controls most aspects of life while sanctioning the use of violence against those who transgress religious law. In some of these literary dystopias bio-capitalism joins religious fundamentalism in total control over bodies and spaces. Finally, inequality and difference in power features in all of these fictional futures: whether it is inequality in basic resources like water or access to health care, mobility in space, or employment opportunities. The underlining concerns of these dystopias may represent anxieties related to loss of the nation-state, or taking this loss for granted articulate personal anxieties about the future. Perhaps the best starting point to examine these issues is to look at older nationalist concerns as they are given new dystopian form.

THE SEA ABOVE US

Amnon Rubinstein's *The Sea above Us* begins with the spectacle of tourists from the future looking through the glass bottom of a cruise ship at the green city of Tel-Aviv that has been completely submerged under water for years. The main point of view on Tel-Aviv is thus nostalgic. The point of view is nostalgic because Rubinstein's present (the book was written after the second intifada and published in 2007) is already yearning for the Zionist past that is perceived as idealistic, wholly convinced in its own righteousness, untroubled by self-critique as well as still relatively autonomous and unintegrated within global capitalism. After the first scene we transition to the near future where the sea is slowly rising on Tel-Aviv. The city is slowly and then with more vigor forcefully evacuated by the authorities. The main protagonist of the book, Yitzhak Halamish, chooses to die in Tel-Aviv with the great flood, symbolically to die with "his" version of the state. Yitzhak

Halamish the classic Zionist hero is a kind of proxy or alter ego of Amnon Rubinstein himself. Besides his exploits during his youth as the radioman of the *Tiger Hill*, a ship used to save Jewish refugees from Hitler's Europe, his main claim to the reader's sympathy in the present comes from his close relationship with Nelson, a Rwandan refugee who nurses him after his stroke. Nelson who is referred paternally as Jumbo is represented as a very big muscular, happy man, dancing when he walks. He also appears threatening in the night for many Israelis, except for Yitzhak himself. Though portrayed like a loveable and stereotypically racialized bear, both Yitzhak's neighbors as well as his own son dislike Jumbo. Yitzhak is made to win the readers sympathy by treating a black man as a loveable human being. One would think that this would be taken for granted; rather this is celebrated as a special endearing achievement of Yitzhak. The environment around Yitzhak is obviously racist, his son calls Nelson Kushi perhaps the Hebrew equivalent of nigger. At one point in the story, Nelson wonders that the British have shot white people (Jews). We are asked here to be wiser than Nelson and understand British resistance toward immigration as due to their anti-Semitism. This episode and others like it form a kind of screen that hides certain blindness in the book; a blindness about Africans but also a blindness regarding Palestinians. In an *Haaretz* interview with Ari Shavit, Rubinstein arguing against cultural relativism says:

> I am not willing to accept a multicultural approach that says that their [Muslim/ Arab] culture is like my culture. I do not understand how one can talk about cultural relativism in a generation that saw Nazism and Stalinism. I find it perverse that Jews should advocate such relativism. Is it really possible to say that all the narratives are equal? That the Nazi narrative is equal to the Anglo-Saxon narrative? That the Stalinist narrative is equal to the narrative of the French Revolution?[3]

Since his vision for the novel is so much influenced by his political worldview, it pays to analyze this worldview more closely. First, the statement is not really about culture in the anthropological sense or in the sense of "high" culture but is essentially about the moral worth of value laden political perspectives on history, what he calls narratives. Rubinstein asserts an ideological strict binary opposition between totalitarianism and liberal democracy, and he insinuates that Muslim/Arab culture belongs to the totalitarian camp. Constructing these binary oppositions however does entail denial of discrepancies between values, narratives and history, distortions and blind spots regarding the "Anglo-Saxon narrative" and the "French Revolution" narratives themselves. To start with the French Revolution, it is often described that both the Stalinist terror, internal security state apparatuses (secret police), as well as claims for radical social equality all have their roots in the French

Revolution, and thus there are affinities between the French, Russian, and Nazi revolutions that cannot be discounted.[4] In many ways it is strange that Rubinstein mentions the French Revolution at all, that in contrast to the Russian Revolution was never an important part of Israeli culture or world-view. The blindness regarding the Anglo-Saxon narrative is as troubling as it is characteristic for Bernstein's milieu, especially as he chose to write about characters such as "Jumbo." Any true account of the Anglo-Saxon narrative must include the reduction of the North American Indian population from 12 million in 1500 to 237,000 in 1900: the 12.5 million transatlantic slave trade, the subjugation of India, Africa, and the Middle East to exploitative British foreign rule, the invention and utilization of the concentration camp in the Boer wars, and so on. All of these events are cleansed from the Anglo-Saxon narrative that is typified in Rubinstein's unhistorical perspective as basically one of the political and ethical values, essentially of human rights. Indeed, human rights can be seen as an enor-mous contribution to the world, however, they themselves have their origin in Italian Renaissance whose sources and inspiration lie both in the East and West.[5] As much as the positive and moral Anglo-Saxon narrative is decontextualized so are the evils of genocide. At one point Nelson breaks down, cries and tells Yitschak that Yitschak has never asked him (Nelson) about his life. Yitschak asks about his life and Nelson goes on to tell a tragic and gruesome tale of the fate of his family in the Rwanda genocide. This genocide is presented as a kind of primordial and nonhistorical outbreak of a transcendental evil wholly unconnected to the legacies of colonialism in Africa.[6] This presentation creates a close affinity between the Jewish and African victims of genocide but precludes the specific historicity of both genocides that must include Western imperial powers (Germany and Bel-gium respectively). This affinity is sealed when Nelson brings his daughter home and they both sing Zionist songs from her kindergarten. Rubinstein presents Israel as a safe haven for refugees and in a sense blurs the line that separates Nelson, an illegal foreign worker and a well-established "found-ing father" Yitschak. Rubinstein like his main character is unable to see the Others' story in a way that does not project Zionist narrative onto that other. At the very end of the book we get a look back at the time of the flood from a history book written in 2107. We learn that the flood that seemed insurmountable has proved a blessing for Israel:

> Israel resuscitated with new forces. Her strategic situation improved immeasur-ably, and what looked like a disaster turned into a great blessing. We count two majors reasons to this turn:
>
> The first, the strategic balance between Israel and the Arab world changed completely. Oil exports, the source of Arab and Iranian wealth, received a hard blow. In order to rehabilitate the oil industry there was a need to turn drilling in

the earth to drilling under water that necessitated huge investments. Extraction and refining facilities disappeared under the sea, and all of a sudden most of the Arab countries as well as Iran were lacking in economic means. This and more: the sources of water in the delta and the beaches where contaminated all throughout the Arab world and the Persian golf. Only Israel had the knowledge and the ability to build desalinization plants in the needed quantity, in order to replace the aquifers and the wells that got salted. This situation decreased the will of the Arab and Muslim countries to devote from their dwindling resources to fighting Israel.

In Rubinstein's characterization, the flood inaugurates peace not by a two-state solution, but by the destruction of infrastructure of the Arab states. Far from asserting liberal humanistic values claimed before, the economic devastation of Arab societies is represented only as a positive outcome with little thought of its effect on the Arab population. Interestingly the population movement after the second flood is the opposite of a movement toward normalization of a two-state solution that Rubinstein abides by. The population movement toward normalization and a two-state solution is one in which half a million settlers move toward the shore, while here we have a couple of million Israelis moving to the mountains. Perhaps this presentation is a kind of displacement of anxieties dealing with the settlements in the territories. In a fortunate natural catastrophe beyond anyone's choosing Israelis are made to settle in the region. Needless to say, there is no reference in the book to the fate of the Palestinians living there today nor a plausible proposal on how the two peoples are to live together in the same territory. In order to better understand this particular outcome and the way in which natural catastrophe serves national purpose, one must analyze the three main discourses that inform Rubinstein's book.

THREE KINDS OF DISCOURSES: ZIONIST, LIBERAL, AND ECOLOGICAL

Amnon Rubinstein's book represents the juxtaposition of three kinds of discourses: a national discourse, a liberal discourse, and an ecological discourse. Many of the fascinating tensions exhibited in the novel ultimately stem from conflicts between these differing worldviews, each pulling in its own direction. Of the three discourses that Rubinstein employs, a conservative articulation of Zionism is the most fundamental. In fact the other two discourses can be seen as a foil to this dominant one. The main protagonist of the story Ytzachk Halamish is a national hero who courageously helped in the most important task of the nation: saving Jewish refugees from Nazi

controlled Europe. The very structure of the novel uses intergenerational continuity as the main trope of affirming the continuation of the Zionist endeavor.
The novel thus spans five generations. Ytzhack is the grandfather of Libet
who herself is an extremely old grandmother of Ezoz who reads her letter in
the far future. At the end of the book Grandmother Libet writes:

> We live in a different era from that of Izchak Chalmish: his world looks differ-
> ent and foreign and strange. Many misfortunes of health have long disappeared.
> The Israel that Chalimish lived, was characterized by war and terror—and the
> everyday existential problem: how to survive as an island in the sea of hatred?
> All of these have disappeared from the existence of our lives. What is left? The
> basic facts are left: we stayed Jewish, we stayed Hebrew speaking, we stayed
> memory bearing.[7]

A certain kind of Zionism is stressed here, one whose most important
aspects are continuity, memory, and identity that endure through crisis.
Highlighting these particular aspects of Zionism is far from obvious, since
throughout Zionism's history different aspects have been stressed. In its
most dramatic phase Zionism has stressed revolutionary characteristics such
as instating a radical break from the politically passive past, the creation
of a new Hebrew man, political sovereignty, and creation of a just society.
In many ways the ecological catastrophe is introduced precisely to demonstrate the resilient "eternal" non changing character of these three things:
Jewishness, speaking Hebrew, and historical remembering.[8] One can say that
these aspects and the way they are formulated in the paragraph articulate a
recent and new kind of Zionist ideology.[9] Rather than stressing rapture with
the past, negation of diaspora life, rebellion, and revolution, the themes of
Zionism in its formative stages, or such aspects as state building and defense
in its "middle stage," Zionism becomes a tool of conservation and continuity
rather than constructive transformation. In Rubinstein's novel this continuity is perceived to be threatened by both intermarriage from "within" and
by ecological catastrophe from without. Intermarriage presents a particular
difficulty since Rubinstein is as much committed to Jewish continuity as to
the liberal tenants that uphold the freedom and autonomy of the individual.
He also perceives intermarriage as necessarily leading to a decrease or even
annulment of Jewishness. The issue of romantic relationship across nations
that embodies the tension between Zionism and liberalism figures repeatedly in the book. This tension is reveled in two stories: one taking place at
the beach in Tel-Aviv where an Arab boy falls in love with a Jewish girl
and plays mute in order not to be found out as an Arab, the other relates the
unfortunate demise of a relationship between Jewish woman and a German
man during the rise of Nazism in Germany. The fact that both relationships

tragically fail allows Rubinstein to maintain his commitment to the freedom of the individuals, affirmed through the theme of the individual's love against societies norms, but also this failure itself precludes a threat to Jewish continuity. At the same time the very stress and inclusion of two narratives of intermarriage reveals the anxieties regarding the clash of national continuity with the freedom of the individual.

Perhaps even more central to the novel is the relationship between Zionism and the specific ecological threat that structures the whole book—sea level rise. In contrast to degradation of land, air, and water and the depletion of biodiversity, rising sea levels has very little to do with national policy and everything to do with the global effects of carbon dioxide. Indeed Zionism and environmentalism can be conflicted around many issues including a general technological optimism, immigration (and resultant overpopulation), intensive agricultural irrigation, urban sprawl, industrialism, pollution, and degradation due to military operations.[10] However, even though these issues are points of contention in marked contrast to rising sea level, they are strongly within the preview of national policy. Rising sea level is due to carbon emissions worldwide and remains outside the preview of the policy of any one state. Global warming and its consequences transcend any national economic and military interest and are supposed to articulate a global common good. Indeed Rubinstein describes the second flood as a global phenomenon devastating seaside cities and causing catastrophes worldwide. Given its global effects one can wonder what has caused Rubinstein to use a global disaster to tell a national story. Was it because he did not want to use a more local ecological catastrophe that could be leveraged as another kind of criticism against the national project? In fact Rubinstein was using ecological catastrophe as a kind of displacement or ersatz for articulating his security concerns. In an interview with Ari Shavit, Amnon Rubinstein discusses nuclear Iran as security threat:

Shavit: How disturbed are you by this threat?
Rubinstein: I am disturbed to the level of sleeplessness. I don't sleep at night.
Shavit: Do you envisage a nuclear event?
Rubinstein: Yes, absolutely. The new novel I am working on starts in a future in which Tel Aviv lies under the sea. The sea rises and covers Tel Aviv. True, it's not nuclear, but it is a reflection of existential anxiety—a very deep existential anxiety.
Shavit: When you walk in the streets of Tel Aviv, do you have the feeling that the city might not exist?
Rubinstein: Yes, definitely. I feel existential anxiety for everything we have built here. I am a fearful Israeli, a very fearful Israeli. And I am afraid not because of primeval fears. I am fearful because I think that Israel is strong in a very limited way and is very weak in other ways. I saw our weakness in the Yom Kippur War. I saw the planes of our great air force being downed over the Suez

Canal in some sort of Israeli mini-defeat. And now I saw the Israeli weakness when a million Israeli refugees fled from their homes in the North and we were unable to stop the firing of Katyusha rockets for 33 days. So since the war in Lebanon my sleeplessness has become worse. I am fearful for the home. I am afraid that the home will fall. I am fearful for the future of the "third temple" [of the Jewish people].[11]

Existential anxiety is thus displaced from security to ecology. Ecology itself is just a marker of an existential threat whose source is really the future possibility of a nuclear Iran. In itself this shows a somewhat opportunistic attitude toward the ecological crisis that indeed threatens to displace millions of people in the not so distant future. It essentially uses what must seem to Rubinstein as fashionable ecological discourse to deal mainly with anxieties of Jewish continuity in the Middle East. Like many dystopias this one articulates concerns of the present and projects them to the future. It also ultimately serves to reassure readers in the continuity of Jewish existence. In fact the concern regarding continuity and discontinuity in general is symptomatic of Israel literary culture especially among the milieu of Amnon Rubinstein. Amnon Rubinstein (b. 1931), who served as Knesset member between 1977 and 2002, was part of what can be called the modernizing elite of Israel that for many years had a sense of control regarding the national project. Since as we saw many of the dramatic changes that Israel has undergone in economy, politics and culture seem out of control of the elite that Rubinstein is a part of, it is perhaps natural that they will give rise to anxieties of continuity. The sense of lack of control and clear direction and its related anxieties broadens beyond Rubinstein's milieu to envelop subsequent generations as well. A good example is Hagai Dagan's *The Land Is Sailing*.

THE LAND IS SAILING

The Land Is Sailing follows its Hero Elad a post-kibbutznik as he meanders both mentally and physically across biographical and mythic time in Israel. In the novel Elad is on his way to a reunion with his classmates from the Kibbutz. His great hope is to find his lost love that he calls Violeta. His longing for Violeta is inexorably bound with his nostalgic reminiscing of a more youthful innocent Israel. The reunion however ends with an earthquake that fractures the land all through the Great Rift Valley. Due to this upheaval, the land of Israel is split from the mainland and goes on a mysterious voyage that ends up touching the shores of Norway. More than a book about its hero the book is about the land as being captivated, oppressed, and over burdened by religion, myth, history, national claims but also simply by its population.

The land is unyielding stuck in its past, but also in the increasingly chaotic Middle East. The original Zionist love of the land that the hero tries to access through song and poems is inaccessible. The other main characters are either settlers who the narrator sees as violent in their love toward the land or entrepreneurs who are trying to generate a profit out of it, signaling the new capitalist class in Israel. In many ways Dagan is lamenting the passing away of classical "labor" Israel. His sailing away of the land reveals not an apocalyptic political anxiety but actually an anxiety regarding the dynamics of the present that hold the land in their grip. Imri Herzog writes on Dagan's book in *Haaertz,* the land is sailing northward that is to Europe "that will divorce it from its holiness, and take it to cool and northern realms that will subdue the national, religious and racial fires that devour her."[12] Herzog perceptively comments on the way in which the book represents the degradation of olive groves by settlers. Olive trees are, of course, a potent symbol both for Zionist who have wanted to become one with the land as well as have a host of meanings for Palestinians such as family, resistance, national revival, and peace.

The degradation of the olive groves represents a failed attempt of becoming native. At one point the hero gives a ride to a beautiful, young female settler that angers him:

> Just to create bypass roads, on the hills, on the olive orchids that you uproot, at the end will be only "a dress of concrete and cement." (quote from Poet Natan Alterman's famous poem *Song of Morning*)
>
> This is what you want ...
> What is this dress?
> You don't know "We Will Build Land our Homeland," Alterman?
> No, no I don't know.
> You are not Israeli. I don't know what you are but Israeli you are not.
> Right, we are Jews.

The narrator gets angry also because he is envious of the settlers; the traditional connection with the land has been usurped by the settlers. This new connection is deemed harmful by the narrator both for the land and for its Arab population. *The Land Sets Sail* is thus not only about the land leaving the things that oppress her, it is also at the same time about the milieu of the author, the labor Zionists who are distancing themselves from the land, the land sort of "sets sail" in front of their eyes. The historical process of nationalist territorialization, the whole regime of agricultural work, extended field trips, camping both military and civil all designed to imbue Israelis with familiarity and love of the land, this whole regime is starting to reverse itself with the advent of a thorough going globalization that this same milieu has gone through. Global integration is in many ways not only indifferent but in many ways antagonistic to local or national attachment to place. Opportunities materialize whose benefits often override attachments to place. Another way of saying this is that nationalist attachment to place can be disadvantageous in consideration of economic, cultural, and other global opportunities. Essentially this process means a thorough deterritorialization of both work and therefore of lives. The most dramatic change has perhaps taken place among people like the narrator himself who were part of the kibbutzim and Moshavim movement that have experienced a profound attachment and care for place and who are now increasingly part of a global knowledge economy. In the final chapters of Dagan's book the land of Israel is detached along the Great Rift, and sets sail, and ultimately lands near Norway to find its rest in a cool and peaceful place. Both Dagan's and Rubinstein's narratives end with a comforting vision of Israel moving to a more politically stable place. In Rubinstein the stable place is the Middle East that accepts Israel out of weakness, for Dagan Israel simply leaves the Middle East altogether. Both dystopias end with a kind of utopia. In many ways however both outcomes sound unbelievable as a kind of utopian wish fulfillment of the normalization of Israel. In both writers we are preview to a metaphor of displacement. In Rubinstein the displacement is toward the mountains signaling a lack of faith that life in Tel-Aviv can continue in its current liberal-commercial form.[13] From 1990s in fact most dystopian novels have been preoccupied with what can be called a kind of derailment of the Israeli or Zionist project. This metaphor of a social project that progresses on track (the locomotive being a central metaphor for the way progress has been conceived since the middle of the 19th century) provides a central organizing concept for the Zionist project until the 1980s. The wholesale "detracking" felt from 2004 onward has in many ways been prefigured already in polemical post-Zionism and its attendant culture that started in the early 1980s. A sophisticated example of this is Orly Castel-Bloom's well-known novel *Dolly City*, first published in 1993 that we have already discussed under another aspect of re-narration of national identity in a previous chapter. While there we concentrated on parody, here I would like to stress its dystopian aspects.

DYSTOPIA IN *DOLLY CITY*

As we remember *Dolly City* is a story of an abusive mother named Dolly. Told in first person and set in a future dystopian Israel, the novel concentrates on Dolly's violent anxiety regarding the health of her adopted son who serves, as we shall see later, a metaphor for the nation. Dolly worries that he might be suffering from various medical conditions ranging from cancer to missing an internal organ. Her response is repeatedly to "open him up" and needlessly operate on him.[14] She is prone not only to fits of violent anxiety regarding her son, but often suffers from murderous rage and a flat affect coupled with extreme promiscuity. The initial reception of the book was varied; some saw it as expressing the linguistic and even moral deterioration of Israeli literature, while others prized the book as a breakthrough in Hebrew fiction.[15] Two leading Hebrew literary critics Dan Miron and Gershon Shaked claimed Castel-Bloom as the most original of a new generation of writers, urban and non-ideological; her writing resists and scorns social norms and public taste.[16] Following the strongly evaluative response that the book stirred up in reviews, the academic critical reception that followed has usually chosen to interpret it through the conceptual lens of postmodernism. Postmodernist interpretations concentrate on the free play of language (signifier) used in the novel, on the lack of coherent reality, the mixture of high and low linguistic styles, and on the lack of depth or real affect.[17] Some interpretations saw the novel as a parody, a grotesque exaggeration of Jewish/Zionist mothering, an impossible endeavor composed of anxious sheltering, coupled paradoxically with preparing the child to be a soldier.[18]

Post-Zionist interpretations have either characterized the novel as disengaging from the national meta-narrative or as an explicit critique of Zionist claims.[19] However here I suggest seeing the book not as a critique of Zionism in the name of an alternative ideological framework but as expressing a feeling of lost purpose, losing the tracks of the national project itself. It is for this reason that Castle-Bloom chooses this kind of schizophrenic heroine for her novel, a heroine that uses a very special kind of speech and language that indeed reflected a reality whose ideological support has been undermined. The German psychiatrist Carl Schneider characterized the essential attribute of schizophrenic language as derailment (*Entgleisen*) in 1930,[20] a metaphor that likens thought disorder to a train starting off only to be diverted and side-tracked from reaching its destination.[21] Derailment offers a fitting description to the disconcerting effect that language has on the speaker. In *Dolly City* derailment often moves to bodily reality entailing a disjointness between the first and the second part of the sentence: "About a week after I became an unwilling mother, at midnight, I was all ready to go to sleep, but sleep eluded me like a toddler hiding from his parents between the concrete pillars of a parking lot in Ashdod." The metaphor not only revels in comparing very different aspects of reality but the very excessive particularity of this metaphor evokes the absurd. In Hebrew the verb for eluded is "Chamak," while the formation sleep eluded [שינה חמקה] is a conventional metaphor. The narrator Dolly reinvigorates this worn out phrase by over-concretizing it and derailing it. Some metaphors in *Dolly City* express a derailment that seems to lead not to an alternate destination but self referentially to the beginning, for example: "The trains in Dolly city run like pantyhose—if you don't stop them, they'll reach your crotch."[22] This metaphor entails an inversion, a conventional Hebrew metaphor that likens longs tears in pantyhose to "trains." Essentially this is a self-referential likeness, a tautology, the trains in Dolly City run like pantyhose that are often compared to trains. Essentially the sentence says "trains are trains" via pantyhose. However, this psychotic closed circuitry breaks out in the phrase "if you don't stop them, they'll reach your crotch." These metaphors also lead to unexpected and absurd actions, for example: "Someone wrote on the wall, Madness is a ripe orange, and therefore it should be wrapped up and sent to Europe in crates stamped with the word Jaffa."[23] This sentence likens the abstract concept of madness to the concrete symbol of wholesome Israeli produce. The sentence simultaneously refers to madness but also reveals the thought process of madness, the way that madness relates to figurative language. There is a movement from the figurative, taking madness to be an orange, to absurd irrational practical consequences. Castel-Bloom's comparison of madness to an orange is then made both literal and political when this orange is sent as a sort of emblem of Israeli produce abroad. In this sentence Israel exports madness.

Dolly's main obsession is to operate on her son by looking for signs of cancer in her son's body, but toward the end of the novel, Dolly's obsession with cancer is decoupled, released free from both her son and human bodies in general. In a kind of special penetrating vision Dolly can see cancer on non-living objects as well: "And then it hit me: I saw cancerous growths on the blonde women's faces, on the barrels of tar, on the wheels of the buses, on the telephone poles, on the trees, on the wheels of cars, on the newspapers— wherever I looked, malignant, terminal, spreading tumors danced before my eyes."[24] Cancer represents irrational growth of life that resists treatment and control and is a central metaphor for a kind of unplanned Rhizomatic growth of Dolly City itself, an extension and differentiation that have lost all control. In this, cancer is a central metaphor for a dystopian future that comes with no sense of progress, normality, rationality, or meaning. Given that the historical meaning of the present is very much set by having an horizon of a meaningful near future, an abnormal future effects the intelligibility of the present. It is through the portrayal of a senseless, absurd future that *Dolly City* brings us in contact with present that is normally subsumed and hidden under normalizing and moralizing tendencies. Castel-Bloom's dystopian world is expressed mainly through the weather, social structure, transportation, and war. Seasons in themselves are a basic temporal ordering principle creating order in human affairs. All cultures arrange human temporality according to

the seasons, giving meaning, order and direction to the longest experiential
unit of life, the year:

> It was August, snow was falling softly. It covered all the roads and pavements,
> and people were walking about wearing Russian fur hats. I stopped a cab and
> asked the driver to take me to Ben Gurion Airport. At Ben Gurion it was sum-
> mer, the sun beat down on the cosmopolitan heads with calm tyranny.[25]

It is not just that this world is topsy-turvy with snow falling in August,
but there is a spatial inconsistency at work, a "patch work" weather/reality.
Dolly's apartment becomes extremely hot or cold at arbitrary points in time,
and Son starts playing with his own frozen spit. This breakdown of the way we
structure our symbolic space/time entails a relentless exposure to an incom-
prehensibly hostile nature. Social structure too, is arbitrary in Dolly City, the
criteria with which political groups are divided is nonsensical. At the same time
Castel-Bloom parodies the extremely partisan one-sided political perspective
that one can come across in contemporary Israel. We learn that there are two
big parties: Bureaucracy and Procedure. The soldiers of the Bureaucracy party
are called the Trashers. They are "revolting, dirty, unhygienic types, who spend
all their time pickpocketing, coughing, wiping their noses on their sleeves, and
relieving themselves in their pants."[26] The Alrighters follow the Procedure
party: "They are all right—absolutely, gorgeously all right. Every one of the
Alrighters has swum across the Kinnereth dozens of times. They all adore
hiking in Jerusalem, most of them go jogging round the Old City walls every
evening."[27] Castel-Bloom is poking fun here not only at Dolly's ideologically
extreme perspective but also at the Alrighters themselves who are seemingly
oblivious to the realities of their surrounding and who hold idealized views of
themselves and of Dolly City. Then there are the Apostrophers, "whose slogan
is as dumb as their faces. They sing to a Reggae beat: 'The state is me. Please
decapitate me.'"[28] Castel-Bloom is perhaps satirizing the radical left that identifies strongly with the state, but at the same time wants to "decapitate" itself.
This constitutes a lack but at the same time an excess of meaning that renders
habitual ways of generating meaning inoperative. The statement "The state is
me. Please decapitate me" can be interpreted as a typical "Bloomian" sentence
as we saw above, since it starts with the political sublime and ends in brutality.
The sentence also superimposes the saying attributed to Louis XIV "*L'État,
c'est moi*" and the decapitations of the French Revolution that is to ultimate
sovereignty and violent doing away of sovereignty at the same time. However,
the fact that the sentence entails self-negation and suicide clearly points elsewhere, perhaps to the self-negation needed to form the socialist and Zionist new
man. Thus, the meaning of the sentence shifts without settling on any meaningful interpretation. Both the language and behavior of the people of Dolly city

shift aimlessly and often brutally. Movement and human activity in Dolly city are as meaningless and directionless as the politics:

> Dolly city, a city without a base, without a past, without an infrastructure. The most demented city in the world. All the people in Dolly City are usually on the run. Since they're always running there's always someone chasing them, and since there's someone chasing them, they catch them and execute them and throw them into the river.[29]

Traffic, movement, and paranoia are impossibly superimposed, with a reverse logic, where results come before actions, where outcomes determine causes. The basic psychological mechanism is projection: people act/feel and then project causes on the outside that then somehow becomes this projection. The original motive for "running" remains nevertheless inexplicable and stands outside the ability of the text to make it intelligible. The text thus attempts to render a purposeless behavior that cannot be made meaningful. The aimlessness of movements and the directionless of Israeli politics are similar:

> I looked out the window, but how long can you go on looking out of the window at rushing trains? Especially when they're rushing to where these trains were rushing. All the trains in Dolly City rushed to Dachau and back again. Not *that* Dachau, just some old plank with the name Dachau written on it, a kind of memorial.[30]

Castel-Bloom comments here not only on the lack of direction, but on the fictional element to which all this rushing to and fro is directed. Dachau is not the real Dachau, signaling that all this hectic activity is somehow directed at a shabby simulation of the real thing. Activity and movement are politicized, and at the same time this political telos is rendered nonsensical. As a critique of contemporary state response to the Holocaust, the statement signals the illusionary and at the same time threadbare character of this simulation. It expresses a general lack of purpose, activity, or action with the politico-religious aspect of memorialization. Just as movement and transportation is linked to a senseless political telos, so sexuality, the traffic of bodies is similarly directionless and lacking in meaning:

> I looked out at the ceaseless movement of this city, at the frenzy of the traffic, at the fury of the buses forced to wait for all the lost, senile old ladies to get on, at the conductors who spent their breaks fucking the drivers on the moldy backseats.[31]

The description elaborates the well-known analogy between traffic and sexuality, their commonalities in movement and in contact. Sex and traffic have all lost their meaning and direction. Like traffic, sex is mechanical and senseless. Sexuality is a violent, sudden, and arbitrary meeting of bodies in Dolly City; it does not come about through closeness nor does it create intimacy. Finally, war is the ultimate absurdity of directionless and destructive behavior of senseless death and injury. Near the end of the novel the sky becomes covered with French Air Force planes:

> The descendents of the Gauls, the comrades and successors of Saint-Exupery, had arrived with their most up-to-date weapons to wipe out the inhabitants of Dolly City, and thousands of animals were parachuted down, dogs and jackals and foxes infected mainly with rabies, but also with typhus and other serious diseases. The animals spread through the city like swarms of locusts, and people began to vomit and fall twitching to the ground.[32]

Castel-Bloom parodies both the means and the ends of war. The motivation for the attack, we learn, is "to wipe out the entire population of Israel, filling the whole of the coastal plain with gleaming white lavatories of the finest export quality."[33] These motivations parody economic incentives for war; replacing the population with white lavatories with no people to use them. War is absurd and it shatters our usual sense making on many levels, it joins the lowest to the highest, the lavatories are the "finest export quality" and defecation descends specifically from the heavens: "the French began dropping shitbombs on us, there was so much shit flying around that it was hard to understand where they were getting it all from."[34] War is symbolized by the lowest in the body but also as the disfigured body. The body, the source of our stable sense of identity, becomes a set of autonomous partial objects. As a result of an atom bomb, "People came in without heads, but with eyes. Some of them came in without legs, but walking, with shoes full of mud. And the funniest of all were the ones without waists, whose upper and lower halves were connected by association."[35] Just as war arbitrarily reconfigures the human body so are its happenings an arbitrary joining of events. When Dolly relentlessly tries to ascertain if her son is in fact alive she is finally told that he was sunk by the Belgians who have mistaken his ship for a French ship. Son by chance went out to sea on a raft to look for mine-bearing fish and survived, but war itself is presented as something defying direction and progress.

In *Dolly City* Castel-Bloom's chaotic derangements pleasurably but also painfully disrupt the conceptual schemas of progress that have habitually supported the intelligibility of our experience. The eruption of drives into language, the derailment of the sentence, the cutting up of the body, and the arbitrary nature of social arrangements all destabilize national progressivist ways of making sense of the world. Up until the 1990s nationalist secular ways of making sense of the world have been the central way that the people of Israel conceived of and participated in modernity. This book argues that this way of understanding the world though nationalist modernization has received an irrevocable blow in the 1980s and 1990s. This blow was delivered by an ideology that combines liberalism, multiculturalism, and globalization. However, these three ideologies split apart many of the things that went together in secular nationalism. Progress is now, not in the hands of the nation-state, but in the hands of a global techno-capitalism. There is no collective project of cultural renewal. Culture comes under the preview of the different "tribes" of Israel, its different communities and in the hands of the commercial market. The tie between culture and modernization is lost; culture becomes either identity or market. The undermining of this combined economic and cultural view of progress has left a deficit in the imagination of a better future among many mainstream Jewish Israelis. The receding worldview of secular nationalism portrayed in dystopian fiction essentially means the receding horizon of engagement with modernity and modernization. We must better understand the relationship between modernization and the nation-state in order to theorize the predicament that we are in today.

CONTEXTUALIZING ISRAELI DYSTOPIAN VISIONS AND THE ATROPHY OF MODERNITY

Modernity, that has reached most of the world through secular nationalism, was predicated on the legacy of technological, economic, and political modernization. Having roots both in antiquity and in the early modern period it has actually "took off" through the twin revolutions of the long 19th century, the French Revolution and the Industrial Revolution.[36] Both forces became global in the late 19th century when almost all the globe was colonized by Western Europe. By the mid-20th century all countries in the world strictly adhered to the tenants of modernization, stressing from the first, technological innovation in agriculture and industry, economic and political modernization and public ownership of means of production. With this combination came various kinds of utopian visions for the future. Israel like other nations was seen as making great strides toward both empowerment and equality, creating a new kind of man and a new kind of culture. Such visions of the future have been essentially dismantled and devalued through the 1960s to the 1980s. From the combined vision of political, cultural, societal, scientific, and technological development, it is only technological innovation that is believed to make progress in the future. Technological innovation itself is also not mainly perceived in a rational planned manner but through an "irrational," and "wasteful" process in which thousands of small firms are founded while only a few of them survived. Technological innovation and the abundance of goods that it provides have also been devalued, as they are seen to contribute to the degradation of the environment and contribute to over population. A combined future horizon of societal and cultural conceptions of progress, freedom, and plenty has diminished. In the social realm progress was conceived as a push for equality and collective ownership of means of production. Israel's main societal innovation the Kibbutz has been dismantled and marginalized mainly because its means of production (agriculture) has become irrelevant in global information capitalism. Of central significance for this book is the breakdown of progress in culture with the advent of multiculturalism and postmodernism. Starting in 1970s all cultural production has been relativized. This relativization stands in marked contrast to previous times. During the time of secular-nationalist modernization, two genres were deemed especially privileged and especially valuable: realism and modernism. Realism, the major genre of the 19th century, was seen as extremely valuable since it gave an emotional and experiential perspective on societal problems, on the consequences of modernization and state-building processes and their impact on human lives. Through realism one was made to truly feel what is wrong with society and attempted to correct it. Modernists have perceived themselves almost as a kind of technical artistic advance in comparison to culture before them. Through experimentation they sought to empower words, colors, and sounds to their utmost extent. They were certain that their music, painting, and literature signaled an advance over religious, bourgeoisie, and romantic culture that they have sought to replace. Significantly both realists and modernists positioned their cultural production largely outside of religious tradition and outside of the market. The realist was essentially a concerned member of society who has undertaken the task of holding up a mirror to that society. His or her novels communicated with fellow citizens on societal issues. Novels as commodity or more bluntly said selling books was not the sole priority. Even when the drive to sell books existed, it existed with other more powerful drives such as to take up the mantel of social critique. Modernists were even more distant from the market, and have articulated themselves explicitly against it.[37] They predominantly sought recognition among their peers. In form, their experimentation was deemed inscrutable for the masses. In content, their "masochistic" taste for the extreme, the negative and the abstract, for madness, alienation, perverse sexuality never endeared them on broader audience who were looking for culture as a kind of compensation of either positive mirroring or idealistic identification. As both the role of social critic who mirrors societal problems and experimenter in words sounds and colors declined, writers responded increasingly to public tastes and market pressures. The decline in realism and modernism is in fact a reflection of the decline in the combined paradigm of modernization as the twin progress of society and technology. Realism in fact can be seen as the cultural avatar of a belief in societal progress, modernism is its technological avatar committed to progress of the technique of art. It should be noted that these complete or total modernization projects were not viewed without ambivalence and concern even by those who undertook them. In fact dystopian visions of rationally administered iron cage have been highly prevalent in both fiction and theory. One can even see key thinkers of the late 19th century and 20th century as dealing exactly with these concerns; Max Weber's concept of the iron cage, Heidegger's works on technology, Max Horkheimer and Theodor Adorno's critique of instrumental rationality, Hannah Arendt's concept of totalitarianism, and Foucault's critique of the discourses of criminology and psychiatry are all saturated with a concern of totalizing and controlling modernity. Novels like Aldous Huxley's *Brave New World*, Yevgeny Zamyatin's *We*, George Orwell's *1984*, and Anthony Burgess's *Clockwork Orange* have created impressive visions of suffocating and rationally controlling totalizing modernity. However and rather dramatically from a certain point in the early 1970s the future does not seem to threaten with rationalization. The fear of a rationally, autocratic planned society has imploded together with its utopian counterpart. The decline or implosion of the totalizing modernization paradigm itself has caused not only freedom and playfulness (postmodernism), diversity, fragmentation (multiculturalism), and the return of religion but also disorientation. Marketization has essentially splintered the joint conception of societal and cultural progress. Society is to be conservative, economy is to be progressively technocapitalist, and culture either religious or commercial. From the perspective of total modernization this constellation seems hybrid, strange but mostly importantly temporally disorienting. Full, total, or whole modernization presented a relatively simple time orientation. Even though there have been anxieties and apprehensions, in the main, it was oriented toward the future. When looking at the past it was likely to celebrate those social, technological, and scientific events that seemed to contribute to this march of progress. The postmodern time perspective is complex and is in fact committed to what is called uneven development.[38] Predominant postmodernizing viewpoints are committed to several articulations of the past that they see as not only having validity in the present but has having a kind of eternal validity for the future as well. They also split their worldview into moral, political, and economic. In terms of morality and culture they ultimately go back to an ethics articulated either by the original axial age from about 8th to 2th BC century when the ethics of Confucius, Buddha, Plato, and Hebrew prophets first articulated itself or its secondary breakthrough in Judaism proper, Christianity, and Islam. In terms of society, politics and economy it is often committed to 18th century conceptions of liberalism and political economy. At the same time it is avidly technologically optimist happily adopting technologies of the 21st century without

necessarily taking on the underlining assumptions that go into technological development such as experimentalism, a mathematical/natural view of
the world, or progressivist optimism. The constellation described above is
quite global. The changes toward this constellation are taking place
(although in different ways) in places as different as India, Israel, East
Europe, and South America.[39] However the move to this composite, complex worldview is often disorienting and disconcerting to those who were
socialized on the modernization paradigm. The new postmodernizing way
of seeing the world contains both internal tensions and tensions between
it and the world it attempts to describe. A classic internal tension, for
instance, exists between religious worldview and capitalism. Related are
the destabilizing effects of the latter are often difficult to account for
within a worldview predicated on 18th century liberalism and religion.
From the point of view of what can be called liberalist-traditionalist, some
of the effects of techno-capitalism simply seem "uncontrollable" or
"ungovernable." Thus for both the "total" modernizers and for the liberalist-traditionalist we live in times that are difficult to conceptualize.
Modernizing elites like the secular nationalists are unclear as to why their
project was abandoned, they are likely to downplay its deleterious effects
on various others, as well as be surprised by the way they lost hegemony
to traditionalist liberals. Traditionalist liberalism since it thinks that the
end of history has arrived after the cold war is unclear as to why "history"
with its attendant volatility is continuing, what is the source of instability
in the world. Its main explanatory framework is to divide the world into
those good subjects who are successfully mimicking the liberal traditionalist precepts (e.g., Asian Tigers) and irrational bad subjects who are not
(Middle Eastern and European fundamentalism). Uneven development,
the discrepancy between relentless modernization of technology and
economy and an attempt to "freeze" or govern society under liberal traditionalist tenants necessarily leads to rifts and crisis. Economic crisis,
environmental degradation, increasing inequality, joblessness and crime,
religious fundamentalism, and terror seem to come from nowhere to the
liberal traditionalist or are quickly moralized. Since state and society are
not truly committed to offset the negative effects of global capitalism
including its use of nature as costless source, unemployment as result of
outsourcing and robotization, and the rising discrepancy between income
based on wages and income based on capital, the effects of all of these
process are then felt and experienced as dystopia. In addition to dislocations that are affecting the center of the world system, the Middle East in
whose realities Israeli fiction is ultimately situated experiences another
layer of dislocations that are characteristic of the semi-periphery of the
world system.[40] Thus the Middle East not only suffers both under the

general disruptions of contemporary global capitalism, but also has not benefited from its fruits. It has not successfully implemented global integration for both internal reasons of bad governance as well as a subordinated position in a postcolonial world. In fact together with Africa, the Middle East seems to be a place that was most adversely affected by postmodernization. Its progressive projects (Arab socialism and nationalism) have been the ones that have most dramatically collapsed or were defeated. Though not experiencing the radical collapse of some of its neighbors both socialism and secular nationalism have largely folded in Israel. The entire region is unstable as it transitions into an unclear paradigm. It is in this context that real and ideological struggle over the meaning of Israel take place. Within the secular-nationalist paradigm with its attendant anti-colonialism, Israel was seen by many Palestinians and Arabs as an extension of the colonialization of the West. As a secular nationalism, Zionism itself was a revolt against the West. First of all, a revolt against growing forces of ethno-nationalism in Germany that precluded Jews from assimilating and later on an active struggle for independence against the British mandate. For both sides the conflict was about independence. With the demise of socialism and the steep decline of secular nationalism, the conflict took on new meanings for both sides. Instead of a future vision of a progressive nation-state both sides have shifted their focus on traumas of the past, the Holocaust and the Nakba, and on religious revival. Mainstream culture that was built on a secular-nationalist mentality has experienced a kind of deficit. As long as there was a rational progressive future horizon the costs and violence of the conflict were seen as the cost of reaching political independence, legitimacy, and societal and cultural progress. After globalization all of the above have come to be questioned. This essentially means that for the secular mainstream the violence of the conflict does not connect with viable frameworks that can provide it with meaning. The violence of the Arab-Israeli conflict thus becomes more nonsensical and inexplicable. What's more for many writers and filmmakers the attempt to come to terms with the conflict is already happening in a post-national context, not just in the sense of the decline of national sensemaking, but by essentially global production and viewpoint taken on the conflict itself. As we shall see, most filmmakers who have undertaken a global view of the conflict; their films are almost always coproduction between Israel and Europe, using foreign film crews and regularly narrate their stories with a US or Western European audience in mind. As I will try to show it is because of this kind of coproduction and co-consumption that none of the events of the Arab-Israeli conflict has captured the imagination more than the second intifada. It is to narrative and filmic representations of the second intifada that we turn to next.

NOTES

1. Noy and Cohen, *Israeli Backpackers From Tourism to Rite of Passage* (New York: State University of New York Press, 2005).

2. R. Grosglik and U. Ram, "Authentic, Speedy and Hybrid: Representations of Chinese Food and Cultural Globalization in Israel," *Food Cult. Soc. Food, Culture and Society* 16, no. 2 (2013), 223–43.

3. Ari Shavit, "Book of Revelations." Haaretz, Mar 01, 2007.

4. Talmon, *The Origins of Totalitarian Democracy* (Boston, Beacon Press, 1952).

5. Samuel Moyn, *The Last Utopia: Human Rights in History* (Cambridge, MA: Belknap Press of Harvard University Press, 2010).

6. The rigid demarcation between the sides was essentially a legacy of colonial Belgium. In 1935, Belgium introduced identity cards labeling each individual as either Tutsi, Hutu, Twa, or Naturalized. While it had previously been possible for particularly wealthy Hutu to become honorary Tutsi, the identity cards prevented any further movement between the classes Philip Gourevitch, *We Wish to Inform You That Tomorrow We Will Be Killed with Our Families: Stories from Rwanda* (London: Picador, 2000).

7. Ibid., 233.

8. Interestingly this brings the writer closer to classical Jewish writing than to more recent Israeli literature. See Alan L. Mintz, *Ḥurban: Responses to Catastrophe in Hebrew Literature* (New York, NY: Columbia University Press, 1984); David G. Roskies, *Against the Apocalypse: Responses to Catastrophe in Modern Jewish Culture* (Cambridge, MA: Harvard University Press, 1984).

9. One of the unique aspects of conservative nationalism that makes it unlike any other political ideology is the way in which it creates a compact between the generations of the living, the dead and those that will be born, another important articulation of conservative Zionism can be read in Ari Shavit's My Promised Land that ends exactly on the same note of Israel as the hope of Jewish continuity rather than its transformation.

10. For a review of the conflicts between Zionism and Political Ecology Alon Tal, "Enduring Technological Optimism: Zionism's Environmental Ethic and Its Influence on Israel's Environmental History," *Environmental History* 13, no. 2 (2008), 275–305.

11. Shavit, "Book of Revelations." Haaretz, Mar 01, 2007.

12. Herzog, "A land looking for new Mythology." Haaretz October 21, 2007.

13. An anxious premonition regarding the end secular, liberal and economically thriving life in Tel-Aviv seems to animate many of the dystopian novels. A good example is "the third" by Yeshai Sarid, see שריד ישי, השלישי.

14. In clinical terms, Dolly suffers from Münchausen syndrome by proxy, where one exaggerates, fabricates, and/or induces physical or mental health problems in others and usually expresses itself in child abuse. J. Stirling Jr and American Academy of Pediatrics Committee on Child Abuse and Neglect, "Beyond Munchausen Syndrome by Proxy: Identification and Treatment of Child Abuse in a Medical Setting," *Pediatrics* 119, no. 5 (2007), 1026–30.

15. For an overview of Orly Castel-Bloom reception and early work see, Tseviyah Ben-Yosef Ginor, "Involuntary Myths: Mania, Mother, and Zion in Orly Castel-Bloom's 'Ummi Fi Shurl,'" *Prooftexts* 25, no. 3 (2005), 235–57; Shyarts et al., "Hebrew Prose: The Generation After," *Modern Hebrew Literature*, no. 15 (1995), 6–9.

16. See Miron, "A Workshop for a New Language of Fiction" Haaretz 19 January, 1994; Shaked, "Literature Then Here and Now" (Tel Aviv: Kinneret Zmora-Bitan Dvir, 1993).

17. For Postmodernist Accounts of *Dolly City* Smadar Shiffman, "Orly Castel-Bloom and Yoel Hoffmann: On Israeli Postmodern Prose Fiction," *Hebrew Studies* 50, no. 1 (2009), 215–27; Bartana, "Where are We?"; Weisman, "Post Modernism 'Ready Made.'"

18. Smadar Shiffman, "Motherhood under Zionism," *Hebrew Studies* 44, no. 1 (2003), 139–56.

19. Todd Hasak-Lowy, "Postzionism and Its Aftermath in Hebrew Literature: The Case of Orly Castel-Bloom," *Jewish Social Studies* 14, no. 2 (2008), 86–112.

20. Andrew Sims, *Symptoms in the Mind an Introduction to Descriptive Psychopathology/Andrew Sims*, (Philidelipia: Elsevier, 2008).

21. The use of the journey metaphor or transportation in general in giving shape to abstract phenomena, like mental illness, is analyzed in George Lakoff and Mark Johnson, *Metaphors We Live By* (Chicago: University of Chicago Press, 1980).

22. Castel-Bloom, *Dolly City*, 77.

23. Ibid., 122.

24. Ibid., 62.

25. Ibid., 29.

26. Ibid., 77.

27. Ibid., 77.

28. Ibid., 77.

29. Ibid., 76–77.

30. Ibid., 49.

31. Ibid., 55.

32. Ibid., 151.

33. Ibid., 151.

34. Ibid., 152.

35. Ibid., 152.

36. Eric Hobswarm makes this forceful argument in his "long 19th century" trilogy E. J. Hobsbawm, *The Age of Revolution, 1789–1848* (Cleveland: World Pub. Co., 1962); E. J. Hobsbawm, *The Age of Capital, 1848–1875* (New York: Scribner, 1975); E. J. Hobsbawm, *The Age of Empire, 1875–1914* (New York: Pantheon Books, 1987).

37. Pierre Bourdieu, *Distinction: A Social Critique of the Judgement of Taste* (Cambridge, MA: Harvard University Press, 1984), 1–55.

38. Though they are related I am using a new concept of postmodernization rather than post-modernism. Since modernism (in art, literature, film etc.) itself was just an aspect of a global project of modernization.

39. Though China for example may not adhere to 18th century conceptions of liberalism, the return to Confucian values of harmony, relationally and hierarchy are becoming increasingly welded to the practice of global capitalism and technological development. See Daniel Bell, *China's New Confucianism: Politics and Everyday Life in a Changing Society* (Princeton, NJ: Princeton University Press, 2008).

40. Immanuel Maurice Wallerstein, *World-Systems Analysis: An Introduction* (Durham, NC: Duke University Press, 2004).

Chapter 7

The Conflict beyond Nationalism
The Second Intifada in Film and Narrative

Though many dramatic events have come to pass since that time, including operations Cast Lead, Pillar of Defense, as well as the 2014 Israel-Gaza conflict, it is the second intifada that has been most thoroughly rendered in media and film. There are several reasons why this might be the case. The creation of meaning through culture and narrative discourse takes events and transforms them. Narrative imbues them with highly condensed meanings, emotional valence through identification, suspense, and surprise. Works also implicitly or more explicitly embody a certain ideological perspective. Aesthetic production in film "lags behind" the events themselves; it is a costly operation both in terms of terms of the time it takes to process events into appealing narratives as well as the time it takes to secure funding from the European Union and to actually produce the film. A related reason for the prominence of the second intifada in Israeli cultural production is that suicide bombings within Israel in a post-9/11 world have caught the imagination of the West much more than anything that takes place in the territories. It is this mediation of the conflict as something that is vaguely similar to 9/11 that sets the basic framework of the rhetoric of these films and explains the popularity of the second intifada as subject matter. One can perhaps divide the narratives of the second intifada into two kinds: narratives that purport to represent the events of the conflict itself and narratives that show the aftermath of the conflict in terms of its effects on people. While this does not map directly to the fiction vs. documentary divide, fiction films do usually tend to present the conflict in real time, that is, in the dramatic present, while documentaries often deal with traumatic aftermath of the violence that has taken place. Both kinds are very selective in the way they relay events, usually ones that fit easily or highlight story like attributes of the conflict. Suicide bombing, for instance, is a highly dramatic event that arouses suspense and dread before the act takes place, and raises questions after the event has taken place especially if the narrative withheld information at the beginning. Films like *Paradise Now* make effective use of suspense and drama before the bombing, while films such as *The Attack* take place after a bombing and are built as a kind of detective narrative toward understanding its causes. While some films deal with suicide bombing, others deal with the acts of violence done while being a soldier and the personal consequences of taking part in this violence. Such films include internationally well-known films like *Waltz with Bashir* to lesser-known documentary films like *To See If I Am Smiling* and *Z32* that explore in detail the very different consequences of taking part in violence. Another theme that has proved highly prevalent is the plight and loss of mothers. Because of the love between mothers and their children is deemed above politics and society, it is mainly mothers that we follow as they sort out their anxieties and sorrows over youngsters participating in the intifada, soldiers who are serving or those that have been killed. In documentaries such as *Encounter Point*, *One Day after Peace*, or *To Die in Jerusalem* we are preview to the process of mourning over their deaths and the attempt to mobilize this loss in creating meaning, closure or political mobilization. A good place to delve deeply into the way that the second intifada has registered most prominently in the Western and global mind is to start with suicide bombing. As I claimed before suicide bombing has figured in film and documentaries not only because of its dramatic potential but also because the events of 9/11 have dramatically introduced suicide bombing to the West.

THE ATTACK

The Attack (2012) directed by Ziad Doueiri is a film that deals with a Palestinian suicide bombing from the perspective of an assimilated Palestinian living in Israel. The film is an adaptation of the best-selling 2006 French novel *L'attentat* (2006) by Yasmina Khadra a pseudonym of the Tunisian author Mohammed Moulessehoul. Very early in the film we are surprised by the sound of a detonated bomb, during the film we work backward with the film's main character Amin Jaafari to find the reason for this violence. We first meet the main protagonist Amin Jaafari, a highly assimilated and successful Arab surgeon in Tel-Aviv, winning a life achievement award. The film accentuates the Western face of Tel-Aviv by establishing shots of the corporate, business like Sourasky Medical Center and down town Tel-Aviv. Amin's wife Siham is missing from the ceremony because she is visiting family in Nazereth. The following day, a bomb goes off near the hospital where Amin works. The victims are brought to the hospital on his shift. That night, his nephew, Adel, comes to his house. He acts suspiciously and claims he forgot some things the last time he was over. He hurries out as quickly as he had come in, carrying a duffel bag. At about three in the morning, Amin gets a call from his friend at the hospital. He is informed that the police found Siham's body at the bombsite. Her injuries are consistent with those of a suicide bomber. Amin is then interrogated and tortured by the Shin Bet. He refuses to believe that she was indeed the bomber until he receives a letter from her with her apology. The letter is postmarked from Nablus. Amin then goes on a voyage, a "kind of heart of darkness" journey, to find out what made her do this. He asks his family, but none of them knows anything. He chases after Sheikh Marwan, who encourages people to become suicide bombers, but the Sheikh refuses to see him. Amin finds the car, that the police has previously asked him about, behind his family's house. He begins to suspect his nephew, Adel, who had acted strangely at his visit to the house. After meeting a Christian priest who praises Siham's actions, he comes face to face with Adel. Adel explains that Siham had been an active member of his cell for a while. It had been her idea to commit suicide bombing. Adel gives Amin a tape with footage from the bombing. Amin goes back to his home and life however he cannot fit in. His best friend (a colleague female doctor) accuses him of not helping the investigation against those who have participated in the bombing. The film ends with Amin watching Siham's video as she tries to call him on the phone before she goes out for her suicide-bombing mission. The final shot of the film is of Amin standing against the Tel-Aviv skyline not knowing where to go. Amin's loss is represented as a wholly personal loss. The ending of the film thus reveals an instructive failure to successfully combine the private and the public. First and foremost it is Siham's, less than wholly credible, transformation from middle-class respectability to a terrorist blowing herself up for the Palestinian cause.[1] But perhaps more crucially the way that the film represents the aftermath of her death, is through the prism of romantic loss. This prism with its attendant structure of feeling is associated with an almost gentle sorrow and a recognition that both love and beauty are doomed to pass from the world, is quite incongruous with the terror associated with suicide bombing and its very public (either nationalist, religious) meanings. Though taking a long journey, from urban professionalism to the "heart of darkness" of the occupied territories, Amin and perhaps his viewers never cross to the other side. Since the act of suicide bombing is viewed as brutal terrorism in the West and as martyrdom among a portion of the Arab and Muslim militants world, the death of a suicide bomber is an essentially contested political event between the two parties involved.[2] Starting with a basic perception of the bombing as a terrorist act with horrific results that he experiences as a doctor, Amin partially empathizes with those who advocate such actions toward the end of the film. The film engages in a compromise formation or a kind of displacement and tries to evade difficult political questions. Instead of judging the bombing and Siham's death politically as terrorist abomination and evil or as necessary national sacrifice, her death is framed as romantic one. Romantic discourse is used as a kind of masking discourse. Instead of being confronted with a political choice we are called to empathize with the loss of a loved one. The film that is geared toward a Western audience is caught between wanting to represent its protagonists in an attractive way while at the same time choosing suicide bombing as its topic. It is perhaps for this expressed reason that the film from the very beginning chooses Amin and not Siham for its main protagonist and why we ultimately see Siham not as political person but as a lost lover. Still though the script is careful to show both sides in a favorable light and uses romantic tropes to displace the act of bombing itself, both its production and its reception have been fraught with political problems. The director Ziad, for instance, had to transgress legal boundaries in order to shoot in Tel-Aviv. In an interview he states:

> I thought about it and I knew I would get some shit for it, but I went ahead and did it anyway. I was concerned about the law a lot more than how people were going to react. When I hired a lawyer a couple of months ago, he said that legally I'm losing the case. There are no loopholes in this harsh 1955 Lebanese law that says you cannot go to Israel and you cannot be in contact with an Israeli citizen anywhere in the world. I'm an American citizen also, but I'm still a Lebanese citizen when I go back. The lawyer said there's no precedent for the case—no grayish area.[3]

After the film has been completed the Doha Film Institute and the Egyptian company that funded the film asked that their names will be taken out of the opening credits. When asked why he thinks they did so Doueiri says, "I've somehow committed a breach by showing the Israelis in a sympathetic way."[4] In another interview Doueiri says that the funders said "You show Israeli kids being blown up, but you don't show any Palestinian kids being blown up."[5] The film has been banned in Lebanon and in most of the Arab world. Perhaps a representative view is given by Farid Qamar who claims that the very start of the film is highly biased, it portrays a refined environment of Israelis (high-end hospitals, awards, etc.) versus a suicide bomb which kills thirteen, including children, "Already the lines are clearly drawn: A clash of civilizations between the barbaric Palestinians and refined Israelis—and yet Doueiri insists that the film does not take sides" Later on Farid writes, "The reaction of the occupation to the attack is limited to a short interrogation with the husband—that's all! Israeli planes do not strike Palestinian villages and no houses whatsoever are demolished, as is usually the case."[6]

Ziad Doueiri has claimed that he did not aim to make a political film but a film about love and yet at other interviews he says "We've tried armed resistance, and it did not work … but when you win intellectually, when you win artistically, culturally, when you make movies that get seen, and you tell your story and you're honest about telling your story, you're more likely to create change."[7] Indeed filmmakers like Ziad who deal with the conflict often find themselves walking a very tight rope. They are rejected by Arab society as collaborators with the Zionist enemy while in the West they are under suspicion for harboring sympathy for terrorism. Usually this has the effect of depolitizing them entirely. However depolitization is not always effective or long lasting. When asked about the way in which the conflict is represented in the film Ziad Doueiri says, "The conflict is stronger than you. If you think that you can live in this bubble and isolate yourself from what's going around, it will eventually come back to you. This is the idea that we're using, which is slightly different from the book, because in the book he dies in Palestine. The book takes a little more the side of the Palestinians. In my film it's much more complex. Amin is rejected in both places. I feel that in my own personal life too."[8] Undeniably filmmakers like Ziad are left with little space to articulate their vision that is essentially humanistic. Almost all Arabs who live or work in the West share this problematic position. This position, this specific impossible space was created by the juxtaposition of the conflict, taking place under globalization. In past conflicts, perhaps most characteristically in the cold war, the populations, economies, trade, and production were relatively separated between the warring parties. In the globalized world today, this is no longer the case, conflict does not occur between geographical sides but inside an economically and culturally integrated world system.[9] Cultural production in general and national art films of the world are coproduced with the West especially with Europe.[10] The breadth of political expression of someone from the Arab world, who depicts the conflict and who wants his or her film to succeed is thus severely limited. Many filmmakers indeed engage in an ideological zigzag when they represent the conflict especially in regard to suicide bombing that is contested both in the West but also among Arab and Muslim populations. There has been a decided world shift regarding the meaning of such acts of violence since the 1960s. In the 1960s many third world peoples and first world intellectuals saw such acts as falling under the rubric of anti-colonial and national liberation struggles.[11] In the last thirty years they are seen not as a strategy of national liberation but as strategies of intimidation in winning more adherence to political Islam.[12] The filmmaker needs to avoid identification with suicide bombing as means for political liberation but cannot represent acts of terror without bringing anything of their political motivation. Thus both in terms of its origination and in terms of its aftermath Palestinian violence creates difficulties in representation. These problems of political representation are endemic for a postcolonial, postnational world. Even more difficult is the process of representation and the generation of meaning for Jewish Israelis who have experienced loss, a loss that has changed its meaning since the 1980s and has changed the experience of bereavement on many levels. In order to understand these new difficulties that surround making meaning out of loss both of soldiers and of civilians, we must examine the changes in relationship to death and bereavement that have articulated themselves since the advent of individualism and the decrease in collective nationalism that has taken place since the 1980s.

POLITICS OF BEREAVEMENT AND THE
MAKING OF A CIVIL SOCIETY

Hypersensitivity to soldiers' lives on the part of the Israeli generals is a relatively new phenomenon. Historically causality sensitivity has its roots in the first Lebanon War of 1982 that was perceived by the public as the first war of choice (not a necessarily defensive war). For the first-time bereaved parents were to openly question military and political policy. The four-mother's movement, for example, was so influential that policy makers such as Ehud Barak saw it as the ultimate cause for the withdrawal from Lebanon. This was an entirely new phenomenon. Just a decade ago in the Yom Kippur war, bereaved parents tried to silence the general public critique on how the war was handled. They saw this critique as lacking in respect for the sacrifice that they and their sons have undertaken. Indeed, the fallen soldiers essentially belonged to the state; they were bereaved as a collective loss. Traditionally each fallen solider has died a hero's death and every sacrifice has been justified. Death by friendly fire, suicide, and other accidents, though common, were never spoken of. After the Yom Kippur war, memorial books began to acknowledge the cause of death that for most soldiers has been a sudden non-heroic exposure to enemy fire, either in tanks or in the air. Parents often began to see their sons' deaths as unnecessary and to demand an explanation from the military authorities regarding the exact circumstances of this death, a rational for the decisions that lead to it.[13] Various interpretations for this change have been suggested. Some have concentrated broadly on a general loss of prestige of the Israeli army. Lamenting the death of Itzchak Rabin, Chief of Staff of the IDF Amnon Lipkin-Shahak said:

> How far we are, O captain, from the days when a military uniform was a source of pride and self-respect. During the past year, as a result of a process which commenced long ago but which has gained momentum, [we have seen] soldiers and officers, conscripts, professionals and reservists, walking around in our midst with an almost apologetic look on their faces.[14]

Shahak's lament has been interpreted as a case of Webarian routinization of charisma.[15] Shahak's generation dealt charismatically with existential threats to a new state, while the younger generation has less enthusiasm for it and simply takes the state for granted. While there is a certain plausibility to this interpretation, one should not discount the changing function of the Israeli Army, that has transitioned from defending Israel against conventional armies in decisive wars, to the unclear, interminable goal of first policing and then fighting against small groups of armed militants and civilian populations in the territories. With this interminable goal, sacrifice has indeed become "unsatisfying" and lacking in meaning. This sort of dissatisfaction can be expressed by saying that if only their sons were to die in what is conceived of a just war they would have acquiesced with their loss. Another interpretation would posit that at least implicitly sacrifice itself has become unacceptable. Israeli society has transitioned from an "enlisted" society to a more marketized civil-commercial society. In an increasingly liberal market society value inheres in individuals and families not in the people or the state. Sociologist Yagil Levy has written "the rise of the market society, which reduced the motivation for sacrifice, undermined collectivist-nationalist commitment and symbols, and nurtured the new 'conditional ambience'; namely the ideological and material conditions that both conscripts and reservist placed in the requirement for sacrifice."[16] What sociologist Yagil Levy calls a "conditional ambience" is a result of a decrease in collectivist values that have created a vacuum of meaning around sacrifice. Levy is essentially correct to look at market society as the cause of this development. This conditional ambience that ultimately comes from the articulation of both liberal and commercial values is mediated by peers, teachers, and parents who have become much more ambivalent about army service. In fact as we shall see, parents have been involved as parents of soldiers in many of the antiwar protest movements in Israel. However, though they may confront the army and government, it seems that at least in some cases a deeper truth emerges. This truth is that they themselves feel partially responsible for injury or death of their loved ones. This uncomfortable truth has expressed itself repeatedly not so much in the media (where its implications are still viewed as dangerous) but in Israeli literature and culture. From the extremely prevalent use of the motif of Isaack's bindings in Israel poetry, used to convey the guilt of the father sacrificing the son, to the critical plays of Chanoch Levin that examines parental guilt and responsibilities. Parental guilt has resurfaced continually in Israeli culture.[17] More recently it has expressed itself powerfully in the novel and film *Beaufort*. In the film a prominent left-wing reporter Gideon Levi is interviewing a bereaved father called Amos:

> *Gideon:* Are you angry, are you looking for the people who are at fault?
> *Amos:* I blame only myself.
> *Gideon:* What do you mean only yourself, why you?

Amos: One can blame the army, the generals, but these generals are not really responsible for my son. They don't even know him. I am responsible for him. He is my son I educated him. It seems that I have educated him in a bad way.

Gideon: It is really surprising what you say, since in Israeli society it is the usual to think that a child who volunteers to an elite unit, it's a sign for a good education.

Amos: When I was a kid my parents gave me the feeling that I am the most precious thing in the world. A precious stone that must be guarded with cotton balls. In this moment when I am speaking to you, I have no idea where my sons are. One came back from a trip to South America, the other is still a solider an officer, and Ziv I know where Ziv is, he is, in the grave. It seems that I did not make them understand how much their lives are important. That if something happens to them, a whole world collapses, crushes. That is the role of the parent. I feel that I abandoned my son.

Gideon: But what do you mean Amos that you have abandoned your son? How can one safe guard one's child but also to allow him the amount of freedom that is rightfully his?

Amos: Just like you teach child not to run to the road. Instill in him an instinct for fear.[18]

This is a call for another kind of socialization by a father who represents the middle-class Ashkenazi establishment. If such socialization becomes universal, it will threaten the very foundation of the IDF, as a people's army. Such attitudes are disturbing to the military establishment. Parental ambivalence and the interminable goals of the army have caused a change in its priorities as they relate to IDF casualties. Traditionally the first value of the IDF ethical code is "Tenacity of Purpose in Performing Missions and Drive to Victory" and is defined as follows: "The IDF servicemen and women will fight and conduct themselves with courage in the face of all dangers and obstacles; They will persevere in their missions resolutely and thoughtfully even to the point of endangering their lives." The fourth value of the ethical code "Human Life" reads as follows: "The IDF servicemen and women will act in a judicious and safe manner in all they do, out of recognition of the supreme value of human life. During combat they will endanger themselves and their comrades only to the extent required to carry out their mission."[19] Though the value comes at the fourth place it has become the first value informing decision-making.[20] This has been a direct result of greater parental involvement and pressures exercised on the IDF to become accountable for the death of sons. When soldiers do die parents are increasingly faced with the problem of providing meaning and sense of their loss. In times that are increasingly both individualized and globalized the meaning of death is not easily subsumed under the heroic national ideal, and parents are faced with the difficulty of generating significance from their loss. Israeli culture in film, television, and literature has been increasingly attuned to the travails and hardships of meaning making. It is to several representations of bereaved mothers that we turn to now.

BEREAVED MOTHERS ACROSS BORDERS

Encounter Point follows Israeli bereaved mother Robi Damelin and other bereaved parents and siblings as they participate in the bereaved Families Forum, an initiative undertaken to bring together Israeli and Palestinian families that have lost loved ones due to the conflict. David Damelin, an idealistic MA student at Tel-Aviv University, was shot and killed while he was doing reserve duty at a checkpoint in the territories. When David was called to the reserve he had doubts about whether he should go, but decided to do what he conceived of as his societal duty. He was killed by a Palestinian sniper, who as a small child saw his uncle killed by an Israeli soldier. The film follows several Palestinian and Israeli families as they participate in dialogue to find solutions for the violence. *One Day after Peace* documents Robi Damelin on her trip to South Africa. Damelin's goal is to learn about the Truth and Reconciliation Commission (TRC). Like the Bereaved Families Forum in Encounter Point, the TRC aimed to bring about peace and reconciliation. The TRC did this by uncovering the truth about human rights violations that occurred during Apartheid and granting amnesty to those who came forward and confessed their crimes. Damelin's goal is to find sources of inspiration, perhaps even a model that could serve Israelis and Palestinians in their peace making. More specifically she is looking for the way in which bereaved families involved in the conflict have sought to achieve reconciliation and reach closure. She meets with bereaved South African mothers who lost their children to the Apartheid regime and speaks with them of their losses. Some of them are still angry and are unwilling to forgive those who have killed their children while others have found peace with those who had done them so much wrong. Perhaps more relevant is her meeting with Ginn Fourie, a white woman who has lost her daughter in 1993 in the Heidelberg Tavern Attack that was carried out by the Azanian People's Liberation Army (APLA). Fourie has joined with the man responsible for her daughter's death to form an organization to help the freedom fighters of the APLA. Damelin contemplates meeting the Palestinian who shot David and questions herself on how honest she was with herself about the possibility of reconciliation with him. The film ends with the freeing of Israeli prisoner Gilad Shalit in exchange for the release of one thousand Palestinians imprisoned in Israel including the person who has killed David. As a viewer of the film one cannot help but constantly wonder to what extent does Damelin see the situation in Israel as analogues or different from the situation in South Africa. There is also an interesting slippage between the core lessons learned from TRC that are not relevant to her situation since the TRC was mainly about individuals who have been part of the South African security apparatus, who have come forth and related their wrong doings in exchange for amnesty. It is this coming open about the crimes of Apartheid that allows for a kind of reconciliation that aims to prevent a scenario of revenge against whites. The testimony given by freedom fighters for the violence they have committed was wholly secondary to the process and did not have concrete political aims rather it originated from psychological needs for closure for those whites that have suffered from violence. The forgiveness of whites toward "black" violence was a peripheral aspect of the TRC. Still as the film progress it comes to concentrate more and more on "black on white" violence in order to procure a fitting analogy to Damelin's quest. Thus the film turns to discuss the violence perpetuated by Brian Madasi a solider of the APLA who participated in the Heidelberg Tavern Attack. At one point Brain says:

> Even in Geneva, in Switzerland the cause of the oppressors was declared a crime against humanity. Now the question is how do we defend ourselves from that crime, right? Now, the armed struggle was the solution.

In the court while both Brian Madasi and Letlapa Mphahlele (his commander) stand trial, the prosecutor claimed:

> The legitimacy of targeting white civilians, that by typifying white civilians in the manner in which you did carte blanche, you would have violated international law.

Letlapa Mphahele answers:

> I think this point must be made clear once and for all. We did not attack white civilians, but we destroyed European invaders, dispossessors, because as far as I am concerned, he who benefits by crime is guilty of that crime. And every white person in this country benefitted from the crime of dispossession, benefitted from the crime of colonialism, benefitted from the crime of apartheid. But now you want to extract yourselves from this crime.

Later on in the film however he says that the forgiveness Fourie offered him released him from the "prison of inhumanity," he is thus in the position where he thinks his actions are justifiable but still need forgiveness. Purely logically if his actions have been fully justified, fully excusable there would be nothing to forgive.[21] However this is not the case. An action can be justified from the perspective of the agent but still in need of reconciliation. The killing has created a kind of rapture with a fellow human being, both particular and general forgiveness is sought to make good this rapture. From the perspective of the victim one looks for a principled overcoming of resentment, a kind of difficult reorientation of the victim, of the wrong doing toward the person who has wronged him.[22] Perhaps the best metaphor is Brain Madasi's comments on Damelin's process of healing:

> I know, she's got that scar inside her heart. Sometimes to heal a scar, you must always touch the scar. So that you get healed. When you touch the scar it's healing, it's a healing. Slowly by slowly you get healed. So, by meeting Ginn on another side of the coin. It's also a healing to her, it's also healing to me. Because I know for a fact where did we meet, and I can't run away from that fact.

Forgiveness itself is both a kind of reorientation and a kind of healing. Forgiveness is a process that must be engaged repeatedly. In the film we see Fourie both claiming that Brian Madasi did immeasurable harm to his cause by killing her daughter, calling his act a "dastardly affair," and telling him that on that day "you ripped my heart out." At one point in the film Damelin asks a white woman who has lost a child in South Africa what forgiveness is for her:

> *Fourie:* Forgiveness is a process in which you take a principle decision, to give up your justifiable right to revenge.
> *Fourie:* Oh, Yes.
> *Damelin:* By the way, I don't know what revenge is, what? I should go out and kill a hundred Palestinians?
> *Fourie:* No, you should fight to keep him in jail.

Thus Gin Fourie inadvertently reveals that this thought of fighting to keep the person who has killed her child in prison has been on her mind (this idea did not come from Damelin and she is visibly surprised by it in the film). It was also a long and very difficult process that leads her to this point of forgiveness. She describes the first moments of recognizing that Letlapa is not who she has imagined him:

> Because I had pictured this severe evil person. And I wasn't hearing that at all. It would have been much easier to have a devil with horns and a tail, than to be impressed with the integrity of the person who's killed you daughter … it is difficult to explain and so it was easy to forgive him.

One of the difficulties that Fourie, Damelin, Latlapa, and Madasi face is the attempt to reconcile the political with the personal. The concept of forgiveness is not classically invoked on the level of conflict between anonymous players. The root of the use of forgiveness is between people who know each other and who have hurt each other self-interestedly on a personal level. Mphahlele the director of military operations of the Azanian People's

Liberation Army did not aim to kill Gin Fourie's daughter. As he claims his actions were a retaliation for the killing of the five black children who were shot at the Eastern Cape. Essentially he was sending a violent message to the society that has dispossessed, exploited, and did long-term structural and systematic violence to his community and people. When watching the film one gets the feeling that it represents the events on the "wrong" level of description, the level of stories, persons and families forcing a collective story to be told as a story of individuals. Individual people and families are not ideally the right level to represent these events. Several researchers have commented that Apartheid and occupation are structural, impersonal kinds of violence.[23] Like other forms of modern organized violence they are initiated and carried out by a great multiplicity of agencies and institutes. Like any modern endeavor, division of labor is highly intensive and thus constitutes forms of essentially alienated impersonal violence. Terror attacks and shootings are also an impersonal kind of violence. Growing up in this structural imbalance and violence both sides are surprised at how literally personable and relatable the other side is, how easy it is to grow affectionate to all of those involved. Nonetheless, however much the participants are personable, their loss and guilt is ultimately impersonal and political. As they go through the process of bereavement, moral reckoning and the search for meaning they must return to political and impersonal meanings of what has happened. These types of documentaries are highly individualist; they force collective events with collective meaning into the mold of personal family drama.[24] In fact it can be read as the privatization of social conflict itself. The ability to relate to a story that features collectives is discounted from the first. Much of the audience's identification with Damelin and Fourie is due to the fact that they, like most of the viewers, lead private largely nonpolitical lives. They have not conceived of their world as a world in which they could be victims to systemic collective kinds of violence. In their private world such tragic losses are relatively unexpected and are thus difficult to comprehend. The people who have committed the violence against them have come to suffer and to expect systemic violence. The meaning of Damelin's and Fourie's loss is difficult to construct. This is as we have seen due to a variety of causes. First globalizing, liberalizing, and individualizing, Israel has created relatively privatized conceptions of their interests. Like other globalizing citizens those living in Israel often have living abroad as an option that they keep on their mind even if they have no concrete plans of realizing it.[25] The commercial atmosphere that reigns in media and street life often stands in contrast with the idealized images of soldiers that were prevalent in the past. Parents take a "helicopter" approach to their sons and daughters military service and are greatly involved in all facets from being accepted into the right unit in the beginning of service to contacting commanders regarding specific requests and grievances later on. However, though they are highly involved, the importance of military service has declined generally. Moreover, in a globalized world, death in the sacrifice for the national cause has become almost unacceptable. It is in this context of the difficulty in generating meaning out of death that Damelin's actions are intelligible. It is the difficulty in finding meaning in their loss that drives Damelin's activism. Perhaps because Damelin has some family background in political activism in South Africa she was able to quickly re-politicize and re-signify her situation. Her first political act was to preclude her son's death from being appropriated into Israeli right-wing discourse and the cycle of retaliation. It is precisely in order to disrupt the cycle of retaliation that she is willing to forgive the person who has killed her son. The empowerment of her political voice stems from a certain tradition of the political mobilization of motherhood in Israeli society. Indeed, her political activity can be seen as an extension of the tradition of activist mothers that started in Israel with the Four Mothers movement. Their intervention in the public sphere in the political discussion regarding war and peace is based on their unique "authority" as mothers, those who have created, cared for, and nurtured children until they became adults. As such they perceive themselves as being special advocates for the value of life itself. Their discourse conflicts with the very "rational" political realist discourse of the security establishment, a discourse that though affected by human loss of life is mainly concerned with balance of power, stability, security, and deterrence, the latter being the most important concept in Israeli strategic thought. As advocates on behalf of life itself, they have had a great influence on decision-making and on the way that causalities are perceived in Israel. However, while her actions and message are highly intelligible in the Israeli context they are not easily translatable when presented to Palestinians. This is the case because reconciliation and forgiveness were given and sought in South Africa after the regime change and political rights have been attained. Palestinians conceive themselves as a people lacking political autonomy and sovereignty. The shooter who has killed Damelin's son has reacted in surprise to Damelin's letter and essentially said that he shot a solider of the occupation, he did not see any relevance in Damelin visiting him. For him such a meeting would generally fall under the rubric of normalizing relationships with Israelis, something that according to many Palestinians should occur only after an agreement has been reached and not before. Thus, actions that have certain meaning in Damelin's Israel (breaking the cycle of retaliatory violence) have a wholly different meaning in Palestinian society, that of normalizing relationships while occupation is still taking place. Indeed, kinds of symmetrical recognition cannot take place while more fundamental asymmetry is in effect. The symmetry and asymmetry in

Palestinian-Israeli relations is the main theme of another film dealing with bereaved mothers *To Die in Jerusalem.*

TO DIE IN JERUSALEM

In a similar way to *One Day after Peace*, *To Die in Jerusalem* follows an Israeli mother Avigail Levy whose daughter, Rachel Levy, has been killed by a suicide bombing by a strikingly physically similar girl Ayat al-Akhras on March 29, 2002. Indeed their pictures side by side were featured by *Newsweek* in which there is an uncanny similarity between the two dark haired girls.

With the help of the producers of this HBO documentary, Avigail Levy attempts to meet with the mother of Ayat. Avigail wants to convince her to renounce terrorism publicly in the name of universal ethics, family love, and humanism. In this her motivations are both similar and different from Damelin's. While Damelin is seeking a beginning of reconciliation and is willing to forgive the assassin of her son, Avigail is seeking a renunciation of violence from Palestinians without any references to the problems that Palestinians face. In their different ways both are attempting a kind of push for grassroots coming together that bypasses official politics. *To Die in Jerusalem* narrates the way in which both Levy's family and the al-Akhras family have dealt with their loss while at the same time shows their difficulties in meeting. The mother of Ayat, Um Ayat, is only willing to travel with her husband while the father of a terrorist cannot get a visa to Jerusalem. Avigail then attempts to meet with them in the camp but gets cold feet when night falls on their way to Dheisheh camp. Finally, the two women meet using satellite television. The conversation does not go according to Avigail's plan. Though Um Ayat did not know of her daughters plans and would not permit her to carry out such an attack, she is unwilling to renounce what her daughter has done after the fact. Her support for her daughter's actions strongly polarizes audiences perhaps more than any other representation of the conflict.[26] The audience in a way is asked to decide whether they find Avigail's request legitimate or whether they view Um Ayat's denial of this request persuasive. In my experience of showing this film in university and college classroom in the United States, this judgment can be articulated as outright simple anger but also a kind of disappointment. Typical of those who empathize with Avigail's demands is the harsh or subtler judgment of Ayat al-Akhras. For example, Dennis Ross who dealt with the conflict as a professional politician said of Um Ayat that she "just can't cross that threshold at a human level even though you can see she feels it." He called her "a prisoner of the context she lives in."[27] Others who have watched the film had more sympathy with Um Ayat and have seen Avigail demands as unreasonable given the situation of occupation. In Um Ayat words Avigail "demands submission not peace." In fact what the film shows is a kind of conceptual confusion of Avigail when meeting Um Ayat. This ideological and political confusion that bereaved Israeli mothers find themselves in is typical when they meet Palestinian mothers. Like many efforts of reconciliation this attempted meeting is arranged by a third party either from Western Europe or the United States. Though the meeting is initiated by the West and Israel and puts the Palestinians in the reactive position, Israeli mothers often find themselves disoriented. The confusion arises because bereaved mothers in Israel largely make sense of their experience through a particular national discourse that does not lend itself to globalization and cannot have the same meaning for Palestinians. Though the experience and meaning of bereavement has changed, it's still very much influenced by the classical nationalist discourse that provides a framework of meaning for the loss. As I argued before, in its classical nationalist stage, bereavement was the result of acts of war between armies and was viewed as a meaningful contribution to the creation and defense of the state. As we saw earlier in the chapter, this meaning was eroded both by the changing nature of IDF activities, by the rise of individualism, the increasing stress on the market economy, by the erosion of national identity, and by the fact that causalities in operations/acts of terror are most often civilians. Still, bereaved mothers are accorded an honor in Israel for having paid a steep price for the life of the nation. As Damelin says in the film "You know, I love Israel, it's my country. I paid a very high price by losing my child." It is for this reason precisely that Israeli media will often pay special respect to the views expressed by bereaved parents. However, this price and this respect are unrecognized by Palestinians whose aims and interests are often diametrically opposed to Zionism. When Israeli mothers come to Palestinians who have from their point of view been involved in acts of legitimate resistance, there is no self-evident recognition of the value of this bereavement.[28] There is often recognition of the pain of the loss, but a refusal to accord this loss with a covert sense of honor and a refusal to apologize. In many senses both mothers are blind to the kind of nationalist recognition that the other side gets for their loss. Avigail Levy the Jewish-Israeli mother is looking for a repentant Palestinian mother who would apologize for what her daughter did but the Palestinian mother never does:

Avigail: I want to talk to you as a mother. I want you to listen to me mother to mother.
Um Ayat: I feel you—you are a mother and I am a mother. You've sacrificed as I've sacrificed. But you are not living under an occupation. You are the occupier.

Avigail: If you go to this way we never going to live in peace.

Um Ayat: I invite you to come live with us to see our conditions. And see how we live. The crimes are beyond description! Killings—bombardments—demolitions! In front of our home a car with two people inside was attacked by missiles. That made her [Ayat] go mad!

Avigail: My daughter never, never would kill someone for nothing.

Um Ayat: Because you daughter had it all and wasn't under occupation. *Because you're not living under occupation—under oppression. Under the crimes of the occupation! You are talking from a position of comfort. We talk from a position of hardship.*

Avigail: You don't do nothing to solve the problem you just complain. You cry all the time like a baby. You have to start from yourself to start from you.

An argument ensues between the precedence of ethics and the primacy of politics. The Israeli mother would like the Palestinian mother to declare that what her daughter did was categorically wrong, an illegitimate act of senseless meaningless brutality. She would like Um Ayat to denounce the act. Um Ayat contextualizes the suicide bombing as a result of legitimate resistance to the violence of occupation. In her conceptualization both she and the Israeli mother are victims of occupation. The interview is a kind of microcosm of the conflict. The Israelis would like a categorical repudiation of violence from Palestinians, while for the Palestinians violence against Israelis is resistance, the only way that the lack of rights and suffering and violence of occupation is registered in Israel. The Israeli mother looks at the situation from an ethical personal perspective. She would like to establish a "mother to mother" connection that will cause the Palestinian to rebuke violence. The Palestinian woman says "you want surrender not peace" revoking violence in her view means total acquiescence with the situation of occupation. In general, the Israeli mother denies political being to the Palestinian mother while the Palestinian mother refuses to acknowledge a general ethical restriction on killing.[29] However on many other levels the relationship between these two women is not symmetrical and they occupy very different positions. One difference is the degree of freedom of expression afforded to them. For Um Ayat freedom to express herself is more constrained than Avigail's. Um Ayat is indeed in a difficult rhetorical position. From the mainstream point of view of her society even talking with Israelis is a kind of normalization of the occupation. Without even taking into account her own personal convictions, she would have found it extremely difficult to wholly renounce what her daughter did as this would go against her own society, and would also cancel the few symbolic and material benefits afforded to her as a mother of a Shahid, a martyr. At the same time she cannot take even partial responsibility for these actions as this will entail a reprisal by the Israeli army that would demolish her house and indefinitely imprison other family members. On the face of it Avigail has more freedom to choose her response. She has all the spectrum between seeking ways for retribution to offering forgiveness (which as we saw was what another bereaved mother Robi Damelin sought to do). It is unlikely that she would suffer socially, materially, or physically from any choice along this spectrum. On a more general level however, both mother's behavior and communication is severely restricted by national and religious ideology. To Avigail, her existence in Israel seems self-evident. She grounds it both as a natural fact and as religiously motivated at the same time. At one point of the film she says to a Palestinian suicide bomber in prison, you have your Koran and we have the Bible that promised Israel to us. Like many Jewish Israelis she has not met many Palestinians nor is she used to hearing their point of view. Um Ayat also thinks exclusively through a mixture of national and religious ideology. Her fixation on the going back to the houses that Palestinians have lost in Jaffe in 1948 can preclude thinking of more likely solutions that take the power inequality with Israel into account and which might result in an improvement of her situation. Again, though Abu Ayat's wish to visit Al-Aqsa Mosque is understandable, it's exceptional from a more neutral or realist point of view that would prioritize physical and economic security. Though Avigail is relatively unable to think outside the box; she does make an effort to transcend national and religious lines, however this attempt itself is fraught with ambiguity. At one point both mothers are discussing the meaning of the loss. Avigail is trying to undermine the meaning accrued to the loss that Um Ayat has experienced. She says:

> I had a dream. My daughter came to me. But you know when I saw my daughter I saw your daughter too, and she was not happy. She wanted to tell me something. I could not understand what she wanted to say. My daughter said to me, I know that you remember me all the time, and I know that you can see me all the time but I don't expect from no one to remember me, and I want to share with you this feeling because you see now, movies and everything, everything will go tomorrow, and whoever stays is me and you. We are going to stay with our pain. You are not going to receive your wishes and I am not going to receive my daughter back.

Avigail then makes a plea for the future beyond nations in which both mothers work together for peace while asking Um Ayat to renounce violence, essentially to renounce what Um Ayat considers legitimate resistance to occupation. Um Ayat rejects this demand and says that Avigail is asking for surrender not peace. The conversation thus ends on the note of what can be construed as a straightforward disagreement. The conversation though it has ended with what can be perceived as relatively clear disagreement was in fact far from simple and took place as an expression of two different but interrelated and tightly linked levels: the national-religious level and the level of personal bereavement. While the national and religious aspect of their loss is at least partially explicated above, it is worthwhile to look at its relationship with bereavement as psychological and social process and to tie it in with meaning making in post-national, post-secular times.

Bereavement has been conceptualized by Freud and others as a process of decathexis, the process of withdrawal from pleasurable attachment to a loved object "Each single one of the memories and expectations in which the libido is bound to the object is brought up and hyper-cathected, and detachment of the libido is accomplished in respect of it."[30] This process has been viewed as solitary and painful one in which the mourner learns to give up the object of their love. More recently however both psychoanalysts and others have stressed bereavement as a disruption in self-organization that is then dealt with through an essentially interpersonal process in which the mourner seeks both to let go but also to preserve his or her relationship with the lost person and to generate socially constructed meaning from the loss. The generation of meaning both personal and social is a significant aspect of the process.[31] Both mothers went through a process of trying to let go, most importantly focusing on their other children, however they are both looking to preserve a relationship with their daughter and generate meaning from this loss. Both preserving a relationship with the lost daughter as well as generating meaning is not a solitary process. Cultural and social resources are often used in the process of bereavement. For both mothers, most of the resources for dealing with death are national and religious.[32] Judaism has perhaps the most elaborate cultural script for dealing with bereavement, the Shiva.[33] In several ways this cultural script is perhaps more elaborate than the one offered by Islam, were overly expressive articulation of mourning are discouraged, one is supposed to bear the loss quietly and with dignity as it is the will of God.[34] Yet it is clear in the film that in terms of meaning making, Um Ayat holds an advantage over Avigail. Though the film does show Avigail's religiosity, and reveals relatively little of Um Ayat religiosity, Um Ayat and Abu Ayat's discourse is permeated with religious references and it is safe to assume that for both of them religion plays a larger role in everyday life in general and the way they handle the loss of their daughters in particular. Abu Ayat says "Before everything else there is God's will. We believe in God and in fate and destiny. God has pre-ordained all that will happen to all humans." While Avigail says something much more conditional and uncertain "I do believe in God, you know, I do believe that there is something, some power." Avigail, though, becomes more religious after Rachel was killed. She says however, that the more she learnt and drew closer to religion the more it made her nervous "because if there is God why is he doing such a thing?" she adds "there is a sentence in the Tora which says 'even Satan wouldn't create a child murderer, if Satan wouldn't kill how could God allow that? I want to believe because [according] to our religion Rachel is now in the best place next to God.'" Avigail has probably grown up either secular or traditional at most and her belief in God is challenged by her daughter's death. She is perplexed and bothered by the classic question of the theodicy, of why a good God permits the manifestation of evil, in a way that Um Ayat and Abu Ayat are not. Her world and her God are largely unable to make sense of her loss. Not only does she feel a lack of meaning she also feels a lack of connection with Rachel. While almost prostrating herself on Rachel's grave she says "I want to feel you but I don't, I am talking but there is no answer." Her bereavement is constantly threatened by a sense of loss that is not only final and irrevocable, lacking in meaning but also threatens to disappear without a trace. It is this threat of total disappearance that animates Avigail's anger and her guilt. At the grave-site Rachel is plagued with guilt regarding an upcoming trip she has planned with the family. She is asking Rachel to give her her blessing and wish them a safe trip. In comparison Um Ayat but especially Abu Ayat though they talk of this loss as unnecessary, bereave using the discourses and practices of religion. Abu Ayat says "What is better than to be a martyr? You are going to die anyway, today, tomorrow or in a hundred years. To die in dignity and honor is better than anything." Um Ayat says "As Muslims, we are required to perform Jihad for the sake of Allah. …. We are pre-ordained to be martyrs, persecuted, imprisoned. That is Jihad." Though it is not clear to what extent Abu and Um Ayat fully believe in this, this kind of meaning making is available to them, and is not available to Avigail. In a way Avigail is attempting to reorient herself after her daughter was killed. However, one can say that throughout the film Avigail expresses no real resignation about her daughter's death. She remains perplexed and indeed angry though she partakes in many kinds of commemorations and meaning-making activities. The film indeed follows commemorative practices in a parallel manner. We see a giant picture of Ayat at the school and a wooden plank commemorating Rachel. Traditional Palestinian dances in parallel to Israeli rock star Aviv Geffen who comes to play at her memorial. Nevertheless the parallel is just a seeming parallel, on a deeper level there is deficit of meaning in Rachel's death for many different reasons, many of them on the societal level. Though there has been more recent attempts by the state to make victims of terror on par in terms of symbolic value to fallen soldiers, this is very difficult to achieve.[35] Several studies have looked into what is known as the hierarchy of bereavement in Israel, the fact that less honor and even less social and material resources are accorded by the state to those who are called officially "victims of hostile activity."[36] The historical base of this hierarchy is founded on the fact that victims of terror did not sacrifice their security for what is considered the public good of the security of the nation-state. When they died they were private individuals looking after their private interests. Furthermore, Avigail is part of a kind of global Israeli whose nationalism itself became attenuated. The Levy's family has spent much time in the United States and in fact some of its members have US citizenship, something that makes Israel a choice rather than necessity. From Avigail's perspective the film itself can be seen as kind of commemoration. The film that was produced by HBO with an international production crew is essentially a kind ersatz commemoration for a lack in national commemoration. Through the film Rachel will win a kind of permanence, she will not be forgotten. For Avigail the film reveals many of the antinomies and difficulties of dealing with loss whose origin is rooted in collective national struggles in the age of individualism and globalization. Avigail cannot wholly rely on the nation-state to provide meaning for her loss and in many ways her call for a mother-to-mother coalition, coupled with a one directional Palestinian renunciation of violence, reveals the strange in-between character of her political meaning making, half an internationally "motherist" discourse, the other is the relatively antagonistic national discourse. Still the national discourse does not "work" with the Palestinian other, nor could it. The film shows the decline of potency of nationalist discourse and nationalist sense making in meeting with the other in a globalizing world. At the end of the meeting with the Palestinian other, Avigail says to the crew "I didn't understand anything—she didn't understand anything." Her nationalist framework for sense making led her to the expectation that she will force contrition and perhaps even shame Um Ayat. When she talks to an Israeli forum of bereaved Israeli parents she says on Um Ayat's father "I hate him and I'll make it clear that I hate them! Not to go against them, to go with them. We are not going to hug or kiss them. We're going to say to their faces that we don't love or trust them anymore!" This kind of combative talk that perhaps makes sense in the nationalist in-group that shares assumptions and passions breaks down when actually talking with oppositional out-groups like the Palestinians and even with the international production crew. Um Ayat holds opposite assumptions about the Zionist national project while the global production team may care more for the technical, dramatic, and rhetorical aspects of the film, for its distribution and success, than for Avigail's sentiment. In a sense the nationalist conceptualization of Avigail finds itself in a world which is either hostile since it has been victimized by her nationalism, indifferent or exploitative. The self-centered, obsessive, rewarding, and meaning-making aspects of nationalism are challenged as they find themselves facing various others. While there are forces that aim to separate Israelis from the rest of the world, globalization in the avatar of HBO brings the world to Israelis. Coming together often means lack of understanding and a painful process of either recalibration of set assumptions or a more active rejection of the other. In many ways Avigail reactions are characteristics for Israelis in a globalizing age. She is active and relatively enthusiastic about participating in this global HBO production, but at the same time this very global production brings her together with the Palestinian other that challenges her world making. Her reactions are also quite characteristic as they entail both a reaching out toward and simultaneous rejection of the other. The close integration with the world essentially causes a crisis in classic national world making that attempts often unsuccessfully to reconfigure itself in a new environment that entails such close proximity with the other. This book has argued that globalization and proximity of the other, a process that started in the 1990s, has essentially undercut secular national sense making. In the film short meeting with the Palestinian other has proved perplexing and difficult for Avigail. Though they partake in a highly dramatic and intense meeting, Avigail and Um Ayat do not have any sort of relationship with one another. There has been a psychological need among audiences especially international audiences to precisely focus on such relationships. It is to these representations of more long-term relationships that we turn to next.

BETHLEHEM

Set at the time of the second intifada *Bethlehem* tells the story of the complex relationship between an Israeli Secret Service officer Razi and his teenage Palestinian informant Sanfur. Razi has recruited Sanfur when he was only fifteen. Toward the end of the film we learn that Sanfur was pressured into collaboration in order for his father to be released from Jail. Sanfur is useful for the Shin Beth in order to get information on Ibrahim's brother, an important militant in Al-Aksa Martyrs brigades. The film begins as Ibrahim goes into hiding after a bombing in Jerusalem that killed thirty Israelis. We witness the way in which Razi acts as a father surrogate toward Sanfur in order to use him, but at the same time develops feelings toward him. At one point in the film, Razi finds out that Sanfur has acted as a money carrier between the Hamas and his brother Ibrahim. The commander of the Shin Beth decides to use a helicopter to kill Ibrahim the next time Sanfur makes the transfer. In an attempt to save him, Razi suggests that Sanfur go to Hebron during the week of the transfer. The killing by helicopter cannot take place and it is decided that they will kill Ibrahim in the market place where he himself decided to pick up the money instead of Sanfur. Two Israeli agents spot Ibrahim in the marketplace, they try to kill him but fail. A chase develops and he flees into a house hiding in a small attic. Cornered there he resists, but by extorting the family the Israeli army learns of his hiding place and kills him. Neighboring Palestinians start throwing rocks and then shooting at the Israeli soldiers. An Israeli officer is shot and is hospitalized in critical condition. Razi's boss at the Shin Beth suspects that it is Razi who sent Sanfur to Hebron and that it is for this betrayal that they have suffered this injury. In the meantime Sanfur is discovered to be an Israeli collaborator by Badawi another important Al-Aksa militant. Badawi is willing to let Sanfur live only if he agrees to meet with Razi and kill him. Razi in turn wants more information from Sanfur on Badawi. Razi and Sanfur ultimately meet. Sanfur asks to be taken into Israel, but Razi says that it's good that Sanfur maintain contact with Badawi. Seeing no way out Sanfur alternating rage and tenderness kills Razi ending the film.

In many ways the film is about a tragic case of love in adverse circumstances. The relationship between Razi and Sanfur is explicitly a father-son relationship set in the impossible circumstances of the conflict. The father both wants his son to further his own goals and to be his representative in the world but he is also looking after him. The son in this case, lacking paternal love needs love, protection, and material support from the father. On the explicit level the death at the end is built on a partial misunderstanding, Razi would have probably taken him to Israel if he knew his life was in danger. However, ultimately, Sanfur kills Razi because fathers have all failed him. First, his own father has failed him, in his very vulnerability to the Israeli army. By arresting the father (usually done in a humiliating manner in front of the family) the army has traumatically negated the idealized figure of the father. Both Sanfur and his brother Ibrahim can be seen as responding to this. Ibrahim becomes his own hero (in the form of an Al-Aksa militant) while Sanfur became doubly vulnerable to the compassionate father figure of Razi both in terms of freeing his father from jail and thus symbolically "reconstituting" him, and in terms of his real needs both material and emotional. The film essentially shows how the occupation is destructive not only of lives, but of selves and subjectivities that cannot go through proper personal development in this setting. *Bethlehem* is part of a series of films on the second intifada made for global audiences. These films aim at personalizing the conflict and making it explicable to international audiences while at the same time capitalizing on the drama and interest generated by events taking place in the Middle East. It seems as though the international audience wants to see the conflicting sides together in a relationship that is both libidinal and conflictual at the same time. It is to another such representation that we turn to now.

THE GREEN PRINCE AND *SON OF HAMAS*

Mosab Hassan Yousef's biography has been rendered both in the book *Son of Hamas* and the documentary *The Green Prince.*[37] Since there is a live-action film on the way it makes sense to view both film and book together and provide their overlapping biographical background. Yousef was born in Ramallah in 1978, he is the son of Skeikh Hassan Yousef, a central religious leader of the Hamas. Yousef, the younger, was arrested when he was ten for throwing stones at Israeli settlers. He was arrested again when he was nine-teen for possession of firearms. Yousef was held by Shin Bet agents in 1996. In prison he experienced both the Shin Bet interrogation methods as well as saw impromptu interrogations that the Hamas did in the prison courtyard. The brutality of the latter convinced him to become an informant for the Israelis. Upon his release from prison, Mosab got interested in Christianity. By imbuing himself with Christian values he came to loath the violence he associated with Islam, and the way that Hamas members used the violence inflicted on civilian and children to further their goals. Between 1999 and 2007 Mosab worked closely with Shin Bet handler Gonen Ben-Itzhak provid-ing information on his father's conversations with Palestinian leaders Yassar Arafat, Marwan Barghouti, and Ismail Haniyeh and on different plans for suicide attacks in Israel. The documentary *The Green Prince* concentrates on the relationship between Mosab and his Shin Bet handler Gonen Ben-Itzhak, the book *Son of Hamas* tells his biography. The book and the film both fas-cinate readers with the absurd "impossible" situation of the collaborator. It is essentially a story about how the Shin Beth uses violence as well as affection in order to use a person to prevent suicide bombing but which also ruins this person's life. Using pain and extreme social isolation coupled with the bond that is created with the "good cop" handler leads a person to turn against his own oppressed people as well as against his own family. This procedure strips a person of dignity, in a sense it deeply violates their personhood. One can profitably look at the relationship formed in the interrogation as the exact opposite of the goals of a positive or therapeutic relationship, especially as the opposite of psychoanalysis. In psychoanalysis transference, that is the projection of childish feeling and thinking, that have had the parent as their original object, unto the therapist, is used in order to create greater autonomy and personal empowerment. Overcoming these feelings and having a realistic assessment of the therapist is the essence of growth. By contrast in interroga-tion, pain, seclusion, and humiliation are used to infantilize and traumatize. These are done in order to increase dependency, to artificially cause regres-sion and emotional and intellectual dependency in order to better exploit the person. In interrogation these feelings are encouraged as a means to subject

a person to the interest of the handler, an interest that goes against the informant's family, people, and religious community. In Mosab's biography this
process results in discounting his own father and having a new "father" the
Shin Bet handler. *The Green Prince* concentrates especially on this process,
and can ironically be called a tale of two fathers. Mosab starts the film by
saying:

> I came to understand the importance of my father from day one. People used
> to travel from every part of the country to hear his Friday speech at Rammalah
> mosque. See this person with this status, that is serving people, living a humble
> life, helping the poor, not taking advantage of his position that taught me a lot.
> I was always very very proud of him, I saw him as my highest example. If there
> was a God which I could see at that time, a higher authority in my life, it was
> my dad.

It is paradoxically this total identification that will later prove fragile. Later
in the film the father is arrested again and again, leaving the family vulnerable
to an indifferent and sometimes even hostile society and acquaintances. It is
this weakness of the real father and ultimately the weakness of the heavenly
father Allah that makes Mosab turn to Christianity (the religion of the son).
Mosab's turn to Christianity as elaborated more fully in the book *Son of
Hamas* is especially instructive. The teachings of Christ, particularly "love
your enemies," are used by Mosab in order to transcend the self-image of the
collaborator. Instead of viewing himself as someone who has done damage
to his people and family, his self-representation is that of someone who took
Christ's words to heart and has turned the other cheek to his enemies. In a
sense Christianity is used as a defense mechanism. It enabled him to find
a new path seemingly beyond the Jewish-Muslim conflict both in spiritual
terms and in terms of his new life in California. Christianity also helped him
to partially rationalize what he went through, his experience. It is his betrayal
and work for the Shin Bet that irrevocably transformed his life, not his discovery of Jesus's teachings. The taking up of Jesus's teaching was not done in
a power-neutral space, it was done as a process of rationalization of the forced
"choice" to collaborate under torture. This taking up of Jesus's teaching is
part of repairing the self-image and part internalization of the stronger Other
(Judeo-Christianity). These processes necessarily involve self-deception.
As viewers we intuitively understand, empathize, and even feel an intimate
bond with Mosab, though we may not be very clear as to our instinctive
empathy. Perhaps this intimacy is created with the viewers because they too
are in some sense "collaborators," they too have internalized others (parents,
teachers) in situations of radical inequality, but then have creatively reconsti-
tuted their selves in a way that affirms as theirs what was actually imposed
upon them.[38] However most of the viewers have "collaborated" as children

with people who largely had good intentions in relations to them and not with people with opposed interests. They also normally stay within the values and loyalties of their own society. Mosab has shifted his loyalty across enemy lines. These enemy lines are not demarcated between the two nations Israeli and Palestinian but characteristically, in a post-national age, the line is drawn between Islam and the Judeo-Christian West. One of the first lines that we hear in the *Green Prince* is "My father dedicated his entire life for the cause of Islam thinking that the Islamic philosophy and ideology would solve the problems of humanity." The father's ambitions are universal, they incorporate Palestine but also transcend Palestine. Mosab has not become an Israeli or American, but a Christian, another global, universal religion. He has also turned to the lecture circuit in the United States in general and the entertainment industry in California in particular where a live-action film of the *Green Prince* is in the making. This trajectory from Hamas to Hollywood is not as strange as it may sound. Turning to the "other side" and having an interesting narrative to tell means being subjected to the strong pull of Hollywood. In the age of globalization and post-nationalism a strange kind of "tunnel" connects these two extremes, the world of Hamas and the world of Hollywood. Once one flips over from being in a society and an ideology that opposes the forces of globalization in its current form, one is swept up so to speak and finds oneself at the very center of the production of global culture. Once turning to the West, a whole new field of power relations with its possibilities and incentives for action opens up for Mosab, a whole new Western govermentability. In today's ideological culture-clash, Hollywood and political Islam stand as close opposites.[39] In contrast to the cold war era where opposing forces were separated through frontiers and walls, in a highly globally integrated world where space time has dramatically shrunk and where mobility on both sides has created various enclaves and overlapping ethnic and religious groups culture, strict geographical separation is impossible. The prison door of the Shin Bet facility next to your village might lead you to Hollywood.

In many ways a dramatic meeting with the Other has become the classic theme of narrative in the age of globalization. Such meetings have become the staple of literature and film that have moved away from both conception and praxis of a homogenous nation-state. Films that depict the second intifada are built on this general concept. They portray the drama of meeting with the Other. In many important ways these films are all in a sense post-national. They are outside the narrative of the nation-state. They don't even present the Arab-Israeli conflict as based on conflicting claims of nation building. The protagonists of *To Die in Jerusalem* and *The Green Prince* are clearly more situated in the sense making of Judaism, Islam, and Christianity than in competing national claims. All participates, perhaps only excluding the Shin Bet interrogator, are animated by a distinctly post-national religious sensibility. As we saw in the *Green Prince* Islamism is supposed to solve the problems of humanity in general. *Encounter Point* and *One Day after Peace* are also built around distinctly Christian notions of forgiveness and reconciliation not around mutual recognition of nations. These works also display a post-national sensibility in the sense that they bring to a global audience a dramatic and "exotic" conflict of the Middle East.

NOTES

1. Some have commented that Sihem bombing is under motivated in the film. James Buchan thinks that "Sihem's motivations are a riddle, and the Arabs created to explain them are mere incorporations of political postures." While it seems the narrative takes time to let us understand her actions it is true that in general we are dealing more with a political allegory then with realism, James Buchan, "Beyond Belief," *The Guardian*, July 1, 2006, sec. Books, https://www.theguardian.com/books/2006/jul/01/featuresreviews.guardianreview16.

2. I am reformulating Walter Bryce Gallie term "essentially contested concept." Essentially contested concepts are concepts like "social justice," "freedom" that have essentially different meanings to different participants. Likewise political violence has essentially different meanings depending on perspective. For essentially contested concepts see W. B. Gallie, "Essentially Contested Concepts," *Proceedings of the Aristotelian Society* 56 (1955), 167–98.

3. Gerard Raymond, "Interview." *Slant* June 28, 2013, https://www.slantmagazine.com/house/article/interview-ziad-doueiri-on-the-attack

4. John Horn, "Ziad Doueiri's Film 'The Attack' Encounters Opposition," *Los Angeles Times*, June 26, 2013, http://articles.latimes.com/2013/jun/26/entertainment/la-et-mn-ziad-doueiri-20130626.

5. Asfour, "The Effort to Stop 'The Attack,'" *The New York Times*, June 14, 2013, http://www.nytimes.com/2013/06/16/magazine/the-effort-to-stop-the-attack.html.

6. "Ziad Doueiri's 'The Attack': Whitewashing the Enemy," Al Akhbar English, accessed October 16, 2016, http://english.al-akhbar.com/content/ziad-doueiri%E2%80%99s-%E2%80%9C-attack%E2%80%9D-whitewashing-enemy.

7. Asfour, "The Effort to Stop 'The Attack.'"

8. Raymond, "Interview."

9. Most famously 9.11 was undertaken by American born citizens.

10. Chapman, *Cinemas of the World*, accessed October 12, 2016, http://www.press.uchicago.edu/ucp/books/book/distributed/C/bo3536644.html.

11. A good example was Jean Sartre who supported use of violence in decolonization projects, specifically those in Algeria. See Jean-Paul Sartre, *Colonialism and Neocolonialism* (London; New York: Routledge, 2001).

12. This has been the case in the attack against Charlie Hebdo, an irreverent left-wing journal with basically anti-colonial sympathy. This event joins the outrage over the cartoons of Muhammad drawn in Denmark that has no legacy of colonialism in the Middle East.

13. Parents have organized to demand information regarding army accidents and therefore have redefined what was traditionaly a consecrated national loss become a social problem. See Gideon Doron and Udi Lebel, "Penetrating the Shields of Institutional Immunity: The Political Dynamic of Bereavement in Israel," *Mediterranean Politics* 9, no. 2 (2004), 201–20.

14. Stuart Cohen, *Israel and Its Army: From Cohesion to Confusion* (London; New York: Routledge, 2008), 55.

15. Ibid., 56.

16. Yagil Levy, "How Casualty Sensitivity Affects Civilian Control: The Israeli Experience," *INSP International Studies Perspectives* 12, no. 1 (2011), 72.

17. For an in depth literary analysis of these themes see Feldman, *Glory and Agony*; For example, from Chanoch Levin לוין, "מלכת האמבטיה 1970.2010 (התיאטרון אוניברסיטת תל אביב החוג לאומנות)."

18. Joseph Cedar, *Beaufort,* Action, Drama, War, 2008.

19. For the ethical code of the IDF see idfonline, "IDF Code of Ethics|The Official Blog of the Israel Defense Forces."

20. Recently there has been a backlash regarding this trend under the keyword causality phobia attributed generals and decision makers. See Udi Lebel, "Militarism versus Security? The Double-Bind of Israel's Culture of Bereavement and Hierarchy of Sensitivity to Loss," *Mediterranean Politics* 16, no. 3 (2011), 365–84.

21. While this claim has been made by philosophers who study forgiveness, we do not in any way think of Letlapah as being irrational when he seeks and gratefully accepts forgiveness. Perhaps more than anything it shows how limited strict rationality is in this respect.

22. Jacques Derrida, *On Cosmopolitanism and Forgiveness* (Routledge, 2001).

23. For a philosophical rendition of the Holocaust and occupation as forms of structural violence see Adi Ophir, *The Order of Evils: Toward an Ontology of Morals* (New York: Cambridge, MA: Zone Books; Distributed by MIT Press, 2005).

24. For the individualizing effects of Globalization Anthony Elliott and Charles C. Lemert, *The New Individualism: The Emotional Costs of Globalization* (New York: Routledge, 2006), http://public.eblib.com/choice/publicfullrecord.aspx?p=254274.

25. See Arjun Appadurai, *Modernity at Large: Cultural Dimensions of Globalization* (Minneapolis, MN: University of Minnesota Press, 1996), 6.

26. While I was teaching several courses on the film and literature of the Palestinian-Israeli conflict it was this scene more than any other text of film that polarized students and reproduced actual conflict in the author's classroom.

27. Elizabeth Jensen, "To Die in Jerusalem - TV," *The New York Times*, October 24, 2007, http://www.nytimes.com/2007/10/24/arts/television/24die.html.

28. This analysis benefits from paradigms of recognition articulated by Axel Honneth and Paul Ricoeur see Axel Honneth, *Kampf Um Anerkennung: Zur Moralischen Grammatik Sozialer Konflikte*, 1. Aufl (Frankfurt am Main: Suhrkamp, 1992); Paul Ricoeur, *Parcours de la reconnaissance: trois études* (Paris: Stock, 2004).

29. See "Structural Divisions and State Projects" in Ariella Azoulay and Adi Ophir, *The One-State Condition: Occupation and Democracy in Israel/Palestine*, 2013, http://public.eblib.com/choice/publicfullrecord.aspx?p=1035250_0, 203–25.

30. Sigmund Freud, *On Murder, Mourning, and Melancholia* (London; New York: Penguin Books, 2005).

31. For an article that articulates meaning making as a central process of bereavement see Neimeyer, Prigerson, and Davies, "Mourning and Meaning." American Behavioral Scientist 46, no. 2 (2002): 235–51.

32. Benedict Anderson has commented that one of the strengths of nationalism (in contrast to other ideologies such as socialism, liberalism, etc.) is that it gives meaning to death, since the dead person partakes in the eternal nation. When discussing national monuments for fallen soldiers he says:

"The cultural significance of such monuments becomes even clearer if one tires to imagine, say, a Tomb of the Unkown Marxist or the cenotaph for fallen Liberals. Is a sense of absurdity avoidable? The reason is that neither Marxism nor Liberalism is much concerned with death and immortality. If the nationalist imagining is so concerned, this suggests a strong affinity with religious imaginings." Anderson, *Imagined Communities*, 213.

33. For anthropological perspective Simcha Fishbane, "Jewish Mourning Rites: A Process of Resocialization," *Anthropologica. N.S.* 31 (1989), 65–84; For earlier sources David Charles Kraemer, *The Meanings of Death in Rabbinic Judaism* (London; New York, NY: Routledge, 2000), http://public.eblib.com/choice/publicfullrecord.aspx?p=165049.

34. While all monotheistic religions conceive of God as having a divine plan. In Islam there is great stress on resignation to God's plans. "Everyone shall taste death. And only on the day of resurrection shall you be paid your wages in full. And whoever is removed away from the fire and admitted to paradise, this person is indeed successful. The Life of this world is only the enjoyment of deception" (Quran 3:185). For a comparative take on Islam see "The Islamic way of death and dying: homeward bound" Colin Murray Parkes, Pittu Laungani, and Bill Young, *Death and Bereavement across Cultures* (London; New York: Routledge, 1997), 110–33.

35. One way in which the state tries to encourage the parallel is by explicitly devoting commemorative events and sites to both the fallen soldiers and civilian victims of hostilities and terror.

36. Yagil Levy, *Israel's Death Hierarchy: Casualty Aversion in a Militarized Democracy* (New York: New York University Press, 2012).

37. Mosab Hassan Yousef and Ron Brackin, *Son of Hamas* (Carol Stream, IL: SaltRiver, 2010); Nadav Schirman, *The Green Prince*, Documentary, Biography, 2014.

38. In fact that is one of the key insights of Nietzsche, Freud, and Marx. The insight being that our ideologies and belief systems are not transparent to ourselves nor do they reflect reality or real values, but are essentially something that we take upon ourselves in positions of weakness. Thus for Nietzsche, Christianity and socialism are a slave morality undertaken in an inferior position, for Freud one internalizes the superego (values, religion, etc.) as a child under the threat of the father, and for Marx "the ruling ideas are the ideas of the ruling class" thus what we believe is usually a result of the power of the ruling classes over the market of ideas.

39. I am borrowing the notion of closeness of binary opposites from semantic theory.

Conclusion

Contextualizing Israel in a Global Knowledge-Society

Since the early 1970s marketization and privatization have been implemented throughout the world. The market forces that saw their initial rise in the 1970s mark the beginning of the end of socialist experiments in planned economy that were so central to most of the 20th century. This turn to capitalism has happened in extremely diverse circumstances and has expressed itself in decisions made by leaders as different as Margret Thatcher, Deng Xiaoping, Ronald Reagan, and indeed Menachem Begin and Shimon Peres. This global trend is often overlooked or minimized by Israeli cultural theorists and historians who concentrate on the Israeli case exclusively. Often these intellectuals cast it as an unfortunate and relatively contingent change that decision makers or Israeli culture has partaken in.[1] Nationalism and Zionism themselves encourage thinking about these issues as wholly particular to Israel. In contrast to these kinds of representations, the premise of this book is that it makes sense to view the changes that Israeli culture went as it sharply transitioned to what is variously called postindustrial age, information or network society or global knowledge economy. These concepts signal that our time has definitely broken with a past that has been organized around industry and production. One locus of such concepts and perspectives has been the intense theorizing in France between the late 1960s and early 1980s, specifically Lotayrd and Baudrillad. Another has been Italian workerism and post-workerism Raniero Panzieri, Mario Tronti, Toni Negri, and Romano Alquati and American sociologists like Daniel Bell. Awareness of the way that unrestrained industrial production contributes to global warming has also restricted enthusiasm toward production and growth itself. Israel like several other advanced societies is no longer organized around industrial production but around social reproduction, consumption, communication, knowledge, and affective services. Workers and farmers are no longer considered a "universal class" rather they are fastest shrinking sector of society. There has been a shift from a stress on production of material goods to a stress on production and consumption of immaterials such as images and code.[2] Producing these codes and images are what theorist Richard Florida calls the creative class, made up of engineers, computer programmers, media workers, artists, and educators. This class is not only asked to solve existing problems it is often asked to come up with new problems as well.[3] The effects of the knowledge economy are seen everywhere in Israel. It has created a prosperous "first world Israel" around the Tel Aviv metropolitan era where immaterials like software, scientific knowledge, entertainment, and social services are produced in a close integration with global networks. It has also created a largely impoverished peripheral Israel. This stress on immaterial work is indeed a radical break with the past. Perhaps more than any other political movement Zionism was intent on counteracting what it perceived as the immaterialism of religious and business culture (what was called Luftgeschäft—air business) with its stress on material labor in agriculture and later industry. Thus we have a nation transforming itself from idolizing working the land, to a nation idealizing working with code. In a space of one generation society moved from glamorizing material production, being libidinally attached to producing material things, to an almost fully immaterial society based largely on a knowledge economy. This new kind of economy, this new kind of society, is juxtaposed with a tense geopolitical situation in the Middle East and with the return of religion. The knowledge economy is creating a new kind of being in Israel. One that revives the intensities of a reconstructed Jewish past, while firmly existing and even assuming leadership positions in the techno-capitalist present and future. Israel's integration in a global knowledge economy has caused fundamental changes that have left agriculture, industry, the welfare nation-state, and even citizenship itself behind. National secular culture in many of its manifestations from realist novels, modernist poetry, army bands, and communal singing has been superseded by a mix of commercial and religious culture. This mix itself would have been seen as surprising, almost incomprehensible as late as the 1970s. These changes have wholly reshuffled the board in determining the context of lives and culture in Israel. Familiar and seemingly continuous elements such as Jewish religion and ethnicity and the Arab-Israeli conflict have assumed new meaning. New types of seemingly "impossible" kinds of people evolve like the ultra-religious software engineer who codes software for multinationals. Such figures are anti-modern and ultramodern at the same time, belong to the Jewish "tribe" as much as they belong to the world. Today's individuals and today's society seem to be immaterially floating in software, popular culture, and religion, wholly de-territorialized. The economic engine of growth in Israeli society is wholly divorced from the nation-state. Start-ups quickly create one-time value and then are brought by big multinationals. Individual success is ultimately related to integration and to the value added to global networks of producers and consumers. Culture has responded in complex ways to economic globalization. Global entertainment and its local variety can be seen as integral part of economic globalization. Popular television series are part and parcel of globalized entrepreneurship as they get adopted and translated in the United States and Europe. However commercial culture has its own blind spots, its own problems in answering deep needs and wants. While providing short-term excitement and relief it often lacks in providing meaning, orientation, or indeed compensation for life's deeper problems and disappointments. While secular nationalism used to provide these benefits, this is no longer the case. I have argued in the book that what started in the 1990s as a liberal and multicultural revolution has generated a cultural earthquake. Its results are a new-old type of culture. In Israel it has resulted in an eclectic mix of popular commercialism, elite liberal culture produced for Western audience, coupled with a conservative nationalism, and religious revival. It is my hope that this book has provided a complex rendition of these dramatic changes.

NOTES

1. A good example of this relatively narrow national viewpoint is provided by Dani Gutwein who analyzes these changes through the rise of Likud party See Gutwien Danny, 2012, Privatization of Industrial Relations as the Political Logic of Dismantling of the Welfare State in מישורי and מאור, העסקה פוגענית פוגענית; for the cultural privatization, see טאוב, *ha-Mered ha-shafuf.*

2. This has been a major stress of social theory of the 1960s. See Debord, *The society of the spectacle*; Baudrillard, *Simulacra and Simulation.*

3. Florida, *The Rise of the Creative Class.*

Bibliography

"(16) ניר ברעם נואם בהפגנת האלפים נגד חוק הלאום - YouTube." Accessed December 27, 2017. https://www.youtube.com/watch?v=yLg7tE1iM7Y.

Agnon, Shmuel Yosef. *Shirah*. Jerusalem: Shoken, 731.

Aharoni, Yair. *The Israeli Economy (Routledge Revivals): Dreams and Realities*. Routledge, 2014.

Anderson, Benedict R. O'G. *Imagined Communities: Reflections on the Origin and Spread of Nationalism*. Rev. ed. London ; New York: Verso, 2006.

Appadurai, Ajun. "Disjuncture and Difference in the Global Cultural Economy." *Public Culture* 2, no. 2 (1990): 1. https://doi.org/10.1215/08992363-2-2-1.

———. *Modernity at Large: Cultural Dimensions of Globalization*. Minneapolis, MN: University of Minnesota Press, 1996.

Arad, Maya. *Sheva' midot ra'ot*. Hargol plus. Tel-Aviv: Hargol: 'Am 'oved, 2006.

ARISA. *ARISA הקליפ - אירופה לא זה זה פה - צנעני מרגלית עם אריסה*. Accessed October 13, 2016. https://www.youtube.com/watch?v=OFZmcSVHnxs.

Asfour, Nana. "The Effort to Stop 'The Attack.'" *The New York Times*, June 14, 2013. http://www.nytimes.com/2013/06/16/magazine/the-effort-to-stop-the-attack.html.

Azoulay, Ariella, and Adi Ophir. *The One-State Condition: Occupation and Democracy in Israel/Palestine*, 2013. http://public.eblib.com/choice/publicfullrecord.aspx?p=1035250_0.

Barber, Benjamin R. *Jihad vs. McWorld*. 1st ed. New York: Times Books, 1995.

Bar-On, Mordechai. *In Pursuit of Peace: A History of the Israeli Peace Movement*. Washington, DC: United States Institute of Peace Press, 1996.

Baudrillard, Jean. *Simulacra and Simulation*. Ann Arbor: University of Michigan Press, 1994.

Baudrillard, Jean, and Jean-Louis Violeau. *The Ecstasy of Communication*. Translated by Bernard Schütze and Caroline Schütze. Los Angeles: Semiotext, 2012.

Beck, Ulrich, Anthony Giddens, and Scott Lash. *Reflexive Modernization: Politics, Tradition and Aesthetics in the Modern Social Order*. 1 edition. Stanford, CA: Stanford University Press, 1994.

Bell, Daniel. *China's New Confucianism: Politics and Everyday Life in a Changing Society*. Princeton, NJ: Princeton University Press, 2008.

Ben-Yosef Ginor, Tseviyah. "Involuntary Myths: Mania, Mother, and Zion in Orly Castel-Bloom's 'Ummi Fi Shurl.'" *Prooftexts* 25, no. 3 (2005): 235–57.

Berlin, Isaiah. *Four Essays on Liberty*. London; New York: Oxford University Press, 1990.

Bhabha, Homi K. *The Location of Culture*. London; New York: Routledge, 1994.

Bloom, A. *The Closing of the American Mind: How Higher Education Has Failed Democracy and Impoverished the Souls of Today's Students*. New York: Simon and Schuster, 1987.

Boorstin, Daniel J. *The Image: A Guide to Pseudo-Events in America*. 50th Anniversary Edition. New York: Vintage Books, a division of Random House, Inc, 2012.

Bourdieu, Pierre. *Distinction: A Social Critique of the Judgement of Taste*. Cambridge, MA: Harvard University Press, 1984.

———. *Reproduction in Education, Society and Culture*. Sage Studies in Social and Educational Change; v. 5. London; Beverly Hills, CA: Sage Publications, 1977.

Bourdieu, Pierre, and Randal Johnson. *The Field of Cultural Production: Essays on Art and Literature*. New York: Columbia University Press, 1993.

Bourdieu, Pierre, and Jean Claude Passeron. *La Reproduction; Éléments Pour Une Théorie Du Système D'enseignement*. Collection Le Sens Commun. Paris: Éditions de Minuit, 1970.

Boyarin, Daniel, and Jonathan Boyarin. "Diaspora: Generation and the Ground of Jewish Identity." *Critical Inquiry* 19, no. 4 (1993): 693–725.

Buchan, James. "Beyond Belief." *The Guardian*, July 1, 2006, sec. Books. https://www.theguardian.com/books/2006/jul/01/featuresreviews.guardianreview16.

Caryl, Christian. *Strange Rebels: 1979 and the Birth of the 21st Century*. 1 edition. New York: Basic Books, 2013.

Casanova, Pascale. *Le Republique Mondiale Des Lettres*. Paris: Editions du Seuil, 1999.

Castel-Bloom, Orly, and Dalya Bilu. *Dolly City*, 2010. http://public.eblib.com/choice/publicfullrecord.aspx?p=1754293.

Castells, Manuel, and Manuel Castells. *The Rise of the Network Society*. 2nd ed., With a new pref. The Information Age: Economy, Society, and Culture, v. 1. Chichester, West Sussex; Malden, MA: Wiley-Blackwell, 2010.

Cedar, Joseph. *Beaufort*. Action, Drama, War, 2008.

Cinemas of the World. Accessed October 12, 2016. http://www.press.uchicago.edu/ucp/books/book/distributed/C/bo3536644.html.

Cohen, Stuart. *Israel and Its Army: From Cohesion to Confusion*. London; New York: Routledge, 2008.

Cowen, Tyler. *In Praise of Commercial Culture*. Cambridge, Mass: Harvard University Press, 1998.

Debord, Guy. *The society of the spectacle*. New York: Zone Books, 1994.

Deleuze, Gilles, and Félix Guattari. *Anti-Oedipus: Capitalism and Schizophrenia*. Minneapolis: University of Minnesota Press, 1983.

Deleuze, Gilles, Félix Guattari, Robert Brinkley, Gilles Deleuze, Félix Guattari, and Robert Brinkley. "What Is a Minor Literature?" *Mississippi Review* 11, no. 3 (1983): 13–33.

Derrida, Jacques. *On Cosmopolitanism and Forgiveness*. Routledge, 2001.

Doron, Daniel. "Crony Capitalism in Israel." *Wall Street Journal*, October 9, 2010, sec. Opinion. http://www.wsj.com/articles/SB10001424052748704657304575540 221888462554.

Doron, Gideon, and Udi Lebel. "Penetrating the Shields of Institutional Immunity: The Political Dynamic of Bereavement in Israel." *Mediterranean Politics* 9, no. 2 (2004): 201–20.

Durkheim, Emile, Carol Cosman, and Mark Sydney Cladis. *The Elementary Forms of Religious Life*. Oxford World's Classics. Oxford; New York: Oxford University Press, 2001.

Elliott, Anthony, and Charles C. Lemert. *The New Individualism: The Emotional Costs of Globalization*. New York: Routledge, 2006. http://public.eblib.com/choice/publicfullrecord.aspx?p=254274.

Evans, Matt. *Reterritorialization or Deterritorialization? Israel's Gaza Withdrawal*. Vol. 42, 2014.

Feldman, Yael S. *Glory and Agony: Isaac's Sacrifice and National Narrative*. Stanford, CA: Stanford University Press, 2010. http://site.ebrary.com/id/10459536.

Fiennes, Sophie. *The Pervert's Guide to Cinema*. Documentary, 2009.

Fischer, Stanley. "The Israeli Stabilization Program, 1985–86." *American Economic Review* 77 (1987): 275.

Fishbane, Simcha. "Jewish Mourning Rites: A Process of Resocialization." *Anthropologica. N.S.* 31 (1989): 65–84.

Florida, Richard L. *The Flight of the Creative Class: The New Global Competition for Talent*. 1st ed. New York: HarperBusiness, 2005.

———. *The Rise of the Creative Class: And How It's Transforming Work, Leisure, Community and Everyday Life*. New York: Basic Books, 2004.

Freud, Sigmund. *Der Mann Moses Und Die Monotheistische Religion. Drei Abhandlungen*. Amsterdam: A. de Lange, 1939.

———. *On Murder, Mourning, and Melancholia*. London; New York: Penguin Books, 2005.

Freud, Sigmund, James Strachey, Anna Freud, Alix Strachey, and Alan Tyson. *The Standard Edition of the Complete Psychological Works of Sigmund Freud. Volume VIII, 1905, Volume VIII, 1905*. London: Hogarth Press: Institute of Psychoanalysis, 1960.

Gallie, W. B. "Essentially Contested Concepts." *Proceedings of the Aristotelian Society* 56 (1955): 167–98.

Gilman, Sander L. *Jewish Self-Hatred: Anti-Semitism and the Hidden Language of the Jews*. Baltimore, MD: Johns Hopkins University Press, 1986.

Glûzman, Mîḵā·ēl. *The Politics of Canonicity: Lines of Resistance in Modernist Hebrew Poetry*. Stanford, CA: Stanford Univ. Press, 2003.

Gourevitch, Philip. *We Wish to Inform You That Tomorrow We Will Be Killed with Our Families: Stories from Rwanda*. London: Picador, 2000.

Greimas, Algirdas Julien. *On Meaning: Selected Writings in Semiotic Theory*. University of Minnesota Press, 1987.

Grinberg, Lev Luis. *Ha-Histadrut Me-ʿal Ha-Kol*. Yerushalayim: Nevo, 1993.

Grosglik R, and Ram U. "Authentic, Speedy and Hybrid: Representations of Chinese Food and Cultural Globalization in Israel." *Food Cult. Soc. Food, Culture and Society* 16, no. 2 (2013): 223–43.

Grossman, David. *See under—Love*. New York: Farrar Straus Giroux, 1989.

Habermas, Jürgen. *Legitimation Crisis*. Boston: Beacon Press, 1975.

———. *Theorie Des Kommunikativen Handelns*. 1. Aufl. Frankfurt am Main: Suhrkamp, 1981.

Hardt, Michael, and Antonio Negri. *Commonwealth*. Unknown edition. Cambridge, MA; London: Belknap Press, 2011.

Harris, Rachel S.—(Rachel Sylvia). "Between the Backpack and the Tent: Home, Zionism, and a New Generation in Eshkol Nevo's Novels Homesick and Neuland." *Shofar: An Interdisciplinary Journal of Jewish Studies* 33, no. 4 (2015): 36–59.

Harvey, David. *A Brief History of Neoliberalism*. Oxford; New York: Oxford University Press, 2005.

Hasak-Lowy, Todd. "Postzionism and Its Aftermath in Hebrew Literature: The Case of Orly Castel-Bloom." *Jewish Social Studies* 14, no. 2 (2008): 86–112.

Held, David. *Global Covenant: The Social Democratic Alternative to the Washington Consensus*. Cambridge: Polity, 2004.

Hermoni, Matan. *Hibru poblishing ḳompani: roman*. Or Yehudah: Kineret: Zemorah-Bitan, 2011.

Hirschman, Albert O. *Exit, Voice, and Loyalty: Responses to Decline in Firms, Organizations, and States*. Cambridge, MA: Harvard University Press, 1981.

Hobsbawm, E. J. *Nations and Nationalism since 1780: Programme, Myth, Reality*. Cambridge [England]; New York: Cambridge University Press, 1990.

———. *On Empire: America, War, and Global Supremacy*. 1st ed. New York: Pantheon Books, 2008.

———. *The Age of Capital, 1848–1875*. New York: Scribner, 1975.

———. *The Age of Empire, 1875–1914*. New York: Pantheon Books, 1987.

———. *The Age of Revolution, 1789–1848*. Cleveland, OH: World Pub. Co., 1962.

Hobsbawm, E. J., and T. O. Ranger, eds. *The Invention of Tradition*. Past and Present Publications. Cambridge [Cambridgeshire]; New York: Cambridge University Press, 1983.

Hochgeschwender, Michael, and Bernhard Löffler, eds. *Religion, Moral Und Liberaler Markt: Politische Ökonomie Und Ethikdebatten Vom 18. Jahrhundert Bis Zur Gegenwart*. Histoire, Band 28. Bielefeld: Transcript, 2011.

"Hollywood, Creative Industries Add $504 Billion to U.S. GDP | Hollywood Reporter." Accessed December 23, 2017. https://www.hollywoodreporter.com/news/hollywood-creative-industries-add-504-662691.

Honneth, Axel. *Das Ich Im Wir: Studien Zur Anerkennungstheorie*. 1. Aufl. Suhrkamp Taschenbüch Wissenschaft 1959. Berlin: Suhrkamp, 2010.

———. *Kampf Um Anerkennung: Zur Moralischen Grammatik Sozialer Konflikte*. 1. Aufl. Frankfurt am Main: Suhrkamp, 1992.

Horn, John. "Ziad Doueiri's Film 'The Attack' Encounters Opposition." *Los Angeles Times*, June 26, 2013. http://articles.latimes.com/2013/jun/26/entertainment/la-et-mn-ziad-doueiri-20130626.

"Housing Minister Sees 50% More Settlers in West Bank by 2019." The Jerusalem Post | JPost.com. Accessed October 13, 2016. http://www.jpost.com/National-News/Housing-minister-sees-50-percent-more-settlers-in-West-Bank-by-2019-352501.

idfonline. "IDF Code of Ethics| The Official Blog of the Israel Defense Forces." *IDF Blog | The Official Blog of the Israel Defense Forces* (blog), August 1, 2013. https://www.idfblog.com/about-the-idf/idf-code-of-ethics/.

"Im Tirtzu." *Wikipedia*, October 9, 2016. https://en.wikipedia.org/w/index.php?title=Im_Tirtzu&oldid=743327619.

"Interview: Ziad Doueiri on The Attack | The House Next Door." Slant Magazine. Accessed October 12, 2016. http://www.slantmagazine.com/house/article/interview-ziad-doueiri-on-the-attack.

Jensen, Elizabeth. "To Die in Jerusalem - TV." *The New York Times*, October 24, 2007. http://www.nytimes.com/2007/10/24/arts/television/24die.html.

Kahn, Susan Martha. *Reproducing Jews: A Cultural Account of Assisted Conception in Israel*. Body, Commodity, Text. Durham, NC: Duke University Press, 2000.

Kaplan, Eran. "Amos Oz's 'A Tale of Love and Darkness' and the Sabra Myth." *Jewish Social Studies* 14, no. 1 (2007): 119–143.

Katznelson, Berl. *Revolutionary Constructivism: Essays on the Jewish Labor Movement in Palestine*. Young Poale Zion Alliance, 1937.

Kimmerling, Baruch. *Zionism and Economy*. Cambridge, MA: Schenkman Pub. Co., 1983.

———. *Zionism and Territory: The Socio-Territorial Dimensions of Zionist Politics*. Research Series, No. 51. Berkeley: Institute of International Studies, University of California, 1983.

Klein, Melanie. *The Writings of Melanie Klein. Love, Guilt and Reparation and other Works 1921–1945 Vol. 1 Vol. 1*. London: Hogarth Press and the Institute of Psycho-Analysis, 1975.

Kraemer, David Charles. *The Meanings of Death in Rabbinic Judaism*. London; New York: Routledge, 2000. http://public.eblib.com/choice/publicfullrecord.aspx?p=165049.

Kymlicka, Will. *Multicultural Citizenship: A Liberal Theory of Minority Rights*. Oxford; New York: Clarendon Press; Oxford University Press, 1995.

Lacan, Jacques, and Bruce Fink. *Écrits: The First Complete Edition in English*. W. W. Norton & Company, 2006.

Lacan, Jacques, and Jacques-Alain Miller. *The Seminar of Jacques Lacan*, 1988.

Lakoff, George, and Mark Johnson. *Metaphors We Live by*. Chicago: University of Chicago Press, 1980.

Latour, Bruno. *Reassembling the Social: An Introduction to Actor-Network-Theory*. Clarendon Lectures in Management Studies. Oxford; New York: Oxford University Press, 2005.

Lebel, Udi. "Militarism versus Security? The Double-Bind of Israel's Culture of Bereavement and Hierarchy of Sensitivity to Loss." *Mediterranean Politics* 16, no. 3 (2011): 365–84.

Lemish, Dafna, Kirsten Drotner, Tamar Liebes, Eric Maigret, and Gitte Stald. "Global Culture in Practice A Look at Children and Adolescents in Denmark, France and Israel." *European Journal of Communication* 13, no. 4 (December 1, 1998): 539–56. https://doi.org/10.1177/0267323198013004006.

Leruth, Michael F. "The Neorepublican Discourse on French National Identity." *Frenpolisoci French Politics and Society* 16, no. 4 (1998): 46–61.

Levy, Yagil. "How Casualty Sensitivity Affects Civilian Control: The Israeli Experience." *INSP International Studies Perspectives* 12, no. 1 (2011): 68–88.

———. *Israel's Death Hierarchy: Casualty Aversion in a Militarized Democracy.* New York: New York University Press, 2012. http://public.eblib.com/choice/publicfullrecord.aspx?p=865664.

Lyotard, Jean-Francois, and Fredric Jameson. *The Postmodern Condition: A Report on Knowledge.* Translated by Geoff Bennington and Brian Massumi. 1st edition. Minneapolis: University Of Minnesota Press, 1984.

Marx, Karl. *Capital, a Critique of Political Economy,.* Modern Library of the World's Best Books. New York: The Modern library, 1936.

"Melnick Mealem.pdf." Accessed October 12, 2016. http://www.jewishvirtuallibrary.org/jsource/isdf/text/Melnick%20Mealem.pdf.

Mendelson-Maoz, Adia. "AMOS OZ'S A TALE OF LOVE AND DARKNESS WITHIN THE FRAMEWORK OF IMMIGRATION NARRATIVES IN MODERN HEBREW LITERATURE." *Journal of Modern Jewish Studies* 9, no. 1 (2010): 71–87. https://doi.org/10.1080/14725880903263101.

Meydani, Assaf. *The Israeli Supreme Court and the Human Rights Revolution: Courts as Agenda Setters.* Cambridge; New York: Cambridge University Press, 2011.

Mintz, Alan L. *Ḥurban: Responses to Catastrophe in Hebrew Literature.* New York: Columbia University Press, 1984.

Mirowski, Philip, and Dieter Plehwe, eds. *The Road from Mont Pèlerin: The Making of the Neoliberal Thought Collective.* Cambridge, MA: Harvard University Press, 2009.

Morris, Benny. *1948: A History of the First Arab-Israeli War.* New Haven, CT: Yale University Press, 2008.

Moyn, Samuel. *The Last Utopia: Human Rights in History.* Cambridge, MA: Belknap Press of Harvard University Press, 2010. http://public.eblib.com/choice/publicfullrecord.aspx?p=3300882.

Murray, Susan, and Laurie Ouellette, eds. *Reality TV: Remaking Television Culture.* 2nd ed. New York: New York University Press, 2009.

Namdar, Ruby author. *ha-Bayit asher neḥrav = Ruined House.* Or Yehudah: Kineret, 2013.

Ne'eman, Judd. "The Death Mask of the Moderns: A Genealogy of New Sensibility Cinema in Israel." *Israel Studies* 4, no. 1 (November 1, 1999): 100–128. https://doi.org/10.1353/is.1999.0027.

Neimeyer, Robert A., Holly G. Prigerson, and Betty Davies. "Mourning and Meaning." *American Behavioral Scientist* 46, no. 2 (2002): 235–51.

Nevo, Eshkol, and Sondra Silverston. *Neuland*, 2014.

Noy, Chaim, and Erik Cohen. *Israeli Backpackers From Tourism to Rite of Passage*. Ithaca: State University of New York Press, 2014.

"On the Globalization of Literature: Haruki Murakami, Tim O'Brien, and Raymond Carver | Electronic Book Review." Accessed October 11, 2016. http://www. electronicbookreview.com/thread/internetnation/bungaku.

Ophir, Adi. *The Order of Evils: Toward an Ontology of Morals*. New York: Cambridge, MA: Zone Books; Distributed by MIT Press, 2005.

Oz, Amos. *A Tale of Love and Darkness*. 1st U.S. ed. Orlando, FL: Harcourt, 2004.

Oz, Amos, and Fania Oz-Salzberger. *Jews and Words*. Yale University Press, 20.

Parkes, Colin Murray, Pittu Laungani, and Bill Young. *Death and Bereavement across Cultures*. London; New York: Routledge, 1997. http://public.eblib.com/ choice/publicfullrecord.aspx?p=168535.

Peleg, Yaron. *Israeli Culture between the Two Intifadas: A Brief Romance*. University of Texas Press, 2009.

Plessner, Yakir. *Political Economy of Israel, The: From Ideology to Stagnation*. SUNY Press, 2012.

Portugese, Jacqueline. *Fertility Policy in Israel: The Politics of Religion, Gender, and Nation*. Westport, CT: Praeger, 1998.

Qashu, Sayed, and Mitch Ginsburg. *Second Person Singular*. New York: Grove Press, 2012.

Qashu, Sayed, and Miriam Shlesinger. *Let It Be Morning*. New York: Black Cat: Distributed by Publishers Group West, 2006.

Rand, Ayn, and Leonard Peikoff. *The Fountainhead*. Anniversary edition. New York: Signet, 1996.

Rawls, John. *A Theory of Justice*. Cambridge, MA: Belknap Press of Harvard University Press, 1971.

———. *Political Liberalism*. The John Dewey Essays in Philosophy, no. 4. New York: Columbia University Press, 1993.

Regev, Motti, and Edwin Seroussi. *Popular Music and National Culture in Israel*. Berkeley, CA: University of California Press, 2004.

Ricoeur, Paul. *Parcours de la reconnaissance: trois études*. Paris: Stock, 2004.

Roskies, David G. *Against the Apocalypse: Responses to Catastrophe in Modern Jewish Culture*. Cambridge, MA: Harvard University Press, 1984.

Roy, Olivier, and Ros Schwartz. *Holy Ignorance: When Religion and Culture Part Ways*, 2013. http://site.ebrary.com/id/11005191.

Said, Edward W., and Jacqueline Rose. *Freud and the Non-European*. London; New York: Verso, 2003.

"Salman Rushdie Delivers Convocation Address – The Source – Oberlin College." Accessed October 12, 2016. https://oncampus.oberlin.edu/source/ articles/2011/10/18/salman-rushdie-delivers-convocation-address.

Sartre, Jean-Paul. *Colonialism and Neocolonialism*. London; New York: Routledge, 2001.

Schirman, Nadav. *The Green Prince*. Documentary, Biography, 2014.

Semyonov, Moshe, and Noah Lewin-Epstein. "Wealth Inequality: Ethnic Disparities in Israeli Society." *Social Forces* 89, no. 3 (March 1, 2011): 935–59. https://doi.org/10.1353/sof.2011.0006.

Senor, Dan, and Saul Singer. *Start-up Nation: The Story of Israel's Economic Miracle*. 1st ed. New York: Twelve, 2009.

Shafir, Gershon, and Yoav Peled. *Being Israeli: The Dynamics of Multiple Citizenship*. Cambridge; New York: Cambridge University Press, 2002. http://hdl.handle.net/2027/heb.08966.

Shamir, Moshe. *He Walked through the Fields*. Jerusalem: World Zionist Organization, Dept. for Education and Culture in the Diaspora, 1959.

Shapira, Anita. *Israel: A History*. The Schusterman Series in Israel Studies. Waltham, MA: Brandeis University Press, 2012.

Shiffman, Smadar. "Motherhood under Zionism." *Hebrew Studies* 44, no. 1 (2003): 139–56.

———. "Orly Castel-Bloom and Yoel Hoffmann: On Israeli Postmodern Prose Fiction." *Hebrew Studies* 50, no. 1 (2009): 215–27.

Shlomi Avineri. "Post-Zionism Doesn't Exist", *Haaretz*, July 06, 2007.

Shyarts, Yig'al, "Hebrew Prose: the Generation After." *Modern Hebrew Literature*, no. 15 (1995): 6–9.

Sims, Andrew. *Symptoms in the Mind an Introduction to Descriptive Psychopathology / Andrew Sims.*, 1995.

Spangler, Todd, and Todd Spangler. "Younger Viewers Watch 2.5 Times More Internet Video Than TV (Study)." *Variety* (blog), March 29, 2016. http://variety.com/2016/digital/news/millennial-gen-z-youtube-netflix-video-social-tv-study-1201740829/.

Spencer, Herbert. *Progress: Its Law and Cause: With Other Disquisitions, Viz.: The Physiology of Laughter: Origin and Function of Music: The Social Organism: Use and Beauty: The Use of Anthropomorphism*. New York: J. Fitzgerald & Co., 1881. http://catalog.hathitrust.org/api/volumes/oclc/19027637.html.

Spufford, Francis. *Red Plenty*. Minneapolis, Minnesota: Graywolf Press, 2012.

Stirling J. Jr., and American Academy of Pediatrics Committee on Child Abuse and Neglect. "Beyond Munchausen Syndrome by Proxy: Identification and Treatment of Child Abuse in a Medical Setting." *Pediatrics* 119, no. 5 (2007): 1026–30.

Strauss, Leo. *The City and Man*. Chicago: University of Chicago Press, 1978.

Strauss, Leo, and Kenneth Hart Green. *Jewish Philosophy and the Crisis of Modernity: Essays and Lectures in Modern Jewish Thought*. Albany: State University of New York Press, 1997. http://site.ebrary.com/id/10588710.

Strenger, Carlo. *The Fear of Insignificance: Searching for Meaning in the Twenty-First Century*. New York: Palgrave Macmillan, 2011.

Tal, Alon. "Enduring Technological Optimism: Zionism's Environmental Ethic and Its Influence on Israel's Environmental History." *Envihist Environmental History* 13, no. 2 (2008): 275–305.

Talmon, J. L. *The Myth of the Nation and the Vision of Revolution: The Origins of Ideological Polarisation in the Twentieth Century*. London: Berkeley: Secker & Warburg; University of California Press, 1981.

———. *The Origins of Totalitarian Democracy*. Books That Matter. New York: Praeger, 1960.

Tamir, Yael. *Liberal Nationalism*. Princeton, N.J: Princeton University Press, 1995. http://public.eblib.com/choice/publicfullrecord.aspx?p=537710.

Taub, Gadi. *Neged bedidut*. Lirik̤ah. Tel-Aviv: Yedi'ot ah̤aronot: Sifre h̤emed, 2011.

The Cameric Five. Comedy, 1999.

"The Culture of Celebrity | Psychology Today." Accessed December 25, 2017. https://www.psychologytoday.com/articles/199505/the-culture-celebrity.

"The God of Small Things." Accessed October 12, 2016. http://www.nytimes.com/books/00/12/10/reviews/001210.10wilsont.html.

"Top 7 Reasons Israeli TV Shows Are Smash Hits Abroad." Israel21c. Accessed December 13, 2017. http://www.israel21c.org/top-8-reasons-israeli-tv-shows-are-smash-hits-abroad/.

Varoufakis, Yanis, Joseph Halevi, and Nicholas Theocarakis. *Modern Political Economics: Making Sense of the Post-2008 World*. Routledge, 2012.

Wallerstein, Immanuel Maurice. *World-Systems Analysis: An Introduction*. Durham, NC: Duke University Press, 2004.

Walzer, Michael. *The Paradox of Liberation: Secular Revolutions and Religious Counterrevolutions*. New Haven: Yale University Press, 2015.

Weber, Max. *Methodology of Social Sciences*. New Brunswick, NJ: Transaction Publishers, 2011.

———. *The Protestant Ethic and the Spirit of Capitalism*. Routledge Classics. London; New York: Routledge, 2001. http://site.ebrary.com/lib/brandeis/Doc?id=2002712.

Weiss, Meira. "Bereavement, Commemoration, and Collective Identity in Contemporary Israeli Society." *Anthropological Quarterly* 70, no. 2 (1997): 91–101.

Wolfe, Audra J. *Competing with the Soviets: Science, Technology, and the State in Cold War America*. JHU Press, 2012.

Wollaeger, Mark A., and Matt Eatough, eds. *The Oxford Handbook of Global Modernisms*. New York: Oxford University Press, 2012.

Wu, Tim. *The Attention Merchants: How Our Time and Attention Are Gathered and Sold*. Export/Airside edition. London: Atlantic Books, 2017.

Ya'ir, Gad. *Tsofen Ha-Yiśre'eliyut: 'aśeret Ha-Dibrot Shel Shenot Ha-Alpayim*. Yerushalayim: Keter, 2011.

Yousef, Mosab Hassan, and Ron Brackin. *Son of Hamas*. Carol Stream, IL: SaltRiver, 2010.

"Ziad Doueiri's 'The Attack': Whitewashing the Enemy." Al Akhbar English. Accessed October 16, 2016. http://english.al-akhbar.com/content/ziad-doueiri%E2%80%99s-%E2%80%9C-attack%E2%80%9D-whitewashing-enemy.

Žižek, Slavoj. *For They Know Not What They Do: Enjoyment as a Political Factor*. Phronesis. London; New York: Verso, 1991.

Zizek, Slavoj. *Mapping Ideology*. Verso Books, 2012.

Zohar, Uri. *Boys Will Never Believe It*. N/A, 1973.

———. *Einayim G'dolot*. Comedy, Drama, 2009.

———. *Hole in the Moon*. Comedy, N/A.

———. *Peeping Toms*. Comedy, 1973.

———. *Shlosha Yamim Veyeled*. Drama, 1969.

ביסטרוב, יבגניה. ישראל 2007-2020 על דמוגרפיה וצפיפות. חיפה]: קתדרת חייקין ,לגיאואסטרטגיה http://primage.tau. .אוניברסיטת חיפה, קתדרת חייקין לגאואסטרטגיה, אוניברסיטת חיפה, 2007 ac.il/libraries/brender/books/2148435.pdf.

"הטלוויזיה החינוכית: הילדים משכונת חיים." Accessed October 13, 2016. http://www.23tv. co.il/321-he/shchunat_haim.aspx.

"זה לא המילקי, טמבל" *Ynet*, October 11, 2014. http://www.ynet.co.il/articles/0,7340, L-4579465,00.html.

טאוב, גדי. *נגד בדידות: מחשבות*. ליריקה. תל אביב: ידיעות אחרונות, 2016.

———. *נגד בדידות: רשמים*. ליריקה. תל-אביב: ידיעות אחרונות, 2011.

גדי טאוב Taub. *ha-Mered ha-shafuf: 'al tarbut tse'irah be-Yiśra'el*. Tel Aviv]: ha-Ḳibuts ha-me'uḥad, 1997.

"לוין,חנוך."מלכת האמבטיה1970.2010 (אוניברסיטת תל אביב. החוג לאומנות התיאטרון:2010) : תיק הצגה .אוניברסיטת תל אביב החוג לאומנות התיאטרון, 2010

"לפיד:'אנחנו מנסים לשנות את המצב רק התחלנו'" MaarivOnline. Accessed October 13, 2016. http://www.maariv.co.il/news/new.aspx?pn6Vq=11&0r9VQ=GGHLM. מעריב אונליין

ענת מאור. *העסקה פוגענית: הדרה וניצול שיטתיים בשוק העבודה* and ,מישורי, דניאל = *Precarious employment:systematic exclusion and exploitation in the labor market*, 2012.

"מכונת קריאה- דלות החומר כאיכות באמנות הישראלית" Accessed October 13, 2016. http://read-ingmachine.co.il/home/books/1142420759/chapter_chapter_chapter04_6703949.

נץ, רויאל. *מקום הטעם: מסות על ספרות ישראלית: בין צליל להיסטוריה*. מהד' 1. אחוזת בית - ספרים. תל אביב: אחוזת בית, 2008.

"פה זה לא אירופה" Lyrics + English Translation." Accessed October 13, 2016. http://lyr-icstranslate.com/en/%D7%A4%D7%94-%D7%96%D7%94-%D7%9C%D7%90-%D7%90%D7%99%D7%A8%D7%95%D7%A4%D7%94-it-aint-europe-here.html.

פריילינג, טוביה. *תשובה לעמית פוסט-ציוני*. תל-אביב: ידיעות אחרונות: ספרי חמד, 2003.

קשוע, סייד and Miriam Shlesinger. *Dancing Arabs*. New York: Grove Press, 2004.

אור יהודה: כנרת, זמורה-ביתן, .Y (שלת, עפר. *המגש והכסף: מדוע דרושה מהפכה בצה"ל*. המצב הישראלי (סדרה 2003.

שמיר, אילנה. *הנצחה וזכרון: דרכה של החברה הישראלית בעיצוב זכר נופלי הזכרון*. תל-אביב: עם עובד, 1996.

שריד, יש י. *השלישי*. ספריה לעם ; 701. תל אביב: עם עובד, 2015.

Author Index

Subject Index

About the Author

Ari Ofengenden is a professor and has taught on Israeli culture and Hebrew language and literature at Oberlin, George Washington, and Brandeis. He has written extensively on Israeli and Jewish culture, including the book *Introduction to the Poetry of Abraham Shlonsky*. He is the coeditor of *Social Histories and New Materialism in Hebrew Culture* (forthcoming). He has also published articles on Freud and Schnitzler. Ofengenden is the editor-in-chief of the Purdue University Press's Comparative Literature and Culture and series editor of the Purdue University Press monograph series of books in Comparative Cultural Studies.

www.ingramcontent.com/pod-product-compliance
Lightning Source LLC
Chambersburg PA
CBHW032028120726
47901CB00002BA/590